ALL GLORIES TO SRI GURU AND GAURANGA

ENCOUNTERS WITH Divinity

The Path of Dedication Vol. II

Swami B.R. Sridhara

GOSAI
PUBLISHERS

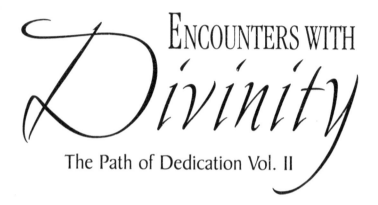

Inquiries, addresses to the secretary
of the publishers, are welcome

Śrī Narasingha Caitanya Maṭha
P.O. Box 21, Sri Rangapatna - Karnataka-571 438, India
E-mail: gosai@gosai.com
Web site: http://www.gosai.com/chaitanya/
or
Śrī Caitanya Sārasvata Maṭha
Kolerganj, P.O. Navadvīpa, Dist. Nadia, West Bengal, 741302, India

Senior Editor:
Tridaṇḍi Gosvāmī Śrī Śrīpāda
Bhakti Bhāvana Viṣṇu Mahārāja

Associate Editor:
Śrīpāda Bhakti Vijñāna Giri Mahārāja

Assisted by numerous ever–aspiring servants
of Śrī Śrī Guru and Gaurānga

First printing: 2005 limited edition 2,000 copies

Printed by Srinivas Fine Arts (P) Ltd., Sivakasi, India
for ŚRĪ NARASINGHA CAITANYA MAṬHA
ISBN 1-932771-80-8

Contents

Preface

It is the duty of every disciple to dive deeply into the nectar of the instructions of their Guru Mahārāja and a disciple should recognize the words of their guru anywhere. There is the story of Aurobindo Ghosh, a famous writer who absconded from the police during India's independence movement in the early Twentieth Century, but was found by a clever attorney who recognized his writings under another name—he saw the same substance in another form.

Sometimes a disciple may not recognize the direct words of their spiritual master or may find the mood and *siddhānta* of their Guru Mahārāja in the writings of another well schooled in their Guru Mahārāja's teachings. In this regard, some devotees have expressed the notion that Śrīla Śrīdhara Mahārāja's statements in the book *Follow The Angels* were not representative of his teachings. However, one who is at all familiar with the teachings of Śrīla Śrīdhara Maharaja (particularly those who are actual disciples of His Divine Grace) will easily see a continuity of thought and emphasis in all of Śrīla Śrīdhara Mahārāja's talks and writings—all his teachings are conservative and penetrating. His teachings are unique in the extent of the depth of his realizations and his profound knowledge of the Gauḍīya Vaiṣṇava *siddhānta*. In one of his earlier works, *Golden Volcano of Divine Love*, Śrīla Śrīdhara Mahārāja states,

> Of course these transcendental topics are very high, and we should not indulge in them carelessly, for if we project mundane characteristics into the higher plane, our future realization will be harmed. Our mundane experience will tend to take us down, so we must proceed with caution. What we conceive of at present is not to be found in the plane of Kṛṣṇa's pastimes—it is a far higher plane of existence than the realm of our experience. Our vision is adulterated. We have only an alloyed conception of the original thing. We must keep this in mind, and with this caution we may deal with these things.

Our personal experience is that the talks of Śrīla Śrīdhara Mahārāja on his veranda in the Śrī Caitanya Sārasvata Maṭha (from which all of his books have been extracted) are consistent with his orthodox approach to all aspects of Kṛṣṇa consciousness. These points are described in greater detail in the 'About the Author' section.

We would like to offer a few words of thanks to Śrīpāda Svāmī B. G. Narasiṅgha Mahārāja for his encouraging words and continuous support in this endeavor to present the poignant realizations of Śrīla Śrīdhara Mahārāja in this written format, without which this project could not have been completed. We feel confident that our readers will benefit greatly from these illuminating glimpses into Gauḍīya Vaiṣṇava *siddhānta*. Having access to an almost unlimited storehouse of Śrīla Śrīdhara

Mahārāja's recorded talks, we plan to regularly bring forth more books in this *Path of Dedication* series.

Further writings of Śrīla Śrīdhara Mahārāja may be found on-line at www.gosai.com/tattva/

Tridaṇḍi-svāmī
Bhakti Bhāvana Viṣṇu

Introduction

To have even the slightest touch with divinity is our greatest spiritual wealth. This is possible when one is drawn into connection with a *sādhu,* the agent of the Supreme Lord. In this publication, *Encounters With Divinity,* the author Śrīla B. R. Śrīdhara Deva Gosvāmī Mahārāja puts us in connection with Divine Conception, Divine Guidance, Divine Manifestation, and Divine Revelation. We cannot but express our humble opinion that his readers are indeed most fortunate to come in connection with this rare and inspiring spiritual wealth.

In part one, Divine Conception, Śrīla Śrīdhara Mahārāja takes us back in time and tells of how his guru, Śrīla Bhaktisiddhānta Sarasvatī Ṭhākura, gave birth to his preaching mission, the Gauḍīya Maṭha. How Śrīla Śrīdhara Mahārāja first came in connection with his guru and how the Gauḍīya Maṭha declared war on *māyā* in a most noble attempt to establish the Kṛṣṇa conception on a universal scale, are also explained.

In part two, Divine Guidance, the spirit of Kṛṣṇa consciousness as well as the vision of guru, the position of *śāstra,* the *sādhu, śrī mūrti* and many other valuable points of guidance to help one develop the proper understanding of the ontological truths of Kṛṣṇa consciousness are presented by Śrīla Śrīdhara Mahārāja in his usual vivid and happy style.

In part three, Divine Manifestation Śrīla Śrīdhara Mahārāja manifests many gems of the Gauḍīya *siddhānta* by explaining the position of Śrī Caitanya, the nobility of *gaura-līlā,* the form of Lord Jagannātha, the worship of *govardhana-śīlā,* the appearance of Ekādaśī and many other sweet and relishable manifestations of Kṛṣṇa consciousness.

In part four, Divine Revelation, the most subtle and sublime aspects of the inner circle of the Supreme Lord's eternal associates headed by Śrī Rūpa Gosvāmī and the soul's gradual entrance into that super-subjective realm of divine *līlā* are revealed by Śrīla Śrīdhara Mahārāja. The feelings of a devotee in separation from Kṛṣṇa, union in separation, and separation from the Lord's devotees are also revealed in this portion of *Encounters With Divinity,* with special emphasis on who is the dearmost devotee of the Supreme Lord.

In *Encounters With Divinity* we find ourselves not only being drawn in connection with divinity, but we find here some of the most sublime experiences of Śrīla Śrīdhara Mahārāja in his own personal encounters with divinity. The words of Śrīla Śrīdhara Mahārāja are indeed non-different from the Supreme Lord as they are 'divinely inspired' in the truest sense of the expression.

It is our most humble appeal that Śrīla Śrīdhara Mahārāja and his readers will kindly forgive us for any mistake that we may have made in our attempt to serve them.

Svāmī B.G. Narasiṅgha
Nandotsava, 28 August, 2005

About the Author

To acquaint our readers with the author we have but to relate some of his transcendental glories. One can easily understand the greatness of an individual by the acts he performs or by the contributions that he makes to society. The glories of Śrīla Śrīdhara Mahārāja are many and they are all deep like an ocean of transcendental nectar.

Śrīla Śrīdhara Mahārāja was not a mundane welfare worker that sought to uplift the bodily condition of a fallen man or that of many fallen and diseased men. Quite to the contrary—the contribution of Śrīla Śrīdhara Mahārāja was to uplift all of humanity to the spiritual platform of Kṛṣṇa consciousness, a rare contribution indeed.

The words of Śrīla Śrīdhara Mahārāja, both on audio tapes and in book format, are perhaps one of the greatest theological treasures of the 20th century. When the transcendental vibration from his lips enters the heart of a sincere seeker of truth, one immediately feels the fulfillment of the innermost hankering of the heart—we want Kṛṣṇa and nothing else.

To compile the complete list of Śrīla Śrīdhara Mahārāja's glories is not possible, but to speak of some of them in terms of what he has said and what he has written is a purifying, and an enlightening experience.

Sri Sri Prabhupada-padma Stavaka

Śrī Śrī Prabhupāda-padma Stavaka is a song of eleven verses composed by Śrīla Śrīdhara Mahārāja that eulogizes the transcendental personality of Śrīla Bhaktisiddhānta Sarasvatī Ṭhākura Prabhupāda. This song is so revered and appreciated by the disciples and grand-disciples of Sarasvatī Ṭhākura that it is virtually sung as a daily *sādhana* in all the Gauḍīya Maṭha temples.

The concluding line to each of the eleven stanzas, *praṇamāmi sadā prabhupāda-padam* (I eternally offer my obeisances to that wonderful effulgence that emanates from the radiant lotus toetips of Śrīla Bhaktisiddhānta Sarasvatī Ṭhākura Prabhupāda) is so sweet that it has become the hallmark of remembering that great *ācārya* of the Gauḍīya firmament.

Srimad Bhaktivinoda-viraha Dasakam

The ten verses *of Bhaktivinoda-viraha Daśakam* (expressing deep separation from Śrīla Bhaktivinoda Ṭhākura) were greatly appreciated by Śrīla Bhaktisiddhānta Sarasvatī Ṭhākura Prabhupāda who commented that, "Śrīdhara Mahārāja has caused Ṭhākura Bhaktivinoda to appear in those verses."

One of the favorites of the *Bhaktivinoda-viraha Daśakam* is the ninth verse that represents the ontological line of the inner substance of Kṛṣṇa consciousness.

"What was sanctioned by Śrī Caitanya Mahāprabhu by His descent, was intimately known only to Śrī Svarūpa Dāmodara Gosvāmī. Sanātana Gosvāmī, the elder brother of Śrī Rūpa Gosvāmī, was attentive to that divine truth, and Rūpa Gosvāmī himself served that very thing with his own hands to the devotees. Raghunātha Dāsa Gosvāmī tasted its sweetness and also added something of his own to its flavor. (He was assisted in doing so by Raghunātha Bhaṭṭa Gosvāmī and Gopāla Bhaṭṭa Gosvāmī.) What was distributed and tasted by Raghunātha Dāsa was protected by Śrī Jīva Gosvāmī, who lent support to its divinity with scriptural evidence. The taste of that divine truth is aspired after by Śrī Śukadeva Gosvāmī, Lord Śiva, and Lord Brahmā who regard it from a little distance with the highest respect. What is that inconceivable ambrosia? The sublime sweet nectar of the mellows relished in the service of Śrīmatī Rādhārāṇī's holy lotus feet. O Bhaktivinoda Ṭhākura, within this world, you fully possess the ability to give us that extraordinary nectar."

Sri Sri Prema-dhama-deva Stotram

Śrī Śrī Prema-dhāma-deva Stotram is a concise description of the *līlā* of Śrī Caitanya Mahāprabhu composed in the Sanskrit *tūṇaka* meter that represents the dancing rhythm of spiritual delight. The verses of *Prema-dhāma-deva Stotram* are based on *Caitanya-caritāmṛta* and other authorized writings about Śrī Caitanya. It describes Śrī Caitanya as Śrī Kṛṣṇa, the Supreme Personality of Divine Truth, permeated with the mood (*bhāva*) and complexion (*kānti*) of His supreme pleasure potency, Śrīmatī Rādhārāṇī. Śrī Caitanya is portrayed as the unlimited ocean of ecstatic love of Kṛṣṇa.

This *stotra* describes some of the most predominant aspects of Śrī Caitanya's divine personality—His transcendental characteristics (*aprākṛta-vaiśiṣṭa*), qualities (*guṇa*), beauty (*rūpa*), charm (*ākarṣaṇa*), compassion (*kāruṇa*), generosity (*audārya*), power (*tejas*), forgiving nature (*kṣamā-śīlatā*), magnanimity (*mahattva*), wisdom (*prajñāna*), conviction (*viśvāsa*), determination (*dṛdha-saṅkalpatā*), self-contentment in ecstatic love for Kṛṣṇa (*svānu-bhāvānanda*), all-encompassing kind love for others (*sarva-jīve dayā*), limitless ecstatic love for Kṛṣṇa (*kṛṣṇa-prema-dhāma-rūpa*), and His compassionate sharing of that divine love ecstasy with others (*mahā-vadānya-kṛṣṇa-prema-pradātṛtva*).

Prema-dhama-deva Stotram is highly regarded for its *siddhāntika* content and especially for its mellow sweetness that transports the listener to the realm of loving devotional service of Śrī Caitanya Mahāprabhu. Paramahaṁsa Śrī Niṣkiñcana Kṛṣṇa Dāsa Bābājī Mahārāja, a dear friend and godbrother of Śrīla Śrīdhara Mahārāja, used to say of this *stotra* that he found in it the very presence of Śrī Rūpa Gosvāmī Prabhupāda, the leader of our *sampradāya*.

Sri Sri Prapanna-jivanamrtam

Śrī Śrī Prapanna-jīvanāmṛtam is, as the title indicates, the life nectar of the surrendered souls and leads its readers to positive and progressive immortality. Śrīla Śrīdhara Mahārāja's introduction reads as follows: "The substance expressed within the ten chapters of this holy book called *Prapanna-jīvanāmṛtam* gives life to the surrendered souls, effecting their eternal growth and nourishment. It is the panacea of the heart and spiritual senses, bestowing those dedicated devotees with mutual happiness by the ever-increasingly newer and newer play of supra-mundane joy (*aprākṛta-rasa*). Lord Kṛṣṇa and His associates are portrayed in their natural pastimes of separation and union, and the line of unconditional surrender as established by scriptures and saints has been elucidated."

The doctrine of *śaraṇāgati* (surrender) is at the heart of Gauḍīya Vaiṣṇavism—indeed, it is the indispensable necessity in the life of a devotee. In *Prapanna-jīvanāmṛtam,* Śrīla Śrīdhara Mahārāja has compiled an anthology of verses in the chapter *Words of Nectar from the Devotees,* delineating the six processes of surrender. Here the processes of *ānukūlyasya saṅkalpaḥ* (acceptance of the favorable), *pratikūlya-vivarjjanam* (rejection of the unfavorable), *rakṣiṣyatīti visvāsaḥ* (confidence in the Lord's protection), *goptṛtve-varaṇam* (embracing the Lord's guardianship), *ātma-nikṣepaḥ* (full surrender), and *kārpaṇyam* (surrender in humility) are illuminated.

Prapanna-jīvanāmṛtam also includes the chapter *Words of Nectar from the Supreme Lord.* Śrīla Śrīdhara Mahārāja says, "Herein, collected from the holy scriptures headed by *Śrīmad Bhāgavatam* and *Bhagavad-gītā,* are words of nectar directly from the lotus mouth of the Supreme Personality of Godhead. This is the nectar to vanquish all sorrow and darkness for the souls surrendered to the lotus feet of Śrī Kṛṣṇa, and also for those aspiring for exclusive love for Kṛṣṇa. It nourishes the lives of the devotees, pleasing their hearts by fulfilling all their cherished desires for devotional service."

Concluding *Prapanna-jīvanāmṛtam,* Śrīla Śrīdhara Mahārāja writes, "Comprised of five nectars (*pañcāmṛtam*) respectively entitled *Upakramāmṛtam, Śrī Śāstra-vacanāmṛtam, Śrī Bhakta-vacanāmṛtam, Śrī Bhagavad-vacanāmṛtam,* and *Avaśeṣāmṛtam* (Prelude to Approaching Nectar, the Nectar of Scriptural Words, Words of Nectar from the Devotees, Words of Nectar from the Supreme Lord, and the Remnants of Nectar), the supreme fruit that gives life to the devotees and delights their hearts has been served in this book."

Sri Sri Gayatri-nigudhartha

Garuḍa Purāṇa states:

artho 'yaṁ brahma-sūtrānāṁ bhāratārtha-vinirṇayaḥ
gāyatrī-bhāṣya-rūpo' sau vedārtha-paribṛmhitaḥ

The meaning of the *Vedānta-sūtra* is present in *Śrīmad Bhāgavatam.* The full purport of the *Mahābhārata* is also

> there. The commentary of the *brahma-gāyatrī* is also there and fully expanded with all Vedic knowledge.

In his Sanskrit commentary on *brahma-gāyatrī (Śrī Gāyatrī-nigudhārtha)*, Śrīla Sridhara Mahārāja has uncovered the steps leading the *gāyatrī-mantra* to the *Śrīmad Bhāgavatam*. The conclusion is:

gayātrī-muralīṣṭa-kīrtana-dhanaṁ rādhā-padaṁ dhīmahi

> The *gāyatrī,* that has sprung from the flute sound of Śrī Kṛṣṇa, only sings the glories of Śrīmatī Rādhārāṇī.

gāyatrī-gaditaṁ mahāprabhu-mataṁ rādhā-padam dhīmahi

> The highest and innermost instruction of Śrī Caitanya Mahāprabhu is to engage yourself in the service of the lotus feet of Śrīmatī Rādhārāṇī through *saṅkīrtana.* Her lotus feet are to be your constant meditation.

Regarding the *Gāyatrī-nigudhārtha* of Śrīla Śrīdhara Mahārāja, Śrīla Bhakti Pramoda Purī Gosvāmī has said, "The explanation of *brahma-gāyatrī,* the mother of all *Vedas,* signifying devotional worship unto Śrīmati Rādhārāṇī, *śrī rādhānudhyāna-para* explanation, which was revealed in the depth of realization of Pūjyapāda Śrīdhara Deva Gosvāmī Mahārāja, possessed with the divine grace of Paramārādhya Śrī Śrīla Prabhupāda (Bhaktisiddhānta Sarasvatī Ṭhākura) upon his head—is deeply appreciated by those fortunate, intelligent devotees who are aware of the relishable beauty of pure devotional service."

Upon the transcendental appearance of *Śrī Gāyatrī-niguḍhārtha* from the pure heart of Śrīla Śrīdhara Mahārāja the Vaiṣṇava world of pure devotees rejoiced and danced in great ecstasy.

The Guardian of Devotion

The *sannyāsa* title of Śrīla Śrīdhara Mahārāja 'Bhakti Rakṣaka' means the Guardian of Devotion and this is something that Śrīla Śrīdhara Mahārāja lived up to in every sense of the word. From our personal experience we can honestly say that were it not for the presence of Śrīla Śrīdhara Mahārāja (after the disappearance of our Guru Mahāraja, Śrīla A.C. Bhaktivedānta Svāmī Prabhupāda) all would have been lost in darkness forever.

After the disappearance of Śrīla Prabhupāda, many misunderstandings and deceitful practices crept in amongst our Guru Mahārāja's disciples. At a time of great unrest and confusion, Śrīla Śrīdhara Mahārāja manifested before our eyes as the Guardian of Devotion and guided the devotees on the path to their greatest fortune.

As the keeper of the storehouse of life's greatest treasure, Śrīla Śrīdhara Mahārāja shared with us the unlimited wealth of Kṛṣṇa consciousness and manifested before us many self-effulgent gems (unrivalled conceptions of Gauḍīya *siddhānta*) to which he was heir. Many of those gems of theological conception have been presented in his books and have in time become *sūtras* (simple phrases with a deep philosophical purport) in the English language. Some of those *sūtras* are: The Search for Śrī Kṛṣṇa— Reality the Beautiful (the ultimate goal of life), *rādhā-dāsyam* (the service of Śrī Rādhā), The Line of Śrī Rūpa, (the ontological position of Śrī Rūpa Gosvāmī), The Golden Volcano of Divine Love (the ecstatic manifestation of Śrī Caitanya

Mahāprabhu as the giver of love of Kṛṣṇa), The Loving Search for the Lost Servant (Kṛṣṇa's loving search for His long lost servant), and *pūjala rāga-patha gaurava bhaṅge* (the motto of the followers of Śrīla Bhaktisiddhānta Sarasvatī Ṭhākura Prabhupāda that put forward the position to be taken by a devotee in the relativity of the Absolute).

Srimad Rupa-pada-rajah Prarthana-dasakam

Just prior to the withdrawal of his manifest *līlā*, Śrīla Bhaktisiddhānta Sarasvatī Ṭhākura Prabhupāda handed Śrīla Śrīdhara Mahārāja over to the holy lotus feet of Śrī Rūpa Gosvāmī by having him sing the prayer *Śrī Rūpa-mañjarī-pada*. The ontological position of Śrīla Śrīdhara Mahārāja became that of the storehouse keeper of life's greatest gift, that of the position of the servant, of the servant's servant, servant in the camp of Śrī Rūpa-mañjarī (*śrī-rūpānuga-varga*). His intense desire for the dust of the lotus feet of Śrī Rūpa Gosvāmī is beautifully expressed in his prayer, *Śrīmad Rūpa-pada-rajaḥ prārthanā-daśakam*.

Śrīla Śrīdhara Mahārāja humbly considered himself as a gatekeeper of the highest conception of *śrī rūpānuga-bhajana* and endeavored unwaveringly throughout his life to be faithful to the ideal and teachings of his Divine Master, Śrīla Bhaktisiddhānta Sarasvatī Ṭhākura Prabhupāda.

Svāmī B.G. Narasiṅgha

Introductory Nectar

(A Lecture given by Śrīla B. R. Śrīdhara Mahārāja at the opening ceremony of Māyāpura Candradayā Mandira, ISKCON, 1973)

This *āśrama* is being opened today. What is its position? In *Śrīmad Bhāgavatam* we find:

vanaṁ tu sāttviko vāso grāmo rājasa ucyate
tāmasam dyūta-sadanam man-niketaṁ tu nirguṇam

> Residence in the forest is in the mode of goodness, residence in a town is in the mode of passion, residence in a gambling house displays the quality of ignorance, and residence in a place where I (the Supreme Lord) reside is transcendental. (*Bhāg.* 11.25.25)

Vana-vāsa means plain living with the minimum of material things to help our life, that is *vana-vāsa.* It is a simple life, plain living and high thinking, but there also we are masters of that little thing, that *sattvika-vāsa.* It is most conducive to our religious life. There is no grandeur of any material enjoyment, etc. That is *sattvika-vāsa* or *vana-vāsa.*

Rājasa-vāsa is a life where one is engaged in various activities in the uplifting of society, the world and civilization. That is *rājasa,* where a maximum amount of energy is spent to improve the paraphernalia where we live to make us comfortable.

Tāmasa-vāsa dyūta-sadanam is a life without caring for any social life, only for the maximum amount of sense pleasure and minimum amount of giving to others, to society or any paraphernalia. It is a reckless life, a life in the clubhouse or hotel—something like that. It is irresponsible life—*tāmasa-vāsa dyūta-sadanam.*

Man-niketaṁ tu nirguṇam—if we spend our life in the house of the Lord, we may live in any amount of grandeur, or anything of the type—but still it is *nirguṇam,* because we are not masters there, we are servants.

In the *vana-vāsa,* we lead so simple a life with a minimum of material things with which we surround ourselves to live, but still there, we are masters to command others. Here we are all servants—everything is to be served. Whatever we shall see, all around, even a tree, even a creeper or even a particle of dust is to be served and is not to be enjoyed or renounced. That is the form of life, a life of worship, a life of devotion. It is not only to please the Lord but also all of His paraphernalia and to see that they are also serving the Supreme Entity. With this idea—to be a serving factor in the all-serving environment of the Lord—this is *man-niketaṁ tu nirguṇam.*

So, we have come here to a *nirguṇa* life, crossing all sorts of relativities of this material world, whatever conception it may be, and to learn that *īśāvāsyam idaṁ sarvaṁ,* the fundamental truth given in the *Īśopaniṣad,* that *īśāvāsyam idaṁ sarvaṁ*—everything here is the presence of the Supreme Entity, the Supreme Lord. With this conception we are to live in such a training house.

I was told that in *Back to Godhead* one gentleman wrote that the so-called universities, colleges, and schools are slaughter houses. I am very much pleased with this idea. Yes. They are nothing but slaughterhouses, and this sort of institution, that our Guru Mahārāja (Śrīla Bhaktisiddhānta Sarasvatī Ṭhākura Prabhupāda) has inaugurated in this world is to uplift us and all *jīvas* toward the worship and loving service of the Supreme Entity. Each is like an oasis in the desert. They are life-giving and not flattering institutions, like so many educational institutions that we find.

Sa vijña mammate jaya—where this sort of training comes, that goes towards the center, towards reality, towards beauty, towards harmony, towards a solution of life, towards nectar giving life—these institutions are only helpful and this is necessary.

Once Madana-mohāna Malaviya, a famous leader in the recent history of India, came to visit our Guru Mahārāja and after listening to his words he told, "Every village should have one center of your Divine Grace." But our Guru Mahārāja answered in return that, "I want to make everybody a temple of the Lord, every human being, every human body I want to make a temple therein, not only villages." So, that was his idea.

pṛthivīte āche yata nagarādi-grāma, sarvatra pracāra haibe mora nāma

With this idea he started his mission, Gauḍīya Maṭha, Gauḍīya Mission. And we are seeing that Svāmī Mahārāja (Śrīla A. C. Bhaktivedānta Svāmī Prabhupāda) by his grace, he is able to spread it around India and throughout the world and different continents. We are very happy to see new faces around us for the preaching purpose and spreading the news of Śrī Bhaktisiddhānta Sarasvatī Prabhupāda, Śrīla Bhaktivinoda Ṭhākura and Śrīman Mahāprabhu, and the vision of Śrī Kṛṣṇa and His beloved.

There are elevationists, there are renunciates, but we are servitors. *Gehaṁ juṣām api manasy udiyāt sadā naḥ*—true to the kindred point of the heaven and the heart. Cloister and the heart, the knowledge of these—but the heart has been made the cloister. The *gopī-bhajana* is to make the heart the cloister. Not that the cloister has a separate place. The heart is the cloister and this is only possible with the Kṛṣṇa conception of Godhead. All will be converted wholesale, every nook and corner. Nothing should be left out. No vacancy should be left out for any other purpose but to devote all respects to the Supreme Entity, to be faithful to the extreme. Nothing should be left. This is only possible in the Kṛṣṇa conception of Godhead (*akhila rasāmṛta mūrti*). All sorts of ecstasy, happiness, and everything of the type can be possible in its divine form when we find Śrī Kṛṣṇa as the Supreme Lord and nowhere else.

One western gentleman told that there are many conceptions of religion in different parts of the world, but we do not find any conception of religion where twenty-four hours can be devoted in the service of the Supreme Lord. Not only engaged on Sunday, not only twice in the day, not only thrice in the day, but every hour and second should be devoted in the service of the Supreme Entity and then nothing will be left behind. This sort of service is only possible in *kīrtanīya sadā hariḥ* and in the *aṣṭa-kālīya-līlā* of Śrī Kṛṣṇacandra Himself in the *mādhurya-rasa.*

Śrī Caitanyadeva came down to this world to preach that, to give that nectarine life to one and all. *Nṛmātrasy-ādhikāritā*—take the Name of the Lord and you will find yourself in His harem one day. For religion, money is not necessary, physical energy in great quantity is not necessary, nor are other helping things necessary. Only try to take the Name sincerely. It should be acquired through the right channel, otherwise there will be some disturbance tampering with it. Trade in the name of religion is also going on here and there, and we should save ourselves from those difficulties by following a bona-fide path.

So, on the day of the advent of Śrī Kṛṣṇa Caitanya, which means serving Kṛṣṇa in all aspects, this laudable attempt is being done in great quantity by our Svāmī Mahārāja. We are very happy to get the chance to attend this function. Svāmī Mahārāja ki jaya!

Part One

Divine Conception

Divine Conception

Bhaktivinoda Ṭhākura pressed Prabhupāda (Śrīla Bhaktisiddhānta Sarasvatī Ṭhākura) to take up the trade of propaganda of Mahāprabhu. At first Prabhupāda did not like it, he thought he would go on with his own life of *bhajana* and the special cultivation, the reading of scriptures and writing. In this way he will pass his life. But Bhaktivinoda Ṭhākura requested and chastised him, "Do you think that Mahāprabhu needs that enjoyment? Without caring for the service of Mahāprabhu, do you want to be a renunciationist? That will be Māyāvāda, apathetic to the duties of Mahāprabhu. That will be Māyāvāda, so don't indulge yourself in such things—indifference to the words of Mahāprabhu." That was Bhaktivinoda Ṭhākura's instruction.

Bhaktivinoda Ṭhākura departed, Gaura-kiśora Dāsa Bābājī departed, and the words of Bhaktivinoda gave Prabhupāda pressure that, "My gurus did not wish that I should simply go on with the studies of philosophy and thoughts with the books, and the Name. They wanted me to do some service for the society, serve this line of Mahāprabhu and show the people what to do." Then Prabhupāda was appealing to the Lord, to Mahāprabhu. "What sort of preaching do You want from me?" When that preaching tendency became irresistible in his heart, he though, "What should I do?"

Then he found a piece of paper that was carried by the wind before him. It was a torn piece of *Śrī Caitanya-caritāmṛta* in which Mahāprabhu requested Sanātana Gosvāmī to take up these four *sevās:*

kṛṣṇa-bhakti, kṛṣṇa-prema-sevā-pravartana
lupta-tīrtha-uddhāra, āra vairāgya-śikṣaṇa

> You will also have to explain Kṛṣṇa's devotional service, establish centers for cultivation of love of Kṛṣṇa, excavate lost places of pilgrimage and teach people how to adopt the renounced order. (*Cc. Antya* 4.80)

Birth of the Gaudiya Matha

So he took it as a divine arrangement that, "I am also to follow the advice Caitanyadeva gave to Sanātana." Then Prabhupāda took up these four endeavors. "Bhaktivinoda Ṭhākura, Bābājī Mahārāja, Mahāprabhu—they all want me to take up these four things and go on with them." But then he thought, "How is it to be practically translated?"

Sakhī-caraṇa Bābu told me that Prabhupāda was almost alone at that time in Caitanya Maṭha. When Sakhī Bābu and Kuñja Bābu (who later became Bhakti Vilāsa Tīrtha Mahārāja), went to see him after the *samādhi* of his Gurudeva, Gaura-kiśora Dāsa Bābājī, Sakhī Bābu told that he was trying his best to make someone understand him. His face became red—of course he was speaking Bengali and they were also Bengalis, but they couldn't understand what he said. Sakhī Bābu told, "Speaking with great emotion, his face became red and sometimes he would slap the table and we felt that he wanted to tell us something immediately. But we couldn't understand properly because we were callous, yet he was not discouraged, and went on with his strong sentiment."

Later in Calcutta in 1933, I also observed that a reddish hue came from his body and face while he was dictating some introductory essays for the Harmonist to the editor, Professor Sanyal. I felt that his face resembled a type of lotus which is white and red. His animated talking inspired the movements of his blood circulation in such a way that sometimes the red color appeared on his face like the petals of a lotus.

So, when Kuñja Bābu joined, Prabhupāda saw him as a divine agent. "I am a philosophically-minded man and may not like any practical connection with worldly people, perhaps this man is sent to make the breech between my philosophical mind and the public mind." Kuñja Bābu practically did that function. He used to bring the public, the educated public to Prabhupāda and manage them. And Prabhupāda would deliver a lecture about the philosophy of Mahāprabhu.

In this way the mission began. Kuñja Bābu took the responsibility of necessary arrangements. He hired a house in Calcutta with the help of four other godbrothers. Four members came for the program and one room was spared upstairs for Prabhupāda.

These four disciples used to supply the *prasāda* for Prabhupāda. In this way the Calcutta *maṭha*, Bhaktivinoda Āsana, began. Then gradually others joined and Tīrtha Mahārāja, the disciple of Bhaktivinoda Ṭhākura, took *sannyāsa* from Prabhupāda. Then, first with one *sannyāsī* and the other three or four, some *gṛhastha*, some *brahmacārī*, the propaganda began. Before that, Prabhupāda and Bhaktivinoda Ṭhākura prepared one monthly *Sajjana-toṣaṇī*, and Prabhupāda continued editing that after him, and gradually he began with the *Gauḍīya*.

Then gradually, *Nadīyā-prakāśa, Paramārthī, Bhāgavata, Kīrtana, Harmonist*—all these periodicals were published. Many batches were sent this side, that side, across the country, to preach the doctrine of Mahāprabhu. In this way the Gauḍīya Maṭha expanded.

Sridhara Maharaja Joins

At first sight I found Guru Mahārāja's attitude was that of complete indifference to the ordinary world. "He does not care for anyone, he is self-sufficient." I had that sort of impression from first sight. Then I began visiting and gradually came to realize that I wanted to stay in such company.

I came from a *brāhmaṇa* family and from a Śākta family also, a *paṇḍita* family who had much experience, and much calculation about *Manu-śāstra, Purāṇa, śruti,* all these things. But why did I leave that paraphernalia and come here? I am a *brāhmaṇa,* my Guru Mahārāja came from a caste which is lower. So, I had some hesitation in the beginning.

One day I was returning from the office and I found a red-colored placard in Chittaranjan Avenue—'Gauḍīya Maṭha Mahotsava for one month.' The address was given near the Pareśanātha Temple. I thought, "Gauḍīya Maṭha must be Mahāprabhu's followers, let me go and see what is there." When I was a law student, through Sureśa Bhaṭṭācārya, I had met the founder of the Bhārata-Sevāśrama, Svāmī Prāṇavānanda. He tried his best to take me into his mission, but I flatly refused.

"My head is sold to Mahāprabhu, so I can't go anywhere else."

He said, "I also have great reverence for Mahāprabhu Śrī Caitanyadeva, but I think the first stage must be Buddhistic abnegation or *vairāgya* and indifference to the world. Second, Śaṅkara's *Vedānta* or *jñāna.* And the last and highest will be Caitanya's *prema*—otherwise people will misunderstand that *prema* to be lust."

I replied, "Yes, what you say is alright—that Śrī Caitanyadeva's *prema-dharma* is the highest, above the Buddhistic and Śaṅkarite conceptions. Bur Śrī Caitanyadeva has not told us, 'First go to the Buddhists and practice *vairāgya,* and then go to Śaṅkara and have knowledge of the *Vedānta,* and then come to Me.' He has told that, "Wherever you are, take the association of a *sādhu* and take the Holy Name." Svāmī Prāṇavānanda was silenced.

I asked him, "If you have any supernatural powers I would be grateful if you could tell me where my spiritual guide can be found." He gave the name of some gentleman, Haranātha and I went to search for him but could not find him. Then I found that placard and went to the Gauḍīya Maṭha. There I found only one gentleman manning the outside hall—the rest had all gone on *nagara-saṅkīrtana.* I had a little talk with that gentleman. I had studied something about Caitanyadeva and other scriptures, but I found that these people representing the *maṭha* had deeper and more sound knowledge than I. Then, the party came back from *nagara-saṅkīrtana* and I found Guru Mahārāja in front with his *daṇḍa.* As soon as he reached the front of the *maṭha,* some disciple came and took the *daṇḍa* from him and gradually he was received there.

In Calcutta I had some interaction. I was waiting after taking afternoon *prasādam.* Prabhupāda was walking on the roof and I was standing there with a greedy look towards that side. Only one attendant was there. Prabhupāda asked through the attendant, "He has come here, perhaps he has something to say." *Kichu vaktavya*? He came and asked me, "Have you anything to say?"

"No, I have nothing to say." He went to Prabhupāda and reported, "He said he has nothing to say."

"He has something to enquire?" He again came and asked. I said, "No, no enquiry."

Again he went to Prabhupāda and said, "He has not come for enquiry." Then Prabhupāda said to him, "He has some purpose for which he has come here?"

Again he came and posed me that question. "Some purpose you have?"

"Yes, when I have come without any purpose, nothing can happen. Of course, I have some purpose."

"What is that purpose?"

I told, "I have come to get your grace, your *prasādam. Āpnāra prasannatā*—I have come for your grace."

Prabhupāda was satisfied, and touched by this he asked me, "Who are you? Where is your home?" In this way there was some discussion and he remarked, "You are fortunate, you have taken birth in Gauḍa-maṇḍala area." I said, "Yes, it is so." Then he offered a small pamphlet, *Gauḍīya Maṭha Ki Korena*—'What Does the Gauḍīya Maṭha Do?' I said, "I already have it." That devotee said, "No, when Prabhupāda is giving it to you, it has a different value. "Alright," so I took it and touched it to my head and kept it. That connection was there. After that I visited the *maṭha* regularly and heard their talks.

The following year I was invited to the appearance observance of Mahāprabhu in Māyāpura. At that time my mother was inviting me to come see her before she went to Haridvāra for the Kumbha-melā. She might not live—her health was not good. I thought that I want to take up the life on this side, so I must give preference here. That is, I avoided the request of my mother and went to the Gauḍīya Maṭha instead.

I attended the birth festival of Mahāprabhu at Yogapīṭha. There I found Prabhupāda delivering a lecture and some judges, advocates had come from Kṛṣṇanagara. They were asking questions and Prabhupāda was answering. And in another place, Bhakti Pradīpa Tīrtha Mahārāja was speaking about the birth ceremony of Mahāprabhu. Bhakti Svarūpa Parvata Mahārāja was collecting donations and writing receipts. There was *kīrtana* in one place with ardent appeal. *Caitanya-caritāmṛta* verses were chanted there. It was a hive of activity. I felt a transcendental happy atmosphere here—all these things captured my mind. But I was still hesitating, what to do?

Then, when I was attending Prabhupāda's lecture, suddenly his eyes came towards me. Prabhupāda remarked, "Oh, this young man has come from such-and-such place. He should be given a little attention." Then many came to me, "Who are you? What is your object?" They gave some attention to me. The next day, after the Gaura-janmotsava ceremony was over, in the morning Prabhupāda was sitting in a canvas chair and so many others were surrounding him. Some were giving *daṇḍavats* and going away—taking leave to go home. Then Prabhupāda began saying, "*Apānarā āmāke vañcanā kariben nā*—You should not deceive me!" Prabhupāda announced. My ear was very acute and I thought, "Where is the question of deception?"

"You came to me with the understanding that you have come for the service of Kṛṣṇa and with that idea I also accepted you as my friends. Now you have attended this particular ceremony only as a fashion and you are going away again, back into family life. I feel that I am being cheated."

"Get Out of the Charm!"

Prabhupāda went on, "If you say 'I have some urgent business, I am coming, I am only finishing a little job.' No, no! There is nothing that should detain you there in your family duties. Even if anyone says that, 'A fire is there, please allow me to extinguish the fire and I will come back.' No! That is also not necessary. What the fire will burn is not your own. Rather, your necessity is to get out of the charm of what the fire burns. All your internal engagement is with Kṛṣṇa. The internal demand in your *ātma*, in your soul, all can be satisfied by Kṛṣṇa—nowhere else. You may find there the wholesale engagement of your self and you should leave this mal-engagement as soon as possible."

He was speaking very forcefully and that captured my heart. "Oh, such a degree to which the service of Kṛṣṇa is so much imperative to us, that even the whole world is reduced to ashes, it is no harm to us." All our demands can only be fulfilled by Kṛṣṇa. This is our relation with Kṛṣṇa. Such an extreme statement of fact, of the spiritual necessity. I won't hear this anywhere else, but I heard it there with such intense necessity for the service of Kṛṣṇa. So I had my determination that, "I shall come here for my whole life!" I decided on that day.

"All of your inner hankering you may fulfill in the holy feet of Kṛṣṇa. Kṛṣṇa can satisfy all your inner hankerings. And this environment to which you give so much importance is your enemy. That has kept you away from Kṛṣṇa consciousness. Your real place, proper home, it is here." So he told this in such a way that I sold my life there in the service of Kṛṣṇa. Such a degree of intensity I have never seen, I never thought it was possible—that in the present world we should serve Kṛṣṇa, not losing even a second. The whole world may be burning to ashes, I do not lose .anything. On the other side, if I get out of that snare, that snare of affection, then I am saved. All my hankerings can be satisfied in detail only in the service of Kṛṣṇa—my inner hankering. Never and nowhere else can that be found. I sold my head there. Everything!

Now the thought came to me, "What's to stop me from coming and staying here?" I cast my glance homeward—father gone, mother living, three younger brothers—they won't be much affected. But my wife will be affected. I don't know why, but a sudden thought came in my mind that, "If she dies, I am free." This thought came. I was attracted by the association at the *maṭha*—so many gentlemanly and educated members, and wholly dedicated to the service of Mahāprabhu. That attracted me the most.

And it was that very day, I came to my quarters and found that my wife was ill. I came home that night, and after three days she passed away. My mother tried to have me marry again, but she could not do so. And within six months she also disappeared in Haridvāra.

So when she passed, I went home and completed her *śrāddha* and after finishing that I came, in the last part of April, to join the *maṭha*. At first, I said that my two younger brothers would finish their studies and take to their vocations, and then I would leave them and join. But Śrīpāda Bhāratī Maharāja and others said that I had a great opportunity.

They pressed, "No, no! Kṛṣṇa has taken your wife, and Kṛṣṇa has taken your mother. He has done enough for you. Really if you neglect to avail yourself of this chance, perhaps some other obstacle will come and this life will be spoiled with no hope." I asked, "What are you saying?" They said, "Come immediately." I took that advice and joined immediately. I was living together with my two brothers in a hostel, and they came with me. They went back crying—I remained in the *maṭha*.

No Defeat Anywhere

I came for the ideal, not caring for the form. The Gauḍīya Maṭha in those days did not have much grandeur. It started in a hired house in Calcutta. The Caitanya Maṭha was almost half-jungle. Many other places were all hired houses mostly. So, there was no grandeur. But the beauty of the thought, the beauty of the idea, that quarter—no compromise in the philosophy. No slacking of this. There was more and more intense earnestness, even until now. That is the truth, the goal, the destination, the point of perfection. Not only within us, but also without. So many different discussions and opposition were there but we didn't think that we were defeated at any time. We were the conquerors and there was no defeat anywhere. I am speaking on these things by the grace of Guru Mahārāja.

In 1926 on Janmāṣṭamī day I first went to Gauḍīya Maṭha, and 1927 on Mahāprabhu's birthday I settled that I would throw myself, my fate, to Gauḍīya Maṭha. In April of 1927 I took *hari-nāma* and in July I got *dīkṣā*. In September of 1930 I accepted *sannyāsa*—three years after.

At first, I was requested to do some service in the press but I had no liking for press work, proofreading etc. I had much liking for the preaching, to go out on *nagara-saṅkīrtana* and preaching. So, next I was sent on a preaching tour. The first stop was in Ḍumurkondā *maṭha* in Bengal and from there to Benares and then Vṛndāvana—we were sometimes doing *nagara-kīrtana*. After that the Delhi *maṭha* was founded and there we did collection from door to door and I was put in charge. The spirit of preaching was very great at that time. Then the Kurukṣetra *maṭha* was established and I was in charge there. Kurukṣetra was a solitary place at that time. First Delhi, and then Kurukṣetra. We also visited Simla and other places for preaching. And much collecting we did—in this way I passed about two or three years. Then again I came back here, every year we came back to the Calcutta *maṭha* for a one month celebration in August.

I was called from UP to join the Madras party. Then I was sent to the South to Rāmānanda Prabhu's place on the Godāvarī River and then Madras. Before that my name was Rāmendrasundara Bhaṭṭācarya, but Prabhupāda converted my name into Rāmānanda Dāsa—he converted my name and sent me in a party with four other devotees to discover the place of Rāmānanda and Caitanya *saṁvāda* on the Godāvarī. In the party were Vana Mahārāja, myself, a new *sannyāsī* Bhaktisāra Mahārāja, Hayagrīva Brahmacārī (later known as Bhakti Dayita Mādhava Mahārāja) and Harijana Brahmacārī, a cook. Vana Mahārāja gave the opinion that the lecture I delivered by his request in Rajamundry at that time— "Was his best speech ever—it was very substantial and impressive."

That divine talk between Rāmānanda and Mahāprabhu Śrī Caitanyadeva is a unique thing in the whole of the philosophical world—a revolutionary revelation about the wealth of the spiritual world. Beginning from *varṇāśrama* it shows the gradual development when coming in connection with God, step by step, how we can approach Him. "This is superficial, this is superficial, this is also superficial—go deeper, go deeper." In this way the progress has been traced there, in the theological development. "Yes, here it begins... go further. Yes, it is also good... go further. Yes, this is a satisfactory position... still further. Yes, I agree, this is the highest. Is there anything else beyond this, above this? Please come out with that." In this way, by gradation it has been given to us—this is very helpful to understand what is theism.

Once, I went for collection when we were building the *maṭha* at the place of *Rāmānanda-saṁvāda*. One man told that, "There is a big *zamindar* who has a case in the court of Justice Balarāma of the Rāmānuja *sampradāya*. If you get a word from the judge, that man can help you substantially." Both Hayagrīva Brahmacārī and myself approached Justice Balarāma and said, "We want money for building Rāmānanda Gauḍīya Maṭha on the banks of the Godāvarī. We are out to collect funds. We are told that one *zamindar* may contribute something substantial, and if you kindly speak to him then we may be successful."

"Do you request me to do this, Svāmījī? His case is in my court and he will expect something from me in return. Would you advise me to do this, Svāmījī?"

I replied, "Yes, because in your *sampradāya* such examples are there for *vaiṣṇava-sevā* and for *guru-sevā*—we hold that this post is given by the Lord to you. And if you utilize your position for the service of the Lord, then there will be no bad consequences. In your *sampradāya,* we find that the Raṅganātha temple was built by dacoits, and one lady, risking her chastity, served the Vaiṣṇavas and guru. So ordinary moral rules have nothing to do with the service of God. It is *sva-janam ārya-pathaṁ ca hitvā*—crossing the law of the country, and even society, the absolute call of service to the Lord should be attended to."

Then he said, "Yes, I shall do it." And that gentleman put a word to the *zamindar* who did what we wanted.

Some time later, the Deities were installed there by Prabhupāda. I founded that *pada-pīṭha mandira,* and a separate *mandira* was established afterwards. We put a plaque there with an inscription:

śāke' bde 'gniguṇā-gamendu-vimite godāvarī-ghāṭake
śrī caitanya-dayānidheḥ pada-yugaṁ bhaktārcitaṁ saṁvabho
śrī siddhānta sarasvatīha paramo-haṁsaḥ padāṅkaṁ prabhoḥ
gaurābde nidadhe yugāśrama-yuge gauḍīya-saṁrakṣakaḥ

At this time, on the banks of the Godāvarī, the feet of Śrī Caitanya (Who is an ocean of mercy) are being worshiped by the devotees. The Lord's footprints have been established by *paramahaṁsa* Śrī Siddhānta Sarasvatī, the protector of the Gauḍīya *sampradāya.*

After returning from the preaching tour from Godāvarī, then I was given *sannyāsa,* by the recommendation of Vana Mahārāja.

Vana Mahārāja came back and told, "He is not a good canvasser but he is a good preacher. He can speak *hari-kathā* well on a philosophical basis, on the basis on the teachings of Śrī Caitanya." And then Prabhupāda gave me *sannyāsa*.

Sridhara, Sridhara

When my *sannyāsa* name was given, Prabhupāda was thinking of my name, and he whispered 'Śrīdhara, Śrīdhara.' I heard it— 'Śrīdhara'—*bhaktyeka-rakṣakaḥ*. Jīva Gosvāmī has given this title to Śrīdhara Svāmī, *bhaktyeka-rakṣakaḥ*. That *ekara, bhaktyeka-rakṣakaḥ* is four letters. Generally Prabhupāda would give 'Bhakti' and then three letters, like 'Bhakti Vinoda.' That was his inner inspiration. 'Bhakti Vinoda,' 'Bhakti Siddhānta,' all three letters. So, *Bhaktyeka-rakṣakaḥ*—many letters. *Bhaktyeka-rakṣakaḥ, Bhaktyeka-rakṣakaḥ*. He pronounced twice, four times, like this and then declared 'Bhakti Rakṣaka Śrīdhara.' That name.[1]

Bagh Bazaar *maṭha* was opened in that year, 1930, in the end of September or beginning of October with a one month festival. Before that the Calcutta *maṭha* was in a rented house in Ulṭādāṅgā. The Deities were moved to the new *maṭha* in a chariot procession.

After that Prabhupāda went on installing those *pāda-pīṭha* in Maṅgalagiri and many other places in the south. Then again I was sent towards Madras side for preaching. Then Prabhupada declared the opening of the Madras Gauḍīya Maṭha, and he put us there and rented us a house. Vana Mahārāja was the leader and the senior *sannyāsī*, and we began preaching there for three or four years.

During this time, Prabhupāda felt that it was necessary to send a party to preach in the west. In his lifetime he could not send anyone to America, but he wrote in the *Gauḍīya* magazine, *'markina-loka'*—that he would like to send some preachers to

America. Before he sent his party to England he consulted with Rabindranath Tagore since he had already gone around the world and was a Nobel Prize winner. Rabindranath thought that Germany had the best prospect for preaching. "The English are too proud because they have a king and we are their subjects. Generally the British have this concept that they are the king-nation and we are the subject-nation, therefore they won't give much attention to our words. America has been polluted by so many other Indian preachers of *yoga* and other things."

Rabindranath did not have much regard for Vivekānanda and the Ramakrishna Mission. When Vivekānanda went to America he used to show many *yoga-āsanas,* especially amongst the women, so Indian *sādhus* had a bad name in America at that time. "The Americans will easily take things up and show appreciation, but the environment is not favorable at this point in time because a few gentlemen have come from India and misrepresented Indian culture—so I don't recommend that you go there. Also the French very easily take something up, but give up that thing just as easily. If you ask my opinion, then, I would say that you should send your men to Germany because the Germans are a considerate people. They have a general appreciation for ancient Indian culture, and whatever they accept, they do not reject it so easily. They are much more stable." So this is what he recommended. So anyhow, Prabhupāda managed to send a party headed by Vana Mahārāja to England and from there they traveled to Germany.

When Vana Mahārāja left for England, I was put in charge of the Madras *maṭha* and the temple was constructed mostly in my time. We stayed there for some time and from there I collected funds from the Rāja of Jaipura (Orissa) for the Madras temple. And there is also a history to this. A new man had been appointed Diwan of Jaipura and that was an *adivāsī* (original primitive inhabitants) area, so the British introduced there a special sort of rule. The Diwan is more powerful than the King. I came from Madras with some recommendation from the officiating Chief Justice, Mr. Ramaswami, who gave a letter of recommendation to the Rāja of Jaipura. Then the Rāja promised to pay the cost of the Madras temple, but the Diwan, a new man, said, "No, no, it is impossible." The Rāja always needed the approval of the Diwan—"He will pay the money to you, not myself. So you go to consult him. I am only giving my signature, but the money will be paid by him, so meet him."

I heard that he was, at heart, an atheistic man, so I hesitated to approach him. "No, you are King, you are master, so you will pay, that is better in this way." But he pressed me very much, "No, you will have to go to meet the Diwan." Then, when I met the Diwan, he said just the opposite, "Oh, no, I am the last man to pay you the amount needed to build the temple at Madras. If you would build it here (Jaipura), then I could consider the case, that there would be some local benefit of a temple here. But if any money we can get in excess, I must give it to help the poor and unfed *adivāsīs* here. That must be used for that cause, but not for this luxury, of constructing a temple, and that also in Madras town. Go there and collect funds and construct your temple there." In this way he spoke. Then I thought that it is a hopeless case, so drastic medicine must be applied. I came out with this *śloka* of *Bhāgavatam*:

vikrīḍitam vraja-vadhūbhir idam ca viṣṇoḥ
śraddhānvito 'nuśṛṇuyād atha varṇayed yaḥ
bhaktiṁ parāṁ bhagavati pratilabhya kāmaṁ
hṛd-rogam āśv-apahinoty acireṇa dhīraḥ

> Anyone who faithfully hears or describes the Lord's playful affairs with the young *gopīs* of Vṛndāvana will attain the Lord's pure devotional service. Thus he will quickly become sober and conquer lust, the disease of the heart. (*Bhāg.* 10.33.39)

"I thought that you want to help the *adivāsīs.* I also want to help the *adivāsīs.* But, your help is in a particular way, my help for them is in another way. It has been told in the scripture by Śukadeva Gosvāmī, that to hanker for a thing, that is heart disease (*hṛd-rogam*)—it is mentioned in the *Bhāgavatam,* the *kāmam, hṛd-rogam,* I want this, I want that, I want thousands, I want crores, millions. That is heart disease and not real. When I was a hog, I devoured a hillock of stool, but my hunger was not abated. When I was an elephant I finished a whole forest, but my hunger was not finished. So hunger can never be finished in this way—I want more and more."

"Many have amassed millions, but still they are not satisfied. So this is heart disease. Śukadeva Gosvāmī in *Bhāgavatam* has given the medicine for this, *vikrīḍitam.* When you can accommodate the Absolute to have His full play, unrestrictively, He has the use, His ownership is with everything, every atom, if you can accommodate such a conception of the environment, of the Absolute, then we can become free of this heart disease." The man was impressed. Tears came to his eyes, "Svāmījī, I believe in God." I said, "Your eyes are giving evidence to that." "I shall pay your money, but not just now. You go to Madras, I shall pay." Then he paid the money and the Madras temple was constructed by that. In this way we served several years there.

My preaching was not that of a false canvasser, but straight dealing—dealing with the plain truth. I did not do any coaxing or use indirect ways, flattery, or sweet words to somehow rob the man—but straight talk, straight dealing in my presentation. My guide was this, "Why have I come here? What sentiment brought me here? I should try my best to represent that to them. This is the cause for preaching—you must appreciate such cause. I have got appreciation in this line, and I don't think that I am wrong." At every moment I think I'm justified to accept this principle and to march on in this line.

Europe Defeated by Asia

The Bombay *maṭha* was opened and for some time I did service there. Vana Mahārāja came to Bombay, returning from preaching in England with two German gentleman, Herr Schulze (later Sadānanda Dāsa) and one other German gentleman.

This German godbrother, Herr Schulze, was taken to a concentration camp during World War II because he had German nationality. At that time, one European gentleman, Walter Eidlitz, was also taken into prison and they were in the same room, both of them stayed for a long time. This Walter Eidlitz wrote in his book *Unknown India,* about his time in the containment camps and his conversion to Vaiṣṇavism. From Schulze he heard many things—he received many instructions about Gauḍīya Vaiṣṇavism and he was converted.

When he came out, Schulze took him to Vana Mahārāja and he took initiation from him. Then he went to Europe and he preached— I heard he was a very eloquent speaker. He preached very widely especially in Italy, Norway and Sweden. Perhaps he took his nationality in Sweden, a neutral country—he lived there and was preaching about Gaura-Nityānanda—so much so that one Bengali gentleman, after attending his meeting in Italy, came here and described that, "You say that the whole world will be converted to Gauḍīya Vaiṣṇavism and this is not impossible because I saw with my own eyes in Italy, this gentleman was delivering his lecture in a big assembly and sometimes in the middle of his lecture he would shout, "*Nitāi-Gaura! Gaura-Nityānanda ki jaya!*" and the whole assembly will cry, "*Gaura-Nityānanda ki jaya!*"

"I saw with my own eyes, this thing in Italy. So I think that when you say that one day the whole world will come under the banner of Gaura-Nityānanda—it may not be impossible," this one gentleman told this. So he was a good speaker and a very energetic man and he was preaching in such a way—I heard this from different sources.

I asked Svāmī Mahārāja, "Have you come across that gentleman who was so much eager for Gaura-Nityānanda? Is he living or dead?" Svāmī Mahārāja said, "I don't know about him. Perhaps he is dead." I had told him already that this man was, "Very energetic and a very pushing man, and he was preaching very sincerely." I got this information from different sources. So I said to Svāmī Mahārāja that, "You please try to find him out and he will help you a great deal perhaps."

This Schulze had much affection for me. When he came I was in Bombay. Vana Mahārāja came with two German gentlemen, this Herr Schulze, a good scholar who was conversant in eight European languages, and the son of a baron.

I was at that time in charge of the Bombay *maṭha* and Svāmī Mahārāja was also there and Madhusūdana Mahārāja, he was also there at that time. I went to receive them from the ship and took them along to our *maṭha*. Then at a round table we took our seat—Schulze, Vana Mahārāja, Svāmī Mahārāja, myself—perhaps four or five, in a round table conference. It was said, "Oh, there, this orthodox fashion doesn't work. That is another type of land. This orthodox formality is blind faith—that cannot be pushed there. They have their own understanding, their own philosophy. They have so many questions which cannot be answered." But I was already a student of philosophy, so I knew both the philosophy of the atheist and of the theist. I had my strong position on the side of the theist. I challenged—"Tell me what are their questions that cannot be answered—they might be atheists of the worst type, but I think I can reply to any of the questions of the atheist class." So the argument began and at last the opposition was defeated.

Svāmī Mahārāja spoke aloud, "Here, Europe is defeated by Asia!" and Schulze, that German scholar, was very minutely watching the discussion. Anyhow, he was able to catch certain points of Gauḍīya Vaiṣṇavism and he had some special affection for me also.

After that, I was freed from there and went with the general party with Prabhupāda, always staying with Prabhupāda and preaching here and there in different places in Bengal. In this way we passed 1936 and 1937. In 1937, in the morning Prabhupāda left. Before this, Prabhupāda wanted me to go for preaching to London, but I told that, "I am not fit, I can't follow their intonation and I can't mix freely with them, so I will pray for the success of that preaching, but I won't be able to show any satisfactory work myself, but, if you order, I must go." Then he sent Gosvāmī Mahārāja instead of me and when Prabhupāda was sick I attended his sick bed.

At that time, some of the *sannyāsīs* showed much reverence to me, "What is this? That which so many persons are eager to take, you reject this chance? You neglect to take advantage of such a position, that you will be a world preacher. You have no hankering for that?" I told, "Yes Mahārāja, I have no hankering for such position. My only humble ambition is that I may be reckoned as a sincere devotee of Mahāprabhu, Śrī Caitanyadeva. No other ambition I have in my mind to become a world preacher and so on. So, this is my nature—I want truth and I hope, I crave for the mercy of the Vaiṣṇavas and you all, that I may not have any ambition but to be the humblest, most humble servant of the Lord and that I may not be misguided."

Sastra-nipuna

In Madras, in *The Gauḍīya*, the leading weekly paper, there was published one calendar. The editor mistook the birthday of Viṣṇupriyā-devī and the birthday of our Guru Mahārāja. Prabhupāda appeared on *kṛṣṇa-pañcamī* and Viṣṇupriyā-devī appeared on *śukla-pañcamī.* One is dark moon and one is bright moon. Viṣṇupriyā-devī is on the bright moon and Prabhupāda the dark moon. But he had it just the opposite. What I read, I read carefully. I caught it, "What is this standard? The basis is off and his philosophy, why *krsna-śakti* has come on the bright moon and the *gaura-śakti* has appeared on the dark moon." I found it just the opposite. I showed it to Vana Mahārāja. "What is this? This is diametrically off."

Another thing. Prabhupāda published *Rāya Rāmānanda.* There it is mentioned that, when Mahāprabhu is going to Vṛndāvana, Rūpa-Sanātana met Him on the way. I knew it clearly that it was when Mahāprabhu was coming back that He met Rūpa-Sanātana. I related, "What is this?" I said, "This is written in the name of Prabhupāda and you did not look out for it? It is just the opposite. When Mahāprabhu was coming back they met and not when He was going towards Vṛndāvana." Then the editor said, "Oh, I can't find out hundreds of mistakes and you are a very great man." I did not relate these and other mistakes to Prabhupāda, but they must have come to his notice, that Śrīdhara Mahārāja detected all these things. So, on the Vyāsa Pūjā occasion, Prabhupāda printed one written address and there he mentioned before my name '*Śāstra-nipuṇa* Śrīdhara Mahārāja'—that he has very deep knowledge of the scriptures.

Before this, I composed a Sanskrit poem about Bhaktivinoda Ṭhākura and Prabhupāda was very happy to read this. When I first showed it to him he remarked, "A very happy style." Then next I heard, he told to Śrautī Mahārāja that, "This poem is so fine, it is not written by him, it is written by Bhaktivinoda Ṭhākura himself, through him. It is very nice." Then once he told to Aprākṛta Prabhu (Bhakti Sāraṅga Gosvāmī), that, "I am satisfied, that after me, what I came to say, that will remain. I find in this *śloka* the *siddhānta*."

Admission to Rupa-manjari Rasa.

In October 1936, some of us went to Purī and stayed in Puruṣottama Maṭha at Caṭaka Parvata, where Guru Mahārāja had a small bungalow. He was very fond of hearing that *śloka* of Dāsa Gosvāmī–*nija nikaṭa nivāsaṁ dehi govardhana tvam*. Every day that was sung before him, and also *Śrī Rūpa-mañjarī-pada sei mora sampada*—this song was sung by Yāyāvara Mahārāja who came there and lived for some time.

At that time, Aprākṛta Prabhu was preparing to go to London for preaching. In Khurda station Guru Mahārāja placed his own garland on him and told him, "If anyone there desires to take *hari-nāma*, I grant you permission to give that."

Then after a month Guru Mahārāja returned to Calcutta, and our party was sent to Cuttack for collecting. A few days later we received the information that his health was deteriorating, and we also went to Calcutta. There, we attended his sickbed. My duty was from 2am to 4am.

Just one day before Prabhupāda's departure he called for me and asked me to chant *Śrī Rūpa-mañjarī-pada* and at that time I was not sitting in the front. I was hesitating, but, I had to chant *Śrī Rūpa-mañjarī-pada*. And the others told that Prabhupāda has given you admission to Śrī Rūpa-mañjarī *rasa*. You have been given admission thereby to the *rasa-sevā* section.

Sri Caitanya Sarasvata Matha

After the disappearance of Guru Mahārāja, the trustees appointed by him made a governing body. The tenth day after his departure a governing body was constructed, but many problems developed which could not be solved, litigation was going on and some stalwart godbrothers had been jailed. I could not leave like a coward, but after a year the case was settled and our godbrothers were released. I thought, "I tried my best to purify the mission according to my conscience but it was not to be," so I left the mission and went outside to try to purify the mission according to my ability. That was my mentality. But many stalwarts said, "No, we can't tolerate the present impure position of the Gauḍīya Maṭha." I was indifferent and they were fighting.

I went to Vṛndāvana leaving the association of the *maṭha*—I wouldn't fight. They tried their best to keep me with them, but I told, "No, it is not possible for me to remain in the association of these worldly elements." Then I went to Govardhana and stayed in Vṛndāvana for a month, finishing the Kārttika vow there. I took *govardhana-śilā* and came here to Navadvīpa and hired a house for two rupees a month. And here I began my life.

On coming from Vṛndāvana I met my previous brother, Mani Bābu and asked him to pay ten rupees to me for a few months. He agreed and he gave two or three months money and with that I came here. Then gradually others tried their best to find out where I was, and at last they found me. Then they began to come and go, and sometimes help me—in this way it was going on. Sakhī-caraṇa Bābu secured this plot with his own money, and here I began my hearts service in that cottage. In 1942, on Ratha-yatra day, I entered the cottage here with *govardhana-śīlā.*

At the same time when I was in the thatched hut, some 40 years back I wrote a poem. We wrote that one day, the flag of Śrī Caitanya Sārasvata Maṭha will flutter very high on Gupta-govardhana, on the banks of Nadīyā. *Śrīmac-caitanya sārasvata maṭhavara*—that poem was on the cover of the *Prapanna-jīvanāmṛta,* which was published in the very house of Svāmī Mahārāja in '43 or '44. Svāmī Mahārāja's sister, Pisīmā, bore the cost to publish that book.

śrīmach-caitanya-sārasvata-maṭhavara udgīta-kīrttir jaya-śrīṁ
bibhrat saṁbhāti gaṅgā-taṭa-nikaṭa-navadvīpa-koládri-rāje
yatra śrī-gaura-sārasvata-mataniratā-gaura-gāthā gṛṇanti
śrimad rūpānuga śrī kṛtamati-guru-gaurāṅga-rādhā-jitāśā

On the banks of the Ganges in Koladvīpa, Navadvīpa
Śrī Caitanya Sārasvata Maṭha stands resplendent.
The flag flies high, singing its glories around the world.
There, the residents chant the glories of Lord Gaurāṅga
and aspire to serve Śrī Śrī Rādhā-Govinda
in the line of Śrī Rūpa.[2]

Udgīta-kīrttir jaya-śrīṁ bibhrat—this flag will fly very high, pronouncing the victory of Śrī Caitanya Sārasvata Maṭha. What is the principle held by Śrī Caitanya Sārasvata Maṭha? The internal aspiration for Rādhikā-Mādhava. Caitanya Sārasvata Maṭha is in the line of *rūpānuga.* What is the nature of Caitanya Sārasvata Maṭha? The current flows from Gaurāṅga to Sarasvatī (Bhaktisiddhānta). They are fully engaged in the cultivation of the current that began with Śrī Caitanya, continuing up to

Sarasvatī. Their main business is to talk about Śrī Gaurāṅga and His greatness, His nobility and especially His instructions. And what is their aim? Whatever is recommended and given by Rūpa Gosvāmī and his successors. We are dedicated to that principle—*rādhikā-mādhavāśāṁ,* as anounced by Raghunātha Dāsa Gosvāmī, who is considered to be the *ācārya* of our highest destination. Raghunātha Dāsa recommends what should be our highest goal:

nāma-śreṣṭhaṁ manum api śacī-putram atra svarūpaṁ
rūpam tasyāgrajam uru-purīṁ māthurīṁ goṣṭavātīm
rādhā-kuṇḍaṁ giri-varam aho rādhikā-mādhavāśāṁ
prāpto yasya prathita-kṛpayā śrī gurum taṁ nato 'smi

I am fully indebted to Śrī Gurudeva. Why? He has given me so many things. He has given me the highest conception of the Holy Name of Kṛṣṇa, the highest form of sound which contains the highest form of thought, aspiration, ideal, everything. And next he has given me the *mantra.* The Name is there within the *mantra.* Without the Name, the *mantra* is nothing. If the Name of Kṛṣṇa is withdrawn and replaced with another name, the *mantra* will give the opposite result. The Name of Kṛṣṇa is all in all. And within the *mantra,* the Name is couched in a particular way as a sort of prayer.

So, I was dedicated to this ideal from the beginning. In my poem that was published in '43 or '44, I have explained my position there—my object and my campaign. I am still a servant of that idea to this day. And my Guru Mahārāja also posted me here. He called me from my sleep, and asked me to sing the song *Śrī Rūpa-mañjarī-pada.* So I find that I am there always, and my aspiration remains unchanged for all these long years.

Caitanya to Sarasvati

We named our mission 'Śrī Caitanya Sārasvata Maṭha.' First there was 'Caitanya Maṭha,' and Sarasvatī is our Gurudeva. So Caitanya Sārasvata—this name indicates the line from Caitanya to Sarasvatī, our Gurudeva. It is indicating the angle of vision of our Guru Mahārāja, Śrīla Bhaktisiddhānta Sarasvatī Ṭhākura, about Śrī Caitanyadeva—the way he saw it with his divine eyes. Within that divine dispensation we are to revere, accept and preach. It is available here, and we are concerned with that—from Caitanya to Sarasvatī, the whole of our *guru-parampāra* is covered, considered, cultured and being preached and spread. This is Caitanya Sārasvata.

Also, *caitanyānuga-sarasvatī—sarasvatī* means *vāṇī, vākya*—the words or expressions of Caitanya. *Caitanya-vāṇī* is the real preaching and instructions of Śrī Caitanyadeva—so the substantial meaning is 'from Caitanya to Sarasvatī.' It is the culture of *Śrīmad Bhāgavatam* as viewed by Śrī Caitanyadeva and His followers up to Sarasvatī. This is the object, theme and purpose of our life. Our nature and acquaintance is there. They are our masters, and we are the servants of that group. We want to revere them, to propagate knowledge about them, and to ask people to accept them. Our whole concern is there.

Caitanya-sārasvata is the line of *Bhāgavatam* as enhanced by Śrī Caitanyadeva. Of all the *ācāryas,* Caitanyadeva preached about love divine. Clearly and in a developed, scientific way, only Caitanyadeva preached the fifth end of life—*bhāgavata-prema*—the end of life is to acquire love, affection and attraction for Godhead, for Kṛṣṇa. Kṛṣṇa is the Lord of love and He is the innermost conception of Godhead—the highest conception of Godhead is in Krsna. The *jīva* can have a relationship with Him—the relationship of love—and that is the highest achievement for all souls, ever known to have come down to the world.

Thus, Caitanya Sārasvata is exclusively *caitanyānuga-sārasvata*—*sārasvata* that belongs to the school of Śrī Kṛṣṇa Caitanyadeva. They are believers in Kṛṣṇa consciousness and Caitanyadeva's instructions. *Sārasvata* means that the communication is with sound or words—a treasure of words—here, sound refers to the Holy Names. Their business is with divine sound—their duty is with the transaction of divine sound. And what sort of divinity? The Kṛṣṇa consciousness sound business is their trade—they are engaged in the transaction of the divine sound of Kṛṣṇa—Kṛṣṇa consciousness.

Kṛṣṇa consciousness is a philosophical ontological expression, but Kṛṣṇa Caitanya consciousness means that Caitanya is there. His Name is Kṛṣṇa Caitanya. Śrīla Svāmī Mahārāja called his society ISKCON, but the public has given it a very warm welcome by calling it 'The Hare Kṛṣṇa Movement.' But 'Kṛṣṇa consciousness' is an ontological expression that can be realized by the philosophically-minded. In the Name 'Kṛṣṇa Caitanya'—*caitanya* means 'consciousness'—so 'Kṛṣṇa consciousness' means 'Kṛṣṇa Caitanya.' The Name is there personified.

War on Maya

Yāre dekho tāre kaha kṛṣṇa upadeśa. Once I went to Kṛṣṇanagara court. There the lawyers put to me, "Why do all you *sādhus* come to court? It is very awkward that *sādhus* come to court. Are you not ashamed?" I told him that, "You have a bad conception of *sādhu*. You think the *sādhu* must retire to Haridvāra or the jungle and there he will go on with his practices. That is the conception of the *sādhu* in your court. But you have not seen such a *sādhu* as the founder of Gauḍīya Maṭha. He is not afraid of the *māyā*. He wants to attack the whole system of *māyā* and destroy it." Prabhupāda wanted to attack and be in war with *māyā*. Our Guru Mahārāja declared that we will capture all the centers of activities and paralyze them. "We want to take the *bhāgavata-kathā* there. Nothing should be eliminated. We are not afraid of *māyā*. We want to conquer it, defeat it, to capture all the centers. Why this court should be eliminated from that. We are *sādhus* of that type. We are not afraid of *māyā*, that we shall run away to the jungle and enter into a cave and there we will go on with *hari-nāma*. Hari will stand and all these other things must vanish," I told him.

Gauḍīya Maṭha is not afraid of anything. A Vaiṣṇava who loved the solitary life of *bhajana* once asked our Guru Mahārāja, "Why do you stay in Calcutta? That is the place of Satan, where fighting for selfish interest is so acute. Leave that and come to the holy *dhāma*." But Śrīla Bhaktisiddhānta Sarasvatī Ṭhākura especially chose that place, saying, "I prefer to represent Śrī Caitanya Mahāprabhu's creed in an extremely contaminated place." For this reason, he wanted to send men to the West. "The East is captured by the glamour of Western civilization," he said, "So Western civilization must first be crushed. Then, its glamour will vanish and the whole world will come to join the campaign of divine love of Śrī Caitanya Mahāprabhu." This was the same spirit with which Nityānanda Prabhu canvassed the fallen souls of this world in His attempt to take them to the lotus feet of Śrī Caitanya Mahāprabhu.

No recognition of the *jāti-brāhmaṇas, jāti-gosvāmīs,* these *bābājīs*, the Ramakrishna Mission—all foes, no friend! This is Gauḍīya Maṭha. Single-handed they are fighting with everyone existing in the name of religion or non-religion or hodge-podge religion. Single-handed! Our Guru Mahārāja, on the basis of Bhaktivinoda Ṭhākura's findings, took the sword and declared war against the whole world. That was his characteristic.

So that was the idea of the general, Prabhupāda. I must capture all the important points from *māyā* wherever I see it.

Go on chanting the Name of Kṛṣṇa. Make service to Kṛṣṇa. One day in Allahabad, perhaps that very year Svāmī Mahārāja was initiated, in a park our Guru Mahārāja gave a challenge, "I issue a challenge." As wrestlers challenge anyone to wrestle, in a meadow, two fighters face-off—just as that one who became a Mohammedan from Christian—Mohammed Ali, challenged the world. "I am ready to fight with any person to show that the highest position is occupied by my Gurudeva, Bhaktivinoda Ṭhākura, Gaura-kiśora Dāsa Bābājī, Mahāprabhu. Let anyone come to fight with me to decide—I'm ready!" That he told, "I am ready to challenge anybody and everybody. Let them come and fight with me. I want to establish my Gurudeva on a throne, in the highest place."

With so much force he came. Just as river comes from the hill very forcibly, the current is very fierce when it comes. So Prabhupāda began such wholesome *pracāra* (preaching). Let the enemies come with all their points of argument and we shall dissolve all that. Say what you have to say. From the lowest atheist to the so-called theist, all come! Only Kṛṣṇa is the highest, and His *bhajana* in divine love, that is the highest. We shall stand for that, we shall occupy it with that. That is the idea.

Deep Knowledge of Bhagavatam

Our Guru Mahārāja wanted to conquer the whole territory of *māyā*. That was his spirit, to attack from different directions. One of the moderate leaders of the time, a pro-Hindu, when he came to the Calcutta *maṭha,* he appeared to have some knowledge of the scriptures and also of *Bhāgavatam.* When he heard our Guru Mahārāja speak, he asked many questions and said that, "I can't imagine these two things that I find here—such deep knowledge of the *Bhāgavatam* and such appreciation at every stage of argument—reciting and giving quotations from the

Bhāgavata. Whatever the subject matter of discussion, a *Bhāgavata śloka* is given in support of that—so much deep knowledge of *Bhāgavatam* I have never seen before nor conceived.

"And another thing, a daily religious paper, I can't conceive that daily a religious paper is published." Prabhupāda answered that, "We are talking about Vaikuṇṭha—that unlimited world. And this world is *māyā,* which means the limited world. So many daily newspapers are going on with the subject of this limited world. In the unlimited world there is only one daily newspaper and that is inconceivable to you? There is so much news." Influenced by the discussion of our Guru Mahārāja that man started publishing books in his own way, but he was not successful in that matter.

The books of the Gauḍīya Maṭha however are of a different kind. They are based on scientific principles with *hari-nāma.* It is mentioned in the *śāstra* that the smallest amount of Kṛṣṇa consciousness can purify remaining *anarthas*—it is so powerful and disinfecting that the least connection of Kṛṣṇa consciousness can purify miraculously. But it must be proper Kṛṣṇa consciousness to purify—the *nirguṇa,* the highest class of *nirguṇa* conception. Like a small homeopathic dose can work miraculous cures immediately—instantly, any man from the lowest class may be fit for the highest duty of a *brāhmaṇa.* If there is *sat-saṅga,* with the association of the *sādhus,* by their combined force any bold attempt may be taken up.

Friends to Help Me Preach

We heard from our Prabhupāda: "So many friends have come to me to help me in the discharge of my duty. I should do all these things myself, but because I am not fit for that, Kṛṣṇa has sent so many friends to help me in that action." This is the real conception of a Vaiṣṇava in our *guru-varga.* We are told to see things in this way. When we look to the real plane we find that everyone has a separate soul—by nature everyone belongs to Kṛṣṇa only and none else. So each has come to help under a different garb—in a different color they have come to do the service of their Lord. The *svarūpa-śakti* is engaging those of different status to help in the discharge of Her duty to serve *kṛṣṇa-līlā*—to be used in *līlā*. Everything is for Himself, in Hegelian language, for Itself. Everything is for Himself. So that is sacrifice—to sacrifice everything for His satisfaction. That is the main current of thought and purity. The highest type of purity is there—surrender to the Autocrat. When the Autocrat is the absolute good, beauty, love, and harmony—don't be a miser dealing with Him. Wholesale giving, realizing that we are His property, He is our Master, to make or mar—He is in a position to do anything He likes with us—such a Master.

Surrender of such quality can save us, give us eternal life and healthy life. We must live and breathe in such an atmosphere where He has full right over us to make or mar—we belong to Him. This realization must be of such a degree of purity that the degree of holiness will also increase accordingly—purity and holiness are of the same order. Ordinary purity is not purity proper, it must come to the standard of holiness, divinity. *Tat-paratvena nirmalam*—purity is *nirmala*. *Tat-paratvena*—as much as we realize that we are meant for Him, according to that degree the purity will increase. *Sarvopādhi-vinirmuktaṁ*—what is otherwise, that must be removed. *Tat-paratvena nirmalam*—an innermost understanding that we fully belong to Him—a type of slave. The purity is there—as much as we have faith in Him, that is the standard of purity—so much it is pure and divine and holy. It does not mean that that realized position is an abstract one. *Hṛṣikeṇa-hṛṣikeśa sevanaṁ bhaktir ucyate*—all the constituent parts of your spiritual body will be utilized. They are not your enemy—the enemy is in the nature of engagement, not in those that are doing some function, not there. They should not be eliminated at all. But only the nature should be changed. Everything will be gold. From iron it will be converted into gold—from mud it will be converted into gold. But everything will be retained. Only the nature is to be changed. The dreadfulness or danger is only with a conception of a secondary interest—a conception of separate interest from that of the absolute center of absolute good. That is to be eliminated, nothing else. Everything will be kept intact and utilized to its fullest satisfaction and fulfillment. Everything has its real and highest fulfillment, only the connection should be established.

What is Not Madhurya-rasa

Our Guru Mahārāja did not emphasize the worship of or install Deities of Gaura-Nityānanda, only Pañca-tattva and in other places he established the pure *mādhurya-rasa*—Mahāprabhu and Rādhā-Govinda. Everywhere he installed Mahāprabhu, both combined with Rādhā-Govinda and separate.

rādhā kṛṣṇa praṇaya vikṛtir hlādinī śaktir asmād
ekātmānāv api bhuvi purā deha-bhedaṁ gatau tau
caitanyākhyaṁ prakaṭam adhunā tad-dvayaṁ caikyam āptaṁ
rādhā-bhāva-dyuti-suvalitaṁ naumi kṛṣṇa-svarūpam

The loving affairs of Śrī Rādhā and Kṛṣṇa are transcendental manifestations of the Lord's internal pleasure-giving potency. Although Rādhā and Kṛṣṇa are one in Their identity, They separated Themselves eternally. Now these two transcendental identities have again

> united, in the form of Śrī Kṛṣṇa Caitanya. I bow down to Him, who has manifested Himself with the sentiment and complexion of Śrīmatī Rādhārāṇī although He is Kṛṣṇa Himself. (*Cc. Ādi* 1.5)

Ekātmānāv api bhuvi purā—in ancient times Rādhā and Kṛṣṇa divided Themselves for a particular *līlā* but—*caitanyākhyaṁ prakaṭam adhunā tad-dvayaṁ caikyam āptaṁ*—again They have combined. *Rādhā-bhāva-dyuti-suvalitaṁ naumi kṛṣṇa-svarūpam*—the Potency and the Owner of the Potency are very closely embraced. The Predominator and the Predominated tendency are present, with an extraordinary ecstatic feeling. Kṛṣṇa is overpowered by the Potency and He is searching after Himself—*kṛṣṇasya ātmanusandhāna*. The influence of Rādhārāṇī over Kṛṣṇa is that Kṛṣṇa is transformed into a devotee, and He is searching Himself. Sweetness personified, is tasting Itself and becoming mad.

Guru Mahārāja preached exclusively this *mādhurya-rasa*, but with great precaution. What is not that thing, he perhaps used ninety per-cent of his energy to preach that this is not *mādhurya-rasa*, the negative side. To clear away the negative side, he had to spare in his words, 'gallons of blood' to teach that this is not that *rasa*. *Neti neti*, this is not that thing, this is not that thing.

And whatever he did—*pūjala rāga-patha gaurava bhaṅge*—his whole life in a nutshell is expressed in this, his own expression. *Pūjala rāga-patha*, the very nature of the *sampradaya* is this.

pūjala rāga-patha gaurava bhaṅge
mātala hari-jana viṣāya raṅge

Pūjala rāga-patha gaurava bhaṅge—the whole tenor of his preaching expedition was *pūjala rāga-patha gaurava bhaṅge*. The *rāga-*

patha is above, on our head. That is the goal. We are to go there. But before that you have got charm for many things, the grandeur. You should try to learn that which is at present charming to you, learn to utilize that for the service of that great domain of love. The majesty, the awe, the wealth, the reverence, what is grand to you, what attracts you most, all these things, put them into the service of that Lord of love and beauty. The Absolute is beauty, love and harmony, an autocrat, and everything should be sacrificed for Him. Learn this!

Whatever you come in connection with, sacrifice it into the fire to establish that Lord of love. For His least satisfaction, all this grandeur may be put into the fire. Learn this. Don't try to attempt to get Him within your fist. That was the whole tenor of his preaching.

Don't Venture to Run

Rūpa Gosvāmī has classified *mādhurya-rasa* in *Ujjvala-nīlamaṇi.* In *Bhakti-rasāmṛta-sindhu* he gives the science of general devotion, general *bhakti* and the gradual development of *bhakti.* And the highest position which comes to *mādhurya-rasa,* it is finished there. *Bhakti-rasāmṛta-sindhu* is the first part. And then the second part is *Ujjvala-nīlamaṇi.* There, only *mādhurya-rasa* has been dealt with in detail. I have not gone through it, but only *Caitanya-caritāmṛta,* and other literatures.

We did not venture to enter into the details of *mādhurya-rasa.* Our Guru Mahārāja did not like it. But it will come irresistibly within you as you go on with *śravaṇa* and *kīrtana. Pūjala rāga-patha gaurava bhaṅge*—the full conception is so high. When it comes, it will awaken within you. It won't be awakened by any other person. An example was given by Gaura-kiśora Dāsa Bābājī Mahārāja. Bābājī Mahārāja used to live in a very small hut on the banks of the Ganges. Another gentleman, imitating him, erected a similar cottage nearby, and externally he used to show renunciation like Bābājī Mahārāja. Eating, not eating, taking bath, some days not taking bath. In this way he was showing some physical austerity. Then Gaura-kiśora Dāsa Bābājī remarked one day to one *sādhu*. "Only by entering a labor room, a girl does not produce a child." It is a mere imitation, but many things are necessary beforehand.

Our Guru Mahārāja told that it is not an easy thing. It is the highest of the high. So don't venture to run toward that. The day will dawn by the grace of the Lord when you will not be able to resist that thing. That tendency is within you, so go on. *Iṅha mālī seṅce nitya śravaṇādi jala*—the duty of the *mālī*, of the disciple, is to pour water onto the root, and there will be natural growth. Then the fruit will come down, and you will taste it.

So don't venture to rush into that. *Ujjvala-nīlamaṇi* is a book where only *mādhurya-rasa* has been dealt with in detail. And in a short way that is given here and there in *Caitanya-caritāmṛta*, in a well-guarded way. We will approach from there and whatever little we have heard from the lips of our Guru Mahārāja—whatever we have heard, that is enough, and one day we may be allowed to enter that domain.

The *mañjarīs* are there and different departments, so many things are there. That is on our head, and we are hoping that is on the upper side of our attainment. But do not unnaturally enter there. Everything will be spoiled. We are not ready to spoil our fortune. Whatever we have, there is much more there, so much more. There is no greater prospect for mankind to reach, so why should I be so much ardent and impatient to spoil my prospect? Don't spoil it! What we have, that is enough food. And if we do not find any food, then to try to find it will be treachery. Eagerness is good, but rushing is foolish and the devotee's tendency should always be to go to the lower service.

Tend to Lower Service

Śrīla Raghunātha Dāsa Gosvāmī says, "I want the service of a servant, and I want to show my reverence towards *sakhya*, friendly service."

sakhyāya te mama namo 'stu namo 'stu nityaṁ
dāsyāya te mama raso 'stu raso 'stu satyam

> I am not fit for confidential service, I always try to revere that, and I shall try, if I am accepted, to do the lowest service. If I get that engagement, I am rewarded more than anything. (*Vilāpa-kusumāñjali* 16)

So, full satisfaction should be the attitude. But Kṛṣṇa will take him up, "No, serve Me in this way," and we have to do that. According to the *rasa* it is such. Those that are eternal friends, don't think like this. They are part and parcel, and surcharged with Yoga-māyā—with the spirit of that particular service of that particular level. Kṛṣṇa is pleased by the aggression of the friends—He's pleased when they are manipulated by Yogamāyā. But we should not be puffed up in that way—we are beginners and not *nitya-siddhas*—we are in the line of *sādhana-siddhas*. We have not yet come to realize, so our nature should be tempered by what Dāsa Gosvāmī Prabhu is teaching. Always try to go downwards.

Mahāprabhu was satisfied with Emperor Pratāparudra when He found that the king had engaged himself in the very menial service of a sweeper. The king performed the service of a sweeper—this attracted Him most. Mahāprabhu Himself engaged in the *guṇḍicā-mārjana* (cleansing of the Guṇḍicā Temple). Jagannātha was coming to Guṇḍicā, so Mahāprabhu and His party collected the dust from the temple in His *uttarīya* and threw it outside, and then washed the temple.

Nothing is neglected but we are attracted—with that low, menial service, we may attract the attention of the high. Nothing is insignificant when it is connected with Him. Still, there is gradation. In the beginning of ones service we must always have a sincere tendency to go towards the lower side. By Kṛṣṇa's will we will be accepted for higher satisfaction.

The tendency of the servitors will be always towards the lower side—"I like the position of a servant, and not the service of a friend." That should be the normal tendency of a devotee. Even in that world, there should be no ambition. One must be the servant of the servant of the servant of the servant—it is not an exaggeration, but it is the real thing. We should find this sort of substance within us, then we are safe and in a good position. So, *tṛṇād api sunīcena taror api sahiṣṇunā*—one can never be deceived if they do not deceive themselves.

Abode of High Sentiment

Prabhupāda had a place at the Bhāgavata Press in Kṛṣṇanagara, where he was publishing the *Caitanya-caritāmṛta.* There was one gentleman, Rāma Gopāla Bābu, an M.A. in law, who was the manager there. He was a very sound and well respected educated man. He told me that once he came to the press and there Prabhupāda was proof reading a particular portion of *Caitanya-caritāmṛta* where the *vṛndāvana-līlā* is mentioned. In this section, Kṛṣṇa has gone to Mathurā and Lalitā-devī, as representative of the *gopīs,* approaches Kṛṣṇa there. She is describing the position of Rādhārāṇī and chastising Kṛṣṇa—some poetry was perhaps written by Prabhupāda himself and he was seeing the proof of that portion which was in the press.

Rāma Gopāla Bābu told me that he looked at Prabhupāda's face and saw so many facial impressions of different types coming and going away, and he was suppressing them. Automatically so many sentiments and feelings were visible on his face but Prabhupāda was trying his utmost to suppress them. Rāma Gopāla Bābu said, "I noticed this in his face and I became his disciple." This incident brought him to Prabhupāda's feet. Such feelings were visible on his face when he was correcting the proofs of that part of *Caitanya-caritāmṛta.*

He was trying his best to suppress these emotions in the unfavorable public environment. "Not only the *siddhānta,*" Rāma Gopāla Bābu told, "But that show of personal expression on his face, the feelings which I found in him, that took me to his feet." That abode of high sentiment.

You Want to Hear Krsna-katha

He also related that once, with another gentleman, he approached Bhaktivinoda Ṭhākura in his retired life and that gentleman requested Bhaktivinoda Ṭhākura to say something about Kṛṣṇa—*kṛṣṇa-kathā.* Bhaktivinoda Ṭhākura was in self-meditation. Then when he came out from his inner contemplation, he said, "Oh, you have come to hear *kṛṣṇa-kathā* from me? You want to hear *kṛṣṇa-kathā?*" Many feelings and sentiments developed in him.

Rāma Gopāla Bābu told that what we observed, that what he has written in that song, *kṛṣṇa nāma dhare kata bala*—all these divine sentiments we could trace in him. Sometimes there was a thrilling sensation, hairs were standing on end and sometimes sweat, sometimes shivering and sometimes much vigor was shown. "You have come to hear about Kṛṣṇa from me." In this way he began speaking *kṛṣṇa-kathā*—with so much emotion.

Analysis of Madhurya-rasa

Mādhurya-rasa considerations are for the higher students of devotion. Analysis of *mādhurya-rasa* is found in the *Ujjvala-*

nīlamaṇi, which is a supplement to *Bhakti-rasāmṛta-sindhu.* And Viśvanātha Cakravartī Ṭhākura has written another book, *Ujjvala-nīlamaṇi-kiraṇa,* which is the gist of *Ujjvala-nīlamaṇi* and *Bhakti-rasāmṛta-sindhu-bindu.* Sanātana Gosvāmī Prabhu has written *Bṛhat-bhāgavatāmṛtam,* and Rūpa Gosvāmī has written the *Laghu-bhāgavatāmṛtam,* a short book. And Viśvanātha Cakravartī Ṭhākura has also given *Bhāgavatāmṛta-kaṇā*—a drop of that nectar. A drop of nectar, a drop of ocean, and ray of the gem—three very short books giving the gist, are composed by Viśvanātha Cakravartī Ṭhākura. One who can go through these three books can have some understanding of the *Bhakti-rasāmṛta-sindhu,* the *Bṛhat-bhāgavatāmṛtam,* and the *Ujjvala-nīlamaṇi,* these three books. They are elaborate and very short.

Rūpa Gosvāmī has also written a small book called *Uddhava-sandeśa.* Here, Uddhava is sent by Kṛṣṇa to meet the *gopīs.* Nanda, Yaśodā, the cowboys, the *gopīs* and Uddhava's experience in Vraja is described there. There are many books, but we must follow the real method of study—otherwise everything will be read and nothing will be obtained. The real process of study is *praṇipātena paripraśnena sevāya,* otherwise it is all book knowledge and no conception. So that will be useless dry labor.

"Everything is underground and I will walk over it." You may think like that, but really I found it to be like this. One may not have the real touch, only the literary portion—the knowledge. In the language of our Guru Maharaja, the honey is in a bottle and we are trying to get the honey—it is useless—between the bee and the honey, there is that glass screen. So intellectualism and the real feeling of participation, are quite different things, and more so, they are mischievous. This should encourage one to know that if *kṛṣṇa-līlā* is not properly approached, then there will be mischief—he will feel encouragement in his experience of the lust utilized for his lady-love and will thereby commit a great offense.

The warning has been given in *Bhāgavatam* by Śukadeva Gosvāmī—if you have no control over your senses don't venture to touch, to come to this area. You will be doomed. Without getting the status of Śiva, Mahādeva, if you drink poison you won't become Nīlakaṇṭha (blue-throated), but you'll have to die immediately. *Naitat samācarej jātu manasāpi*—even mentally we will die. One who has self-control over their senses, their other enemies are sure to die. One who is not Śiva, if they drink poison in their folded palm, they are sure to die. It is the opposite thing—one is by dedication to the Lord, another is by exploitation to the extreme stage—*kāma*. One is the most dense darkness, and the other is the most pleasing sight.

Bhaktisiddhānta Sarasvatī Ṭhākura Mahārāja has written *Vedānta Morphology* and *Rāya Rāmānanda* in English, and Bhaktivinoda Ṭhākura has written *Śrī Caitanya: His Life and Precepts*. And there are many poems also composed by Bhaktisiddhānta Sarasvatī Ṭhākura. Mainly his commentaries are very important to prove and to establish the teachings of Mahāprabhu, Kavirāja Gosvāmī, and Vṛndāvana Dāsa Ṭhākura, etc.

What is our anomaly? We are disappointed if we do not know everything, if there is something lacking. We are ordinary people with an infinite number of desires within us. In our present condition, the tendency to improve is to be praised. We are fallen *jīvas*, but we want to rise up and awaken. We have, in our Guru Mahārāja's words, 'volcanic energy' and it should not be misused. When properly guided it will fetch the most precious thing for us. Proper guidance is the most important thing in the life of everyone—although we have raw materials with us, that is not sufficient.

Ujjvala-nilamani

We are not atheists that think, "If I die before reading the *Ujjvala-nīlamaṇi,* my prospect is gone forever!" Don't think like that! If I am there in the soil, I am safe. One day I must get that. Guru Mahārāja gave me some hints. He gave admission by requesting me to sing the song of Rūpa-mañjarī. I may think that he has given, at least many of our friends told that, "He has given you admission." A gatekeeper, by the name of 'Bhakti Rakṣaka.' They say that I am the protector, but I think that I am a gatekeeper. By this name he has appointed me as a gatekeeper. Who will go in, Prabhupāda wants to see. So, I am not giving passport or visa to anyone and everyone.

We should not omit any step. If one step is omitted then the gap will be there in me. We must closely follow in our progress, gradual process—*ādau śraddhā tataḥ sādhu-saṅgo 'tha bhajana-kriyā.* Sometimes to get to the top quickly, we may be encouraged to omit steps in between, but this will be mourned afterwards. Progress must be solid, not hollow. Whatever I have, I must finish it perfectly. Then I shall go up:

ādau śraddhā tataḥ sādhu-sango 'tha bhajana kriyā
tato 'nartha-nivṛttiḥ syāt tato niṣṭhā tato rucis tataḥ
athāsaktis tato bhāvas tataḥ premābhyudañcati

All these stages we have to pass through, very cleverly and very sincerely. Then we shall find that it is reality.

Otherwise, it may remain in the realm of concoction and imagination—we won't get any strength from this and anyone may come and push me from my position. That won't be—none can shake me or push me out. The energy must be at the disposal of the Supreme Lord, but where is the guarantee? Only the bona-fide agent can guarantee and also to a certain extent the scripture can guarantee, that my energy will reach there—to purify myself and make me sincere, to convert me to a bona-fide seller and purchaser, a customer. My energy will go there, all things will go there and will make me a sincere customer, a permanent customer of that and nothing else. There lies the skill of the agent. With the selection of the proper bona-fide agent, one will feel that his capital is increasing and he is becoming more and more a customer of those goods. It will go to Goloka and the coin will come in dollars, in pounds and in this or that. And a valuable thing will come. More or less everyone of us has the energy. Of course the indolent—those in the *tamo-guṇa* have no energy but still they can also be utilized. A clever devotee may utilize so many things for the service of the Lord. And thereby one day they will also rise up—wake up and go towards Goloka, towards Vṛndāvana. One day they will be able to purchase a ticket for Vṛndāvana. The trees, the creepers, everyone may get the chance for Goloka. We have to know first, how that is the summum bonnum of our life.

A Preachers Responsibility

What is that? Leaving everything aside we shall accept that to be the only goal, our only destination, otherwise everything will be imitation. If that cannot capture my inner heart then everything will be imitation for the time being. That means that I have misconceived the different goals, different destinations. Why shall I feel attraction for Vṛndāvana leaving aside everything else? What scientific reason may be there? What is that thing? Is that reliable? We must have self-analysis. We must put these questions to our own heart. What is the cause? Illuminate everything for I am captured by that idea. Will it endure? If it is real, then why?

I am to explain to others and also in the beginning I shall have to explain it to myself, to my conscience. I must be confident about that, about my movement, my behavior, my tendency, my aspiration. Am I going to deceive myself—setting aside so many demoniac conceptions of reality offered by the materialists, by the so-called renunciationists, so-called spiritualists, imitationists? Omitting all these offers I am going, but I must explain it to my own conscience. Is there any ulterior motive? Am I a hired man of any other school or a real agent of Goloka? If I am not correct then I will mislead many. So I should correct myself—to become a preacher, there is so much responsibility. We must be sincere in our attempt, otherwise the filthy things from outside shall influence us. So I must be clear, sincere to myself first.

If I have it, then I can give it to others. What I have I can give that only. At least I must be a true mediator. Sometimes it is possible that even if I am not perfect still I can give it, by the grace of the *sādhu*. What may come, that may not be contaminated with my filthy heart but may pass through. It is possible sometimes, but not for long—that will gradually convert me. So we must have connection with the agent above—*yāre dekha tāre kaha kṛṣṇa upadeśa.* Some sort of *sukṛti* is necessary there. I do not realize it fully but I have a vague idea that this is good. So I transmit. I cannot make it as my own but only a temporary converser, I hold only a temporary post. For the time being, I am working as a mediator. Apparently these goods seem very good to me. You take it and use it and you will be able to benefit. Take it from there. Sincerity is necessary everywhere.

Yāre dekha tāre kaha kṛṣṇa upadeśa. Here Mahāprabhu assures us that in any way that anyone comes to deal with this thing, he cannot but be purified. These things are of so much intense purity that in the long run it will purify him. *Yāre dekha tāre*—at least give the Name to any and every person. Who can say this? The highest authority only can give such an order. Some goods may be lost, I won't care for that. Go on, give it to one and all. Nityānanda Prabhu was of that type. Distribute it everywhere. No fear of anyone. Distribute it anywhere and everywhere. That sort of high source can give such an order.

Yāre dekha, Mahāprabhu says, Kavirāja Gosvāmī says, "No discrimination whether one is fit or unfit. Inundate all with the flood. Whoever you come across is released. Only when His grace came to such a high degree was I captured. An ordinary course could not cure me, but it was of such a high order that I could not but fall within that jurisdiction. So the meanest of the mean, a person like me has been purified. I can't deny that I am purified. Then it will be blasphemy of the great Name of Nityānanda. I can't tolerate that. Although it may be my pride, my boasting, still I cannot but admit how magnanimous is the great gift of Nityānanda. Only to advertise in the public, to give publicity to all I have come. I venture to say that I have something. I have Rūpa-Sanātana. I have Raghunātha, I have my guru. I have Vṛndāvana, Govindajī, Madana-mohana, Gopīnātha. All these things I have." All these are of concrete interest for the Absolute. Not any local interest, however great it may be in magnitude; self-centered, or family-centered, or village-centered, or province-centered, or humanitarianism—anything that is a part of the infinite. So, we are to understand these things in a general way. The technical words: *anartha-nivṛtti, bhāva, āsakti*—these are all included in this understanding.

The Death Blow to Sahajiyas

A bona-fide student will avoid all kinds of imitation—Sahajiyāism. We have to cross Bhū, Bhuvaḥ, Mahar, Jana, Tapa, Virajā, Brahmaloka, and Vaikuṇṭha to Goloka, step by step. The Sahajiyās take spiritual advancement very cheaply; they are not prepared to pay the real price. But the death blow to them is—

upajiyā bāḍe latā 'brahmāṇḍa' bhedi' yāya, 'virajā,' brahmaloka, ' bhedi' 'paravyoma' pāya—it is necessary for one's devotion to cross these many planes, as the creeper of *bhakti* grows and rises up to Goloka.

But the pseudo-devotees do not care to know what is Paravyoma, what is Brahmaloka, what is Virajā, what is the *brahmāṇḍa*. Without caring to know about these things, they approach any guru, receive some *mantra,* and go on meditating. But if one meditates upon *rādhā-govinda-līlā* in such an ignorant state, instead of entering *rādhā-govinda-līlā* one will become entangled with the ladies and gentlemen of this world. One will become entangled in the domain of lust and will have to go to hell instead of going up to Goloka.

Anurāga, our affinity for the Supreme Personality is not a very cheap thing. We have to understand who Kṛṣṇa really is. Those without dedication should not deceive themselves into thinking they can find Him in the area of the material zone.

Madhvācārya gave one hundred points against Māyāvādism and its so-called renunciation, and our Guru Mahārāja gave *Prakṛta-rasa-śata-dūṣaṇī*—one hundred points against Sahajiyāism, to guard against imitating *kṛṣṇa-bhajana* in material life. So many ways, at every step we have to make decisions to go this way or that. Every moment we are at the crossing, but on the whole our sincerity will guide us. Deception and illusion are there, but the grace of the Lord is also there in the background. He won't allow these agents of deception to misguide us if we don't associate with them.

Necessity of Vaidhi-bhakti

Śrīla Rūpa Gosvāmī says that we must observe *vaidhi-bhakti* (regulative practice) for as long as we can't get admission into the level of *rāga-bhakti* (spontaneous affection).

Dāsa Gosvāmī also says that we shall show reverence to *rāga-bhakti,* but we shall try to live within *vaidhi-bhakti,* with its rules and regulations according to the *śāstra.* But the arrogant do not care for this instruction of the followers of Śrī Caitanya Mahāprabhu.

I have nothing against *vaidhi-marga. Pūjala rāga-patha gaurava bhaṅge*—we are trying to follow the *vaidhi* and always look with our aim towards the *rāga-patha.* Go on with *vaidhi,* but the goal is with *rāga-patha.* That is our aim. Otherwise, why *vaidhi?*

Law is not everything. The law of your society should be accommodating to nurture divine sentiment, otherwise it is no law. Law should promote faith. *Śāstra's* jurisdiction is limited. It is meant only to promote love, and when love comes, it will be free—smooth. Harmonious working is possible only in the area of love. Śrīla Rūpa Gosvāmī says that *vaidhi-bhakti,* devotion under the guidance of *śāstra,* is helpful only to a certain extent. It will help the inner awakening of love and affection and then retire. Law will retire, giving room to the spontaneous flow of love. Law is necessary, especially in the lower stages, but it should make room for free movement in the relationship. Freedom is the highest thing. Free service is *rāga-mārga,* and that is service proper.

Vaidhi means to regulate oneself, but for what? Regulation is not itself the aim or object. But regulation means for something else. We want to regulate ourselves so that we may be free in that land and acquire the position of a free servitor. Regulation has its desired effect.

And what is that? We shall get that spontaneous service. Otherwise, there will be a master, a teacher with a whip to order me, "Do this, do that!" We must reach a place where freely we shall do that thing with our intrinsic urge. It is the success of life, it is there.

There is one party in Vṛndāvana that does not admit the necessity for formal devotion. Many others you will find in Vṛndāvana also. This party claims they have a connection with the Gopāla Bhaṭṭa *sampradāya*—this is Gauḍīya Vaiṣṇavism with a little deviation. They want to begin with *rāga-bhakti*—*anurāga* eliminating *vaidhi-bhakti.*

This is worse than Sahajiyāism. Sahajiyāism formerly accepts everything, but they want easy entrance to do only what comes naturally without work, and they don't admit the necessity for formal devotion. They are lazy in their practice, preferring the enjoying mood to the serving mood, but service means sacrifice. So this atmosphere is dangerous and we should mark with all attention any theistic awakening and take care so that we may not go down again to the depths of nescience. Very carefully we shall try to collect our wealth.

Science of Devotion Proper

Real progress towards the Infinite gives the idea that, "I am nothing, I am in great danger." Progress towards the Infinite is like that. Thinking, "I have it, I am above,"—this is a foolish feeling, a foolish statement. The very nature of advancement is that, "I am low, I am undone, I am the most helpless." The closer we are, the further away we will feel, whereas the further away we actually are from divinity, we may complacently feel we are close. As much as we come into the relativity of the Infinite, we cannot but conceive ourselves to be the lowest of the low. That is the criteria.

The very sign of real progress will show I am nothing, I am the most needy, the most wretched and the most helpless. The negative aspect must be improved to attract the positive. If one point of the negative will say, "I am positive" then immediately it will be rejected, you are under the false control of *māyā.* Rather to think, "I am the meanest of the mean," that will attract the attention of the high. This is the science of devotion proper.

Mahāprabhu was in *samādhi,* falling in the sea, experiencing *kūrma-rūpa* in Jagannātha Purī, and coming back to His senses. Then He related a description of His experience in *samādhi,* all pertaining to this *mādhurya-rasa.* In *Caitanya-caritāmṛta* He relates, when He is coming out of His swoon, "I went there, I saw all these things, but you have taken Me from there." *Pūjala rāga-patha.* We should be mindful of every step and automatically that will take us there. Don't try to go too quickly. Try to keep back and it will forcibly take you there. Your acceptance will come from the higher quarter, not by your endeavor.

In His deep trance, He had experience of that *vraja-līlā,* He expressed that. And these Sahajiyās are trying to imitate these things. They are imitating—by their imagination, by their mundane mind and with their imagination they think they are going to get a touch of that *līlā.*

Even some ordinary mundane scholar said that this *kṛṣṇa-līlā* is *aprākṛta.* We can trace it from the descriptions of the *Caitanya-caritāmṛta.* Kavirāja Gosvāmī has described the *līlā* of Kṛṣṇa, even *jala-keli* (pastimes in the water) in such a way that we cannot take our lusty mind there. He has kept the purity of the *līlā* with his description, and Kṛṣṇa with the *sakhīs* are going on with their play in the tank in the Yamunā. The transcendental characteristics have been maintained there. That *nitya-līlā,* which Mahāprabhu experienced in His deep trance, has been given by Kavirāja Gosvāmī. It is not any mundane thing—we should be prepared for that experience. So much higher we have to reach for a slight experience of those higher pastimes. We must be ready to pay for that, and for that only our Guru Mahārāja came.

Nitai-Gaura-Radhe-Syama

The Sahajiyā followers of Rāma Dāsa Bābājī are also imitators and there is a blunder in their theoretical conception, in that they say '*bhaja nitāi-gaura-rādhe-śyāma.*' That is a most dangerous thing. In Kavirāja Gosvāmī's writings we find that Nitāi is Balarāma.

Rāma Dāsa's guru was Caraṇa Dāsa, who suddenly 'discovered' that Nitāi is Rādhā. So that is the dangerous difference between them and the Gosvāmīs, the higher authorities in our *sampradāya.* Paṇḍita Gadādhara is Rādhārāṇī really and Mahāprabhu is Kṛṣṇa. So these people are a shadow of the real thing. Nityānanda is fully one with Baladeva. But these people say Nitāi is Rādhā.

In a dream Caraṇa Dāsa got this *bhaja nitāi-gaura rādhe śyāma mantra.* But Bhaktivinoda Ṭhākura and Guru Mahārāja said that it is a concoction. It may have appeared in his dream, but that simply proved that he was a false man, not in touch with reality.

Rūpa, Sanātana, Kavirāja Gosvāmī, and Narottama Dāsa Ṭhākura—we must accept their decision, their vision, their estimation. And this *bhaja nitāi-gaura rādhe-śyāma* is an anamoly. What is this? This is against the pure line of devotion, and breaks the *mantra* that is descending, which is a living thing. According to our whim, can we cut it asunder and take a part of that and mix it with another part creating something new? That idea is also not happy.

Caraṇa Dāsa was a little earlier than the time of Prabhupāda. Very earnestly he wanted to have Prabhupāda within his community. Once I heard from Prabhupāda that Bhaktivinoda Ṭhākura was going to Mahāprabhu's temple in Navadvīpa and Prabhupāda was following him. Bhaktivinoda Ṭhākura had gone perhaps a few steps further and Caraṇa Dāsa suddenly came and stood before Prabhupāda, "You are our future prospect"—in this way he began to eulogize Prabhupāda very much. Prabhupāda stopped for a minute or so, then again joined Bhaktivinoda Ṭhākura. He asked Prabhupāda, "What was that man telling you?" "He was saying like this, that you are our future prospect." Bhaktivinoda Ṭhākura told, "Be very cautious, don't be a captive to that man's trap."

The Impure Line

Caraṇa Dāsa's guru was Bhāgavata Dāsa Bābājī, who was a disciple of Jagannātha Dāsa Bābājī. Bhāgavata Dāsa Bābājī was not really pure. Rāma Dāsa Bābājī came in the line of Bhāgavata Dāsa Bābājī and Caraṇa Dāsa Bābājī, and that Caraṇa Dāsa devised that *mantra—bhaja nitāi-gaura rādhe śyāma japa hare kṛṣṇa hare rama*. So this fundamental blunder is there with the *siddhānta*—that can never be encouraged, so we cannot have any connection with them.

Bhaktivinoda Ṭhākura, later took *veśa* from Gaura-kiśora Dāsa Bābājī, and Gaura-kiśora Dāsa Bābājī took *veśa* from Bhāgavata Dāsa Bābājī. Gaura-kiśora Dāsa Bābājī used to hear *Bhāgavatam* from Bhaktivinoda Ṭhākura at Svānanda-sukhanda Kuñja, in Godrumadvīpa. There is a small *pakka* room built there in Godruma where Gaura-kiśora Dāsa Bābājī used to take his seat and hear *Bhāgavata* explanations from Bhaktivinoda Ṭhākura.

Bhāgavata Dāsa was a criminal, who later left that lifestyle and went to Vṛndāvana and took *veśa* from Jagannātha Dāsa Bābājī. But Caraṇa Dāsa, his history is otherwise. He was a *gṛhastha*. Once, there was a riot and Caraṇa Dāsa committed a murder and absconded. In the meantime he went to Vṛndāvana in disguise. Then after twelve years when he was safe from criminal prosecution, he again went home and after a few days returned to Vṛndāvana.

So this Caraṇa Dāsa took *veśa* from Bhāgavata Dāsa and began to preach very forcefully. He was a man of gigantic size and with a high voice he would chant and dance—he created that *bhaja nitāi-gaura-rādhe-śyāma mantra*—all these things. He wanted Prabhupāda also to support him. In the beginning Prabhupāda approached him and asked him, "Where did you get this *mantra*? Is it mentioned in the *śāstra*? You have created a new *mantra*!" So many things were changed, and that man was also characterless.

He said that you should not build a *pakka* latrine, meaning that you need not marry. Whenever there is a necessity to pass stool, wherever you are, you may pass. But don't build any permanent latrine, that is, don't marry. That was his idea.

Sakhi-bheki

Sakhī-bhekī was another aberration of Caraṇa Dāsa. *Sakhī-bhekī* is a type of imitation. They think that, "If I can externally wear the robes of a *sakhī*, that will remind me that I am actually a female." They also get a *mantra* from their guru in the Sahajiyā section—"You are a girl of the age of eleven and your superior is Rūpa-mañjarī, Vilāsa-mañjarī etc. You should conceive of yourself as being in that line and go on. You are a young girl, you are in the association of so many *sakhīs*, you have a particular service—try to do that. Externally you should beg and maintain your life, but internally you should go on thinking like that. Accept the dress of a female and that will help you in your conception that you are a female." That is *sakhī-bhekī*.

There was one *sakhī-bhekī* in Caraṇa Dāsa Bābājī's *maṭha*, whose name was Jayagopāla Bhaṭṭācārya, who called himself Lalitā-sakhī. I saw him, before joining Gauḍīya Maṭh, when I visited Navadvīpa to find a *sādhu* from whom to take initiation. He was a *brāhmaṇa* and a graduate also. His age was at that time about fifty. He was a big figure clad in a lady's dress and was trying to imitate the movements of a woman. Anyhow, one gentleman amongst the visitors there came with a copy of the *Gauḍīya* magazine from Gauḍīya Maṭha. In that paper there was some remark about that *sakhī-bhekī*. Before hearing this article, that *sakhī-bhekī* wouldn't talk to anybody since he was posing as a shy lady. But when that guest read the article from the *Gauḍīya*, then he immediately came out in a mans voice—"Oh, what have they said? That is wrong! You should read another article from *Sonāra Gaurāṅga* magazine by Dr. Rādhāgovinda Nātha. That article is supporting me."

I did not know all these things at that time. I was simply a spectator and listening to all these things. I wondered, "Where is this *Gauḍīya* magazine from? And another magazine is in support of this gentleman"—only this I marked. This man seemed very serious, posing as a very advanced person—but when that criticism came, a man came out from the lady's dress to protest earnestly. "Oh, they are abusing me! They do not know anything! You can see this other article also is there!" I marked his attitude.

Sakhī-bhekī is imitation. In this mundane world we may attain something and satisfy ourselves—it is very easy. We may get a very cheap bargain. We do not want to pay for the object of our desire. *Na hi kalyāṇa kṛt kaścit*—none can deceive you if you do not deceive yourself. To think that this body is all in all is poison to the soul. It is a negative representation to the soul. It is ludicrous—*tamo-dharma.* If only by sacrificing this body of flesh and blood, we can attain Krsna, then at every second I want to accept death millions of times.

Another time we heard that Rāma Dāsa Babājī, Caraṇa Dāsa's disciple, was coming to Kalna and would do *kīrtana.* Some of us went to see him. He was singing and two of his disciples took their seat on either side of him—profuse tears and some mucus were coming from his nose like threads. From both sides his men helped by wiping and cleaning him with a cloth. Sometimes he was shivering greatly—in such way that if one did this for a few minutes their whole body would be damaged. He was moving his neck so forcibly it was a wonder it was not injured. His eyes had a very strange look also.

I had some knowledge of *Caitanya-caritāmṛta,* so I doubted his 'ecstatic symptoms.' Many of my companions were impressed with him, but I said that I thought in this way. Then the time of *ārati* came and he was asked to stop the *kirtāna* and he did so. I wondered how he could stop so quickly—"What is this?" Then, when the *ārati* was going on I approached Rāma Dāsa Babājī in front of the Gaura-Nityānanda Deities and asked him personally, "Who is Nityānanda and who is Gaurāṅga?" He told me, "On the left side is Nityānanda and on the right is Gaurāṅga." I found him calm like a stone. There was no trace of his previous sentiment—not a pinch was present in him. I was surprised that he had suddenly stopped at the request of the priest, and when I approached and questioned him he answered me. I thought, "How is this possible, what is this? When Mahāprabhu was in *samādhi,* He took a long time to come down from that stage—it is not a formal thing like a dress that I shall wear and then leave it. But if it comes to capture the heart naturally, it is very difficult to get out of that feeling, that sentiment. This should really be the nature of that influence. But the man was now in an ordinary temperament, when just a few minutes ago he was in the highest ecstasy of God."

Then when I again came to Gauḍīya Maṭha, I learned that this was all bogus and they were preaching against Rāma Dāsa Bābājī. This show of sentiment was only to capture people. And they also quoted from Rūpa Gosvāmī, that such a show is possible only by practicing imitative sentiments:

nisarga-picchila-svānte tad abhyāsa-pare'pi ca
sattvābhāsaṁ vināpi syuḥ kvāpy-aśru pulakādayaḥ

> Whenever shedding of tears, horripulation etc. are seen in a person whose heart is soft externally and hard internally, and who are habituated to crying, rapture etc. even though they do not possess a semblance of divine emotion—such an imitative sentiment should be known as totally unsubstantial and lifeless. (*Bhakti-rasāmṛta-sindhu* 3.89)

In a drama also one may take the role of Nārada Gosvāmī and chant "Haribol, Haribol" and weep with profuse tears, but it is all artificial. One may learn cent-percent to show these symptoms in the body. Some people can shed tears easily and there are others who can learn the art of doing so. These two classes of people show so many 'high sentiments' to the public. So, it is possible for one to learn this art without a touch of divinity.

We must try to help save the ordinary people from this sham—this show and false exhibition of a high Vaiṣṇava's character. We won't allow such a dog to enter the temple. So, these persons want to imitate and take possession of the position of a Vaiṣṇava. We can't tolerate to see this. Who can remain idle and ignore this? "You fool! You cheat! You want to take the position of our guru. You want to capture the throne of our guru—I can't tolerate this! You must remain outside, you dog!" With this type of courage Prabhupāda came out.

Afraid to Approach Gaudiya Matha

There was one Professor Melville T. Kennedy (who published the book *The Caitanya Movement: A Survey*, in 1925), who was anti-Gauḍīya Maṭha and favored this Rāma Dāsa Bābājī party.

The Caitanya of this Professor Kennedy means the Sahajiyā concept of Caitanya, not the Caitanya of Gauḍīya Maṭha.

That is easy food for the scholars, but Gauḍīya Maṭha is a hard nut to crack. So Kennedy did not approach Gauḍīya Maṭha and accept that they are preaching the ideal of Caitanya. Really they are afraid to approach Gauḍīya Maṭha because they oppose everyone, maintaining that Caitanya's cult is the highest. So Gauḍīya Maṭha is not easy fodder for the western scholars.

Neither do we care for Kennedy's motivation—that out of his own pleasure or the magnitude of his own scholarship, he came to measure anything—we discard this! There is no time to lose, to mix and talk with them, we must have a standard with whom we shall talk—a general standard.

I have nothing to do with this Kennedy. I don't like to hear about him. He is dead already. He supported this Rāma Dāsa Bābājī sect which represents a nasty aspect of Gauḍīya Vaiṣṇavism, and he accepted them as the Vaiṣṇava standard. So Kennedy is judged thereby. He came to accept that party as Vaiṣṇava, representing Caitanyadeva. So it is finished. Why should I use my energy against him?

His book has disturbed the faith of some—they are ill-fated. They were tempted by that thing and they have gone out—many will do so. Coming and going, that is a fashion everywhere. Out of curiosity they come and then after some time they go away. They do not come with a deep inquiry to solve their problem—it is a problem of faith.

Adhoksaja Krsna

When I first came here to Navadvīpa, one boy used to dress as a woman. This foolish person once remarked, "I have seen Kṛṣṇa and not only myself, but I have shown Kṛṣṇa in a tamarind tree on the other side of the Ganges—there is so much evidence. So many men saw Kṛṣṇa and I showed Him to them."

I said, "Why are you cheating yourself? I am told that you are a *brāhmaṇa* boy and coming in contact with these Sahajiyā Vaiṣṇavas, you have become degraded to such a state."

"You see Kṛṣṇa? Kṛṣṇa cannot be seen by these eyes. He is *adhokṣaja.* We have learned something, consulted with saints and we have read some *śāstra, Veda, Upaniṣad, Bhāgavatam, Gītā*—all these things we have gone through. So, don't deceive yourself. You know yourself, that you are still a slave of your senses. You have lust, anger, so many things. You feel it and I also know that. You are not only deceiving the foolish persons, but what is worse, is that you are deceiving your own self." At that time I spoke very strongly, "Why are you deceiving yourself by taking this woman's dress? You have already taken a woman's ego! That full scale ego is within you. By taking up this dress you will simply mix with the women." Very strongly I said this, then he got some impression and after some days he gave up that female dress and shaving his head, came to me. "Now enlist me amongst your disciples."

Kṛṣṇa is *adhokṣaja,* He cannot be seen, and for Him to descend is very, very rare. He comes down from the spiritual sphere to the mental sphere and becomes so strong that when our eyes open they are overflowed with the vision of Him. Then, when He withdraws, nothing remains.

So, it is not so easy, there are so many stages, *ādau śraddhā, sādhu-saṅga, bhajana-kriyā, anartha-nivṛtti, bhāva-bhakti, prema-bhakti*—it is like a mathematical calculation. We can trace in a man, by measuring with this philosophical computer, how much progress is there. Has he got *śraddhā* proper? He will say, "Oh Śiva, Kṛṣṇa, Kālī, Śakti, all are God, all are equal." And that type of man will say, "I have seen Kṛṣṇa." We reject it.

Standard of Seeing Krsna

The standard measurement criterion is there—in what stage one will see Kṛṣṇa and when he has seen Kṛṣṇa, what will be the after-effect? After one has seen Kṛṣṇa, what will be his behavior? All these things should be considered. The Sahajiyās who take Kṛṣṇa, *svayam-bhagavān* Kṛṣṇa, to be in the lower level, we despise them. They are born offenders. Sanātana Gosvāmī and Jīva Gosvāmī have given the calculation, that by elimination of so many things within our area of knowledge we may go to that transcendental side. It is not a very easy affair.

I have not yet seen Kṛṣṇa, but I am on the way, in search of Kṛṣṇa. I have not got Him, not seen Him, but I am in search of Kṛṣṇa and I feel that I am on the real path. What has been said to exist on the path, I have some experience of that. I am on the real path to Kṛṣṇa, that much I can say. But I do not have the audacity to say that I have seen Kṛṣṇa or I am in *līlā* with Him.

All these things I revere and I don't want to take it so cheaply. Cheap Kṛṣṇa I don't want—this market-Kṛṣṇa I do not want. I want to have *darśana* of that Kṛṣṇa as guided by my Guru Mahārāja, either in this birth or hundreds of births after, it does not matter. I am not going to deceive anyone with any wrong statement, but I think I am on the path by the grace of Guru Mahārāja. That I can say and I feel it.

Bhaktivinoda Ṭhākura sings, "I am a resident of Svānanda-sukhada Kuñja," as if he is in *līlā*. His highest ideal is that. He is describing his ideal life—seeing from afar, from a distance. He is describing the feeling within his inner heart, "Suddenly I had a flash, I saw it, and then when I went to mark it in a particular way, it vanished." It is something like that.

If our Lord is gracious, one may get a flash of their ideal. Don't try easy marketing, you will be cheated. Pray. Make yourself ready to pay a higher and higher price. Don't accept any bargain or you will be a loser. Why? We are after the Absolute and the Absolute can never be limited. We say that we are seeking the Absolute, but practically we feel that we want to be master of the Absolute. It is impossible—that sort of aspiration should be crushed, nipped in the bud. In this search you should be willing to die. 'Die to live,' don't be miserly. Try to give yourself completely. Then as much as you will be ready to sacrifice yourself and can successfully do that, then automatically you will find yourself in some other plane. But, as a subject and making Him the object, you will be able to make Him prisoner? Don't try to have a vision of Him—try to become His prisoner.

Keeping your subjectivity you cannot have any contact with Him. Your old self is to be dissolved and your new self will come out and you will find Kṛṣṇa consciousness all around. Then sometimes Kṛṣṇa may be pleased to give you the touch of His existence in different ways. It should not be as though I am an inquirer and I want to make Kṛṣṇa the object of my inquiry—to imprison Him in my imagination—the prison-house of imagination.

When I had not yet joined the *maṭha* I was a law student and the nationalist movement came. Just in the front of the Calcutta University Hall, one gentleman was delivering political lectures, so I left there and went up the hill across the road. There I found a *sādhu* and I asked him in broken Hindi, "Have you seen God? Can you show me God?" The *sādhu* replied in such an inspiring voice, "Don't you see? Don't you see Him? Look at all this, the atmosphere, the trees, the water, the view, all these things. Cast your glance upon the whole of the environment. Can't you feel Him? Can't you see Him?" With so much inspiration he said this, that at that moment I saw that conscious backing. Whatever exists, just in the background, I found some spiritual existence. In such an impressive way he said, "Don't you see Him? Look at the sky, the trees, He is there, He is everywhere. Can't you see? Only He is there."

Negative Hankering

By our continuous engagement we shall come to the stage of seeing Kṛṣṇa everywhere, talking about Kṛṣṇa, hearing about Kṛṣṇa, taking the Name of Kṛṣṇa, taking His *prasādam,* and collecting for Him. In this way gradually we shall enter into the intense feeling of His halo, His luster and gradually we shall come to have a conception according to our capacity.

atha vā bahunaitena kiṁ jñātena tavārjuna
viṣṭabhyāham idaṁ kṛtsnam ekāṁśena sthito jagat
(*Gītā* 10.42)

> Arjuna, what more shall I say to you? Who am I? Everything you can imagine is there in only My negligible part. You are going to inquire about that, it is not something cheap. Then after that what will you do?

Mahāprabhu said, "I am searching after Him but I have not obtained even a little bit of that divine love—*na prema gandho 'sti darāpi me harau.* Otherwise how can I maintain My life, sustain My life without His company, without His grace."

yugāyitaṁ nimeśena cakṣuśa prāvṛṣāyitam
śūnyāyitaṁ jagat sarvaṁ govinda-viraheṇa me
(*Śikṣāṣṭakam* 7)

Yugāyitaṁ nimeśena—one moment seems to me so many light years. *Cakṣuśa prāvṛṣāyitam*—so many tears run from my eyes.

Śūnyāyitaṁ jagat sarvaṁ—the whole world seems to me only a vacant background. *Govinda-viraheṇa me*—because I still cannot get the company of my beloved Lord Kṛṣṇa.

Higher Standard of Devotion

Sometimes a student may say that, "I have given so much and all I want is a little drop, just a touch so I can be inspired to do more. Not that I want to enjoy Kṛṣṇa, but I want some reciprocation—'Yes, I am there.'"

But this is nothing. Taking food, walking, taking bath, dressing, so many comforts we are seeking and what demand are we going to fulfill? Try to calculate everything in terms of the Infinite. No finite thing, however great, can come to the Infinite. The very composition of Infinite is of another type. When you are on this path you will think, "I can't do anything to approach Kṛṣṇa. I have done nothing." That is a unit of measurement towards the Infinite. "I am doing this, I am doing that, I am doing so much, I am paying so much value," that is the opposite way. Those that are really on the path of Kṛṣṇa feel that, "I can't do anything for Him." The whole attitude will be changed. We have been given this idea by our Guru Mahārāja, the nature of the way of real searching.

Once, two *brahmacārīs*, after ten years of service, came to Śrīla Prabhupāda to put some questions, and they were hesitating to speak. Then Prabhupāda himself asked them, "It seems that you want to speak something to me but you don't." "Yes, we came to say something to Your Holiness but we dare not venture." "No, no, say what you have to say." Then they spoke, "For ten years we have come and we are doing service as we are ordered, but so far we do not feel anything about Kṛṣṇa. We do not feel we have made any progress." Prabhupāda asked, "What you say at present, is it true? Are you sincere in your statement?"

They replied, "Yes, what we say is true." He told them, "Then it is alright. You continue, don't be afraid." That was his point. What does this mean?

You have not acquired anything—you are searching for something but you have not obtained anything concrete. That feeling is a good sign. If you should say that I have so much knowledge, so many things, then that is progress in the egotistical way. Instead you must empty yourself. It is a very striking thing.

Only negative hankering for Kṛṣṇa is the measurement of our progress in that way. "I have nothing, I can't relish anything, I am going to be mad, I have not yet obtained any trace of Kṛṣṇa."

This is the way—*viraha-vipralambha.* The other day I was saying, "All risk, no gain," the way is like that. No risk, no gain, but all risk, no gain, the way is like that. You risk everything but you won't get anything, because what in our terms is gain and loss, has captured us on the negative side—we do not know the measurement.

Prepare yourself. Don't be satisfied with anything, thinking, "This is Kṛṣṇa." It is not Kṛṣṇa. *Neti neti neti! Neti*—eliminate the falsity and in the background you will be able to find something real. "It is there. It is with the scripture. It is with the Guru and the Vaiṣṇava, but I have nothing. It is their property all the time, not mine. It won't be my property, it is the property of my Gurudeva." In this way the angle of vision will be set. He is the property of my Gurudeva, the property of Nanda, Yaśodā, they can deal with Him in anyway they choose, but I am a sight-seer. I will be asked by the servitors, "Do this, do this for His service." That position is better for me—not to approach the nearest but serve from far off. I am not fit. We have to take that course, that we are unfit. The unfitness should be the first thing to analyze—the first thing open to us.

We need *śaraṇāgati*, self-abnegation. I must undo what I am, dissolve my ego, then He will reveal Himself. It is difficult to dissolve one's ego, but when the ego is fully dissolved then another ego will come out through service. When we have eliminated the present ego, and come to the very gist of the souls conception, then we find ourselves in a wonderful atmosphere and through service we will gradually enter into it.

We are reminded of the example of one western *sannyāsī*. He was very mad in his dancing to show that he was inspired with *kṛṣṇa-rasa*. I never saw our Guru Mahārāja dance and chant, only soberly talking about Kṛṣṇa. If at any time, any tear was oozing from his eyes, with his controlled mind, he very stealthily removed them. He was very eager not to express any feeling, and if any feelings or sentiments came out, very carefully he tried to conceal them.

That was his nature, not to show. What did Rāma Dāsa Bābājī and other Sahajiyās gain by showing off with mad dancing, shedding tears and shivering? All this show drew the common mob towards them and Prabhupāda had to explain that these things are no real sign of devotion. *Koṭi mukta madhye durlabha eka kṛṣṇa bhakta*—amongst millions of liberated souls, one *kṛṣṇa-bhakta* is hardly to be found. Try to come in the vicinity of the Infinite. We have to cross to the Infinite and dissolve our ego. Hegel said, 'Die.' Learn to die first and die not for this or that but for the Kṛṣṇa conception coming from Gurudeva, 'Die to live.'

The Halo of Radharani

We are wakeful in this material world, but there are others that are completely awake in that plane of faith. This world of matter is underground—it is far away from their conception. This tangible world of exploitation and enjoyment is far away from those who are deeply engaged in the world of service through faith, *śraddhā*.

They believe that even to feel the need to see Kṛṣṇa is a kind of enjoyment. They say," No, we won't disturb His sweet will. Whenever He likes, He may come before us and then we will get the chance to see Him; otherwise not." It is a kind of imposition of our exploiting nature that we should, for our satisfaction, want Kṛṣṇa to stand before us. The devotees do not want that. Mādhavendra Purī was fasting so much that he did not beg for food or his livelihood from others. If things came automatically he would take them, otherwise he would fast. Kṛṣṇa came by and supplied some food to him and said, "Why Purī, do you not beg for your food?"

We think that Mādhavendra Purī was very fortunate that he was supplied food by Kṛṣṇa, but we find an even higher devotion in Sanātana. When Rādhārāṇī came and supplied foodstuffs to Rūpa Gosvāmī for cooking sweet rice, Sanātana Gosvāmī was very much disturbed at heart. "What is this Rūpa? Did you aspire after something for me?" Rūpa Gosvāmī replied," Yes, I did Gurudeva. I thought that if I get some milk and rice, I can prepare some sweet rice which is your favorite and so I could then invite you to take that *prasāda*." Sanātana told, "It is so tasty—I have never had such tasty *prasāda*—it must have some peculiar origin. Who gave you this material? You wanted it, so who gave it you?" Rūpa replied, "A girl came from her family and presented it to me." Sanātana inquired. "Who is that girl?" That girl was never found in the nearby village.

Then Sanātana Gosvāmī could understand that Rādhārāṇī Herself had come and supplied the ingredients. "We are hunting after Her to serve Her and She came to serve us! You have done wrong. What is this? It is just the opposite. What have you done, my brother? You wanted something for me and that was supplied by Her—this is a great misfortune."

Sanātana Gosvāmī was very much disappointed and he went away with that sort of mind. Rūpa Gosvāmī could not take that *prasādam*.

This incident concerning Sanātana Gosvāmī reveals that the higher kind of devotion never requires that Kṛṣṇa comes and supplies us with anything. To impose our will on Him is not service proper. Whatever He likes He will do and whatever He requires from us, we should consider ourselves fortunate if we are able to supply it. All our desires to the extreme should be exhausted and eliminated fully and we should place ourselves at the disposal of the Supreme Lord. It is His nature to supply anything to His devotees, but the devotees do not want the Lord to fulfill their necessities Himself. Pure devotion is like that. Through faith, the devotees think, "He is my Lord and I don't want to have *darśana* to satisfy my lower faculties."

It is a lower class of faith that demands that if I can see Him then I'm satisfied that He exists. Although we have no capacity to see Him, to be the subject and to see Him as an object is a lower kind of faith. The higher kind of faith dictates that He does exist and that He is the cause of everything. The cause is that wherefrom everything is coming, everything is being maintained and everything is, at last, entering into Him. The effect is not everything—the cause is there. What is the nature of the cause? Some say Brahman is the cause, some say Paramātma and some say Bhagavān is the cause of everything—the destination and designer of everything. So try to keep the faith. It is meaningless to search after proof whether or not He exists. Deep faith says He does exist.

Faith is almost non-existent to us in our present condition, but faith is the most substantial thing and it has its superior existence—other things may vanish, but it will stand forever. Faith is the particular potency of Śrī Rādhārāṇī. Kṛṣṇa is ecstasy

Himself—He feels Himself, He tastes Himself, and He enjoys Himself in the distribution of that sort of ecstatic joy to others—however, it is only possible through faith, through *śraddhā*. It is the very nature of the *hlādinī-śakti*, which is represented by Rādhārāṇī in full. Faith can transmit Kṛṣṇa consciousness to the outside world.

Faith is the halo of Rādhārāṇī, the light of which allows others to understand Kṛṣṇa. The negative combined with the positive reveals Them to the outside. All parts of the center negative can expand and transmit that sort of faith, that sort of joy. *Śraddhā* means faith and that peculiar sort of substance is to be understood by us. What is that? It is not a mere abstract substance.

Management is Radharani's Service

In Purī, during the last days of Prabhupāda, three months before he disappeared, I found him dictating his commentary on *Caitanya-bhāgavata.* Some devotees came and inquired about temple management. Leaving that commentary aside, he began to inquire about the financial administration of the *maṭha.* We felt a little disturbed, "Why do they have to bother him at this time, when he is engaged in some deep thinking—giving narrations about the highest world."

But I was told by one of my godbrothers, whom I revered at that time that, "This duty is that of Rādhārāṇī Herself—to manage the domestic affairs of Kṛṣṇa." That explanation touched me deeply. She holds that managerial responsibility for the household of Kṛṣṇa. This is *sambandha-jñāna,* where everything is devotional. And what ostentatiously seems to be the science of devotion, may be otherwise.

In this mundane world Durgā-devī (Mahāmāyā) is in charge of management and may be considered Yogamāyā's representation in this perverted world. Yogamāyā is considered to be the comprehensive potency under Baladeva who is entrusted with the charge of management—to facilitate *kṛṣṇa-līlā* there in Vṛndāvana. *Chāyeva yasya bhuvanāni vibharti durgā*—Durgā is in charge of this mundane world for management, and her higher extension in the positive world is Yogamāyā. Yogamāyā is managing in the transcendental world and her facsimile is cast here in this mundane world. So Durgā-devī says in the *Nārada-pañcarātra*—*tava vakṣasi rādhāhaṁ rāse vṛndāvane vane*—"I am Rādhā in Vṛndāvana!" She is proud to state that, "We are potency, and the potency should not be neglected. We have our extension in Vṛndāvana. There is Rādhārāṇī, of Whom I am the representation. She holds the greatest position in Vṛndāvana, and She belongs to the potency section—the negative side. That negative side is extended up to the highest quarter, so you should not ignore us. Here, I am the favorite of Mahādeva but as my real self, I hold the highest position there in Vṛndāvana."

Prabhupāda said that we are really Śāktas—we are the worshiper of the potency, not just Śākta but *śuddha-śākta*. The original potency is in Vraja, and that is the dedicating Moiety towards Kṛṣṇa. Direct connection is there and indirectly with Kṛṣṇa through Her. This is Rādhā's position.

Followers of Darwin

Bengal is especially selected for *śakti* or Kālī worship. Tantra is there also. They believe we should satisfy our direct controller, the prison superintendent. In *Brahmā-saṁhitā*, Devī is described as the mistress, the controller of the whole of this *brahmaṇḍa*, the prison house where those that lead a regular life are put into prison. They do not follow *īśāvāsyam* or *yajñārthāt karmaṇo'nyatra, loko'yaṁ karma-bandhanaḥ*. They have no recognition of the final authority and they think of themselves,

"We are separately in an independent stage—we are all Śiva." They are put in the womb of Māyā. *Māyā* means misconception. Māyā-devī rules over them and they want to satisfy the goddess who controls this prison house. Thereby their punishment may be a little livable, unless they are given a chance to go up. Sometimes she releases those that are very sincere and shows them the path to go up to Nārāyaṇa. In *Bṛhat-bhāgavatāmṛta* we see Gopa-kumāra was worshiping with the *kāmākhya mantra, śakti-mantra.* Because he was very sincere, Kāmākhya-devī showed him the way towards the higher direction. But generally such worshipers are insincere and they give some offering and want some advantage. They are thinking, "How can this serve me?"

Their liberation is of a particular type, but they are not advised to take to the worship of Nārāyaṇa and then go up. Their goal becomes Śiva—to attain the position of Śiva, the master of the material potency. But one remains in connection with the material potency and gradually he again enters *māyā.*

ye 'nye 'ravindākṣa vimukta-māninas
tvayy aṣṭa-bhāvād aviśuddha buddhayaḥ
(*Bhāg.* 10.2.32)

They cannot secure any visa, but they get a passport. After securing a passport they have to move in the boundary line and without a visa, they will have to again enter here. That is the general case. But in a special case, Māyā-devī recommends them for the visa. "You do it in this way and then you can get the visa, and you will go up to Vaikuṇṭha. Otherwise you may come to the last boundary of this creation and you will have to enter again into the compound." That is the case, if they have faith.

Some of them think that *śakti,* potency, is above everything, and that consciousness is under the potency. Potency is the highest existence and potency produces consciousness. In other words, those who are out-and-out Śāktas, their conception is this. *Puruṣa* and *prakṛti—purusa* means consciousness—*prakṛti* means energy.

Energy in the course of its evolution produces consciousness, and this consciousness is of three types—Brahmā, Viṣṇu and Śiva. Brahmā with *raja-guṇa* is creation. Viṣṇu is *sattva-guṇa,* that is the nature of sustenance and Rudra, *tamo-guṇa,* this is dissolution. Evolution, dissolution and the main type is sustenance with Viṣṇu. Brahmā, Viṣṇu, Maheśvara—three *guṇas,* material qualifications, are produced by the potency.

If any potency, devoid of consciousness, is thought to be the ultimate, it can only be the material potency. That is fossil—that is the Darwin theory. The orthodox Śāktas, whether they know it or not, are followers of Darwin. They believe that matter produces mind, but according to *Vedānta,* it is just the opposite. Consciousness produces it—it is subjective evolution. And there, they have faith in objective evolution, that *prakṛti* produces everything—first the three *guṇas—sattva, raja,* and *tama.* Then the whole creation comes into existence. That is their theory. And those that are almost Vaiṣṇavas, that are sincere, they also have recognition of *prakṛti,* but otherwise: "You are my mother and you gave me the vision of what is what. I can see. Now I can go on accordingly." That type of progress has been shown in *Bṛhat-bhāgavatāmṛta* by Sanātana Gosvāmī.

na hi kalyāṇa kṛt kaścid durgatiṁ tāta gacchati
(*Gītā* 6.40)

Those who are sincere at heart receive real help from the jail superintendent. The authority of the prison house guides them properly. "They are good prisoners and although they have come into this prison house, they are good persons. They should be guided well so they may go and live with their family outside."

Three Classes of Atheists

Buddhists are also of the Śākta type. They believe in force in matter, but not eternal consciousness. The Cārvakas, the Epicurean aspect of thinking, believe that it is only with the combination of some material substances that consciousness has been produced. With the dissolution of the body nothing remains. This is the lowest kind of atheist.

The Buddhists are moderate materialists. They say with the subtle combination of material things, the mind has been produced. And according to *karma* we get physical attraction to objects, and we attain a physical body. The physical body may transform—in the physical world one gets many bodies according to their own *karma.*

So at the dissolution of the body, the *jīva* soul does not end as the Epicurean or the Cārvaka school thinks. But with the dissolution of the mind, everything disappears and nothing remains. This is also a type of atheist. An atheist thinks that the soul is mortal. The soul is really immortal but these fellows say that the soul is mortal. Some say that after the dissolution of the physical body, nothing remains as soul. And the Buddhists say that with the dissolution of the mental body, nothing remains as soul.

And Śaṅkara takes it one step further. Śaṅkara says there is already a light there and that light is focused here and seems to be like a soul. Just as in glass, the sun or moon is reflected. The moon is there—it is reflected in the glass. Remove the glass and there is no moon there. So all the *jīvas* are not different souls but only one soul, like the moon in the sky reflected in so many pieces of glass. So many reflections are considered as different souls. This is Śaṅkara. And the Buddhists? No moon! No soul! Dissolution of the mind means dissolution of the soul. And Cārvaka, the lowest class—with the dissolution of the body—nothing remains!

So there are three sections of atheists according to the Vaiṣṇavas. They are all considered as atheists because they do not believe in the eternal existence of the soul. They are all proper atheists and there is also a classification amongst them, according to their conception and the environment. Christianity and Islam have faith in eternal existence of the souls and also God, but their conception of God, soul and world is of a different type.

Disarm the Scientists

Generally scientists are considered another type of atheist. The scientists usually have bad feelings towards religion, so to convince them, generally we must first disarm them—show them that their methods are faulty. The first point is that with a finite conception, how can you get the Infinite?

Also, one of your scientists may say something and another greater scientist says, "No, it is not so! It is false." A greater scientist can prove that the lower scientist is false. So in different ways we can try to show the proper process of knowledge. Local knowledge cannot guide the central knowledge, but the central thing can drive the local. It can govern the local point. Hegel's theory was, "The reality must be by Itself and for Itself." God has taken everything from the hands of the scientists and left them empty-handed.

The other day, I was told that the scientists are finding new things, and I said, "Yes, they are *finding* new things, but are they *creating* new things or were they already there? They were already there and they are *discovering* them. They are not finding the cause—they are only partly discovering and understanding. But the Infinite is there. The astonishing knowledge of this is outside our understanding and with great attempts we are finding something and thinking that we have created. "I am greater than the Creator of all this!" This is a foolish thing, is it not? Everything is there. All wonders are there. Wonder of wonders! And I discover only one wonder in my experience and I think I am more than God!!! Such foolish persons—scientists! Only one point I am finding out in the finite section, and I boast that I am more than God. What foolishness can be more than this?

Science is nothing! Science is a part of misconception. What is science? They are a group of exploiters! And the worst type of exploiters—exploiting from the mineral substance also. And they will have to pay with interest. For every action there is an equal and opposite reaction—one of their friends has given this warning to them, and this still holds true. For every action there is an equal and opposite reaction. This is not an analytical world. Whatever you desire, He alone will give to you. Action, reaction, you are not the master to loot this universe, you human rouges, this is not meant for your robbing. There is justice.

That is my contribution to the Bhaktivedānta Institute which has been requested by Svāmī Mahārāja to crush the Darwin theory of fossil cause. My contribution is that the origin of things is consciousness and what we conceive as the material world is floating like an iceberg in the ocean. Consciousness is the original substantial thing, and the different types of thoughts and ideas, that this is stone, this is gold, this is tiger—all these ideas are floating in the world, in the ocean of consciousness. I want to assert that. And the Master of the consciousness, like a hypnotist, wants us to see, and we are forced to see like that—we are helpless. That is also in stages. But His will—the Master's will is all important. We are helpless. It is His *līlā,* He represents the one whole, and we are a small part of that one whole. We have some laws of movement, but He is the autocrat, and can change the law—we are designed and destined by Him.

Everything is a subjective evolution of consciousness. There is the subjective eternal domain and this world where our free will is tested. There is also evolution, that is another thing—the eternal *līlā.*

Position in the Infinite

Stop your investigations in this world! Undo your progress and find that the Lord's mercy is with you. Only stop your negative attempt. Your negative enthusiasm should be stopped and you will find that the grace of God is with you. He is everywhere, He is within you also. Try to find Him out. *Tad dūre tad vantike*—the most remote and the most near. He is nearest to you and also the furthest. So stop your energetic searching and enthusiasm on the opposite side. Make yourself self-sufficient. "I can know!" If He directs you to know Him, then you can know. That is the method recommended by the scripture.

The right to making Himself known to you is in His hand, not your hand. So, accept that method to know Him—it is within His fist. He is by Himself and for Himself. You are for Him, He is not for you. You have not created Him, but He has created you. Try to understand your position in the infinite. You are meant for Him, and if you take that attitude first then you will find that He is also for you.

āmi to' tomāra, tumi to' amāra
ki kāja apara dhane
(*Śaraṇāgati,* song 8)

First surrender, saying "I am Yours!" then you will know that He is yours.

suhṛdaṁ sarva-bhūtānāṁ
jñātvā māṁ śāntim ṛcchati

> Only I am the enjoyer of everything, and I am friendly to all. When you can realize that I am all in all, but I am friend to all at the same time, then all the misgivings will disappear in you. *(Gītā 5.29)*

Our interest is represented in our Guardian. We may not know our real interest, but He knows it better. So I should not be afraid of Him, the management is with Him. The Absolute Good is autocratic—that is the best arrangement—the Absolute Good. In autocracy, freedom must be there—then everyone will be benefitted because the center of all power, the Absolute Power is absolute good. There will be no misgivings, no room for apprehension—then his heart will be filled only with peace. You are for Him, He is not for you.

Stealing for Krsna

From the real plane of thinking, no one is a proprietor of anything, but Kṛṣṇa is the proprietor. Generally stealing and cheating is justified if it is really meant for Kṛṣṇa and a Kṛṣṇa *bhakta*. *Asura-luṭiyā kaya, kṛṣṇera bhāṇḍāra*—the demons are looting and utilizing the things of Kṛṣṇa for their purpose. Everything belongs to Kṛṣṇa, so if I steal anything and offer it to Kṛṣṇa or a Kṛṣṇa *bhakta*, that is not stealing in the absolute sense, only in a relative sense. In the absolute consideration, no one is master or owner of anything, even his body, what to speak of property. This body does not belong to the man, it does not obey him.

Everything, *īśāvasyam*—everything belongs to Him. So, "This is mine, this is his, this belongs to a third person," this is all misconception—not absolute consideration, but mis-consideration. And we are to forgo this and realize that everything, including myself, belongs to Kṛṣṇa—everything. And we shall all work for His interest, then that is normal life. *Janma, mṛtyu, jarā, vyādhi*—this is abnormal—the punishment is death, disease, birth, infirmity. All the punishments we are to suffer from are due to this misconception.

Footnotes

1. Prabhupāda conferred upon him the name "Śrī Bhakti Rakṣaka," which means "Guardian of Devotion." And further echoing the statement of the great Vaiṣṇava Preceptor, Śrīla Jīva Gosvāmī—who referred in his Sanskrit writings to the renowned Śrīmad Bhāgavatam commentator, Śrī Śrīdhara Svāmī, as *bhaktyeka-rakṣakaḥ* [Supreme Guardian of Devotion]—Śrīla Bhaktisiddhānta Sarasvatī Prabhupāda gave him the *tridaṇḍi-sannyāsa* title of 'Śrīdhara.' Thus, he became Śrīla Bhakti Rakṣaka Śrīdhara Mahārāja.

2. One day, the godbrother of Śrīla Śrīdhara Mahārāja, Sakhī-caraṇa Bābu, after hearing this verse, told his other Godbrothers, "Śrīdhara Mahārāja has nothing there except a thatched house where he has erected a very long bamboo pole with a flag on top, yet he has composed this grand *śloka*!" Śrīla Śrīdhara Mahārāja responded by saying, "You will see in the future what will manifest here!"

~ Part Two ~

Divine Guidance

Divine Guidance

Some devotees have first initiation, *hari-nāma*, from Śrīla Svāmī Mahārāja and second initiation from another guru, but that is a formal thing. Not everything depends on the relative consideration, there are other things—the absolute consideration. That is relative—formal.

So whom they look to as guru depends upon their connection, to what extent their connection with their Prabhupāda is perfect. If his connection and Prabhupāda's connection are the same, then it is so. But if his consciousness is deviated from that of Prabhupāda, then we may not expect it to be so.

Always the relative, and the absolute consideration—these two sides should be considered. What is given by our *guru-paramparā* follows the absolute consideration, not the relative. In the formal way, we do not find his disciple, then another's disciple—in this sort of order. But the gist, the highest type of substance is found, and that is accepted. The whole *guru-paramparā* is like that. It is fixed.

Wherever we get the highest transcendental realization, we accept that. It is not dependent on the place, the land, or knowledge of English, or philosophy, or this or that. The highest criterion will be what I have understood to be the conception of our goal. But where to trace this? Which way can I go? That is the *guru-paramparā*. Find it in this way.

Rūpa Gosvāmī's and Sanātana Gosvāmī's *dīkṣā-guru* was Vidyā Vacaspati in Navadvīpa. Then Rūpa and Sanātana were both connected with Svarūpa. And Svarūpa was connected with Mahāprabhu—Rādhā-Kṛṣṇa combined. Svarūpa is almost in the same classification as Rūpa-Sanātana. Jīva Gosvāmī's guru was Rūpa Gosvāmī. Raghunātha Gosvāmī's *dīkṣā-guru,* in his previous life, was Yadunandana Ācārya. But Raghunātha was connected again. Raghunātha and Jīva are both connected with Rūpa. Kavirāja Gosvāmī was connected with Raghunātha. And then next is Narottama, who is a disciple of Lokanātha Gosvāmī. Lokanātha Gosvāmī is hardly mentioned in the *paramparā.* And then, Viśvanātha is connected with Narottama. There is no direct connection between them—he is in the middle, down two steps. Narottama's guru is Gaṅgā-nārāyaṇa Cakravartī. Then Viśvanātha. And Baladeva is also combined there—He has some contribution in the middle. And then from Baladeva comes the connection of Jagannātha Dāsa Bābājī.

Then came Bhaktivinoda Ṭhākura, whose direct guru, Vipina Gosvāmī is omitted. So many are omitted. Vipina Gosvāmī comes in the line of Jāhnavā, Nityānanda Prabhu's wife. So many females are in between, ten, twelve or so. They all are omitted. And Bhaktivinoda Ṭhākura is connected to Jagannātha Dāsa Bābājī, his *śikṣā-guru.* His *dīkṣā-guru* is omitted. Then Bhaktivinoda Ṭhākura asked Prabhupāda to take *dīkṣā* from Gaura-kiśora Dāsa Bābājī Mahārāja. So Prabhupāda saw both of them in the same line. And from him we have come—the next generation.

So this was taught to us, against vehement opposition from the *kula-gurus* and these *bābājīs* also. "The Gauḍīya Maṭha does not recognize *guru-paramparā* in reality," that is their general complaint. The *bābājī* class, and the *kula-guru* class, the Gosvāmī class are very loud in their assertion that, "Gauḍīya Maṭha does not recognize the *guru-paramparā,* which is so important for a Vaiṣṇava. They do not care for that." That is the general complaint against Gauḍīya Maṭha.

But our stand is that we are not bound by any flesh connection. We only want the gist of the *paramparā*—wherever that is to be found, I shall bow down my head there. And whatever respectable bodily connection one may have, I have nothing to do with him. No body connection.

Follow the Spirit

We are to follow that spirit and not the form we find there. The physical connection has been ignored and the flow of the pure knowledge has been traced there in that *guru-paramparā.* And we have to believe, if we have faith in such things, then we are real followers of Gauḍīya Maṭha and we must preach this. The Sahajiyās attack us, "Oh, they have no *guru-paramparā,* they are all lost. Who will care for that? They have no guardian! Guardian-less. They are all mushrooms, the Gauḍīya Maṭha. Their guru was a mushroom—all mushrooms! They are kept in the dark! No lineage to be traced. What are they?" That is there *kolahala*—their loud noise.

But the *śāstra* is there. The conversation with Rāmānanda Rāya and other *śāstras* are there. There are the *Ṣaṭa-sandarbhas* through which we have to understand the *Bhāgavatam, Mahābhārata, Gītā* and all the *śāstras.* And where is the substance we hanker for? The good side, the place where we want to purchase a ticket to, is located here. The *Gītā* says, the *Bhāgavata* says, the *Mahābhārata* says, *Caitanya-caritāmṛta* says it is so—with the approval of our heart. *Krīyatāṁ yadi kuto'pi labhyate*—in whatever market it is available, deposit the money and purchase it at once! No haggling over the price, that is the materialists' way. So, anywhere you find it, purchase it at any value. In *Bhagavad-gītā* you will find such a valuable thing, in *Mahābhārata,* in *Bhāgavatam*—here and there such valuable things are possible, it is existing. So wherever you find it, attain it at once!

Succession of the Thought

It is not undetectable. One who has the eye to see cannot but follow this idea. They may say, "I don't see this. Why should I do that?" But we also have *guru-paramparā.*

In the days of Mahāprabhu, they also had *guru-paramparā,* but they left everything and came to the *pārṣadas* of Mahāprabhu—Advaita, Nityānanda Prabhu, Gadādhara. Why did they come? They had their *guru-paramparā* already. *Guru-paramparā* does not mean the succession of the body.

We have to chase the succession of thought of Kṛṣṇa Consciousness, because we are beggars for that. Not for anything else, not for formality, not for the material thing, not for knowledge, *jñāna,* whatever. But for the substance, not for the form. That attitude is shown in our *guru-paramparā,* so we are to follow that.

In history also we find this. In England the main powerful kings are traced, and the others are in the background. Unqualified kings are left in the background. In the lists of presidents or kings, it is everywhere. The non-important persons are in the background. Individually anyone can come and learn their strategy, tactics, and their bravery from Napoleon, from Alexander, from Hannibal. They don't care for the gap between Hannibal, Alexander, Napoleon, and Julius Caesar. The specialist has to learn from that, not from an ordinary general in that period—they won't care. And in research also.

One man said for posterity that after Newton, then came Einstein—all individuals in between will be left out.

In this way, we are indebted to the stalwarts who have given some substantial contribution. We want to keep up their gift for the benefit of all, and for ourselves also. We want the substance, and not the form, to a certain extent. As much as possible, we can show our regard for that form. But mainly we are interested in the substance. The contained, and not the container, but the container may also be regarded to a certain extent. And what is contained there, that will have the most important attention. In our *guru-paramparā* we have accepted that. When you have accepted that *guru-paramparā*, then it is clear.

Vision of Guru

We shall try to see that our intelligence is the property of our Gurudeva—it is not our own. It is there. It shines very beautifully on the head of Gurudeva. We are required to regulate our vision in that way. But it is just beyond my touch, transcendental. We must come very close to Gurudeva, for he has come down, so far. Gurudeva in his personal capacity in *vṛndāvana-līlā*, may be seen as a particular *mañjarī*.

Prabhupāda told once that, "My Gurudeva is Guṇa-mañjarī, Gaura-kiśora. But if I can look at him at heart, in a very spacious way, a very generous way, then I can find Rādhārāṇī in him." The *mañjarī* section represents the partial *līlā*, not the general *līlā*. But he told, "If I look carefully with a broader outlook, I can find Rādhārāṇī in him. *Antaryāmī*—in that way. He is representing Her, his whole heart is devoted to Rādhārāṇī. In that way we can follow. And everywhere it is possible—everywhere we can see that.

Mahāprabhu said to Rāmānanda Rāya, "You are a *mahā-bhāgavata*. Wherever you cast your glance, you find Kṛṣṇa easily." *Yahān tahān rādhā-kṛṣṇa tomāre sphurāya.* We must think of Rādhārāṇī. Deeper insight, eliminating everything. By Her it may be possible for us to think about Her in a more intense and spacious manner. By this we may have some conception of Her. *Vaikuṇṭha-daśā* means this—transcendental view.

But some sort of ecstasy is there that, these so-called concrete things do not capture our mind or our heart, and that which can attract us is more than imagination. So that is reality and this is rubbish. These concrete things are simply rubbish due to their mortal characteristics. This is our opposition.

Soul will have contact with soul—that is natural. When the soul is forced to come into material conception, that is abnormal, that is *māyā,* illusion. So he cannot free himself. The soul is forced to feel like a fossil. What is this? The soul cannot move in its own soil? That the soul is forced to move in the soil of the fossil, is abnormal. The soul must move in its own soil and then it can advance to the higher soil.

Even we are told that in this world the *Kāma-śāstra,* which describes mundane love, there the ladies and men are classified. Generally there are four headings. For the men, *aśvajātiya*—the lowest class, like a horse. Then the next class is *vṛṣajātiya*—the ox-class section, that is a little better. And then *mṛga*—they are second class. Then the first class *śaśaka*—*śaśaka* means rabbit. These are the four classes of men.

Women are also divided into four classes; *hastinī,* the most cruel class, fourth class. Then next higher is *śaṅkhinī.* And the second class is *citrinī,* and the first class division for ladies is *padminī.*

This classification is according to their temperament of gross gratification. In the higher class, their union and their pleasure is only singing, dancing and conversation, not gross sense experience.

And the grossest sense experience, the carnal desire, that is in the lowest category. Accordingly that has been classified as such. So if the fine things satisfy us, that must be of a higher class. The high thinking men are not existing in the fossils' world, they are always busy. People such as Newton and Einstein, are always engaged with fine things, not so many gross things are there.

In this way it may also be conducted on the spiritual side. Their satisfaction therein is with the finer things. They do not require anything gross for their satisfaction. That existence is higher existence. Satisfied with the high ideals, they can live and move. They can retain that position twenty-four hours a day. From here they continue to advance.

But, with a gross mentality, they can't maintain that sort of life in the very subtle world. Those who want the gross things for the tongue, for the nose, for them this sensual attraction is the main thing in their life. Some are more attached towards the tongue, some towards touch, some towards sight—in the level of this sense experience.

But for a higher type of recreation, they find their satisfaction in the higher plane. Our Prabhupāda told, "If I look at my Gurudeva with some aspiration I can find Rādhārāṇī in him." That was his expression. Look deeply at the inner existence.

Guru as Nitya-siddha

A pure *nitya-siddha* devotee (such as Śrīla Bhaktivedānta Svāmī Prabhupāda) may sometimes speak of his previous life (such as that of a medical doctor) but that must be pushed in the background. His brightest duty is awaiting him, to spread this doctrine of love. He was a doctor, who could not only remove and cure physical diseases, but he came to remove the heart disease of so many in this world. That was his purpose.

One important point I want to make clear is that, when it is necessary, for the pure devotees to discharge some divine duties, then their so-called mundane life is merely a plea. Just as the CID (Criminal Identification Department) may take any garment, any shape, any duty, but his main object is to watch.

When they come to this mundane world, the *nitya-siddha* comes with a variegated plea by the will of Kṛṣṇa, but that is not an important thing. The reality is there, and this is only a sham dress for the time being. You see the Pāṇḍavas, and other *pārśadas* of Kṛṣṇa in different situations and with different personalities. Someone is begging, someone is enraged, so many things, but this is somewhat worldly and all this is just to show to the people that these things have no value. This is all *māyā, sattva-guṇa, raja-guṇa, tamo-guṇa*—all *māyā.*

A sacred life according to the standard of this world, is considered to be in *sattva-guṇa,* but that is false. And the life of the dacoit Ratnākara Dasyu (Vālmīki) is very *tamo-guṇa*—that is also false. When the light comes, darkness of any density may disappear in a moment. So, this matters little in the case of the *nirguṇa,* Yogamāyā. Whenever Yogamāyā wants, Mahāmāyā retires.

In prison there is a particular law for the prisoners, for the culprits, but whenever the officer from the higher sphere comes to visit the prison house, wherever he goes, the prison law retires.

Yogamāyā—*prakṛtiṁ svām adhiṣṭhāya, sambhavāmy ātma mayayā*—Kṛṣṇa says, *prakṛtiṁ svām adhiṣṭhāya,* by controlling, not by fighting. Wherever this higher law goes, this lower law is forced to retire. No exertion, no fight is even necessary to remove Mahāmāyā.

api cet sudurācāro bhajate mām ananya bhāk
sādhur eva sa māntavyaḥ samyag vyavasito hi saḥ

What he is doing is perfectly right, cent-percent. You may see some bleak things in the life of a *sādhu,* but if he is a real *sādhu,* in the *nirguṇa* position, then what you see is only a concoction that has no value, if cent percent he is doing the right thing. So this *māyā* is a negative stage, it has no value when any positive thing comes back to it. So, taking Ratnākara Dasyu's case, and Jagāi and Mādhāi's case, in the previous moment, they were great demons, and in the next moment they are great devotees. It is His divine will.

The phenomenal conception has no position before the Infinite divine will. The Infinite divine will is in one place, and this self-condemned misconception is on the other side. What can *māyā* do to Kṛṣṇa?

So in any form, in any way, they may come, but the *śāstra* asks us not to look at the background.

kibā vipra kibā nyāsi śūdra kene naya
yei kṛṣṇa-tattva-vetta sei guru haya

Kṛṣṇa consciousness is absolute. It does not depend on anything. Still, because we have some weakness here, we may try to find a guru from a high family, whose figure is a beautiful one, and has neglected his opulence like Buddhadeva, and is a great scholar. This may be helpful to the disciples. But really this has such a negative value. Otherwise, in *kṛṣṇa-bhakti,* the devotion of the Supreme Lord, divinity does not care for any such grandeur of this false world.

Gurudeva is Never Sadhana-siddha

We were circumambulating Vraja-maṇḍala and in Varṣāṇā there was a camp. Prabhupāda was delivering lectures, and we were all sitting around and listening, and he told at that time that, "Up to my Gurudeva the *guru-paramparā* is coming down, we must not look at them as *sādhana-siddha*—we must see them as *nitya-siddha.*" Gurudeva is never *sādhana-siddha,* because—*sākṣād-dharitvena samasta śāstrair uktas tathā bhāvyatha eva sadbhiḥ.* Gurudeva and the ordinary Vaiṣṇava's position is different. On Ekādaśī, Gurudeva is offered *anna-prasādam bhoga* (grains) on the altar. Other Vaiṣṇavas are not. According to the necessity of the disciple, Kṛṣṇa, Baladeva or Rādhārāṇī are represented in Gurudeva, just as the affection of the child reaches the highest position in the mother and not the grandmother and others.

So, by the special arrangement of the Lord, the maximum well-wisher of a disciple is found in guru. That is not contaminated, it is the purest connection. By the order of Kṛṣṇa, he will have to be present there, and work on ones behalf. So the guru should never be seen as *sādhana-siddha*—he is in the line from the beginning of the *paramparā.* The guru must not be seen as *sādhana-siddha,* but *nitya-siddha.* Otherwise, he will be disregarded. We are asked to see guru as Kṛṣṇa Himself, or His full representative—His delegation is there.

We must come in that connection with this conception—then only will our *bhajana* and our *sādhana* have real impetus. Thinking "I am in close proximity to perfection," my progress will increase. We should not think that something has tampered with the truth that has reached us—that there is some dirt there. There is a certain percent of dirt there? No. The truth, in it's perfect form, is just at the door graciously waiting to take us up. The *śāstra* asks us to see things in that way, and what the *śāstra* says, that is not false. That is true. But if we cannot come up to the mark that is our defect.

sākṣād dharitvena samasta śāstrair
uktas tathā bhāvyatha eva sadbhiḥ

kinto prabhor yaḥ priya eva tasya
vande guroḥ śrī caraṇāravindam

To the Vaiṣṇava, the guru is *mukunda-preṣṭha* (dear to Kṛṣṇa), because they know that the guru is *kṛṣṇa-śakti* of the highest type—the function of guru is there. It is not Kṛṣṇa Himself, so he is *mukunda-preṣṭha.*

The most favorite of the Lord has come as guru to me, and I am just adjacent to that highest purifying dynamo. So, I cannot but be purified. This sort of idea must come within us to really help our progress.

Apparent Suffering

Great devotees may appear to suffer from disease and old age even though it is stated in *śāstra,* that even the reactions to past sinful acts can be destroyed. There are different stages and different valuations. There are some stages where the past reactions are being finished by suffering. And in higher stages, when the soul is awakened and connected with the ecstatic plane, the outward suffering is nothing to them.

Suppose a man, when sacrificing voluntarily for his country, is feeling happiness within and externally he is feeling some sort of suffering. Because he is offering his life for the cause of his countrymen, the external suffering is reduced to almost nothing. Internal joy is everything.

When in the Kṛṣṇa connection ones soul is connected with the plane of Kṛṣṇa, there will be the feeling of ecstatic sentiments—what is only on the surface does not affect us much. Still it is sometimes visible to teach others. Whenever you will find troubles of the Vaiṣṇavas externally, you can understand that internally they are enjoying much happiness. Just as in the case of the soldier—the general is giving his life smilingly.

It is possible. So, there is some sort of happiness within, and externally there is some sort of pain. That is negligible to them. When one has love for ones country then they can ignore bodily misery, then how much more can those with love of God ignore this bodily misery. It is negligible.

So, we shall think that suffering is giving food to me—giving me the chance for serving the Vaiṣṇavas and thereby the Lord will be highly satisfied. A Vaiṣṇava is exhibiting suffering, a disease, trouble in his mind, trouble in his heart—it is by divine arrangement to give a chance to the lower section to serve them. And through that way they will be able to go to the inner and higher plane.

Sometimes an exaulted devotee may experience apparent material difficulties, such as our Svāmī Mahārāja. Before going to America, he was gored by a cow and later during his sea voyage to America he experienced two heart attacks.

So, there are two angles of vision. Firstly, supposing he was an ordinary man. So, *mūkhaṁ karoti vācālaṁ paṅguṁ laṅghayate girim*—Kṛṣṇa entered him and through him did such wonderful work—that is one angle of vision. Secondly, he was a higher realized soul, but he exhibited so many defects externally. He had a wife who was not favorable and a family which was dysfunctional. And he tried his best to do business successfully, but he failed. This was his physical paraphernalia. Then his life was full of struggle. All these were a show that he was one of the members of the mundane world—all may be a hoax. Another standpoint is, as I told, that a man may be *paṅgu* (crippled), but Kṛṣṇa's divine will can also make him dance like anything.

Prabhupada's Last Days

In his last days our Guru Mahārāja liked very much to hear the poems of Dāsa Gosvāmī and Rūpa Gosvāmī—*nija nikaṭa nivāsaṁ dehi govardhana tvām.* The meaning is that Rādhā-kuṇḍa is the highest, but, *pūjala rāga-patha gaurava bhaṅge*—giving respect to the highest position, to the superiors, we shall come down a little. So our pride will be a little checked and we can be in a normal position. I am not in the highest position, but a little lower—I am Vaiṣṇava *dāsa,* not Vaiṣṇava. That is a very advantageous and intelligent position to take.

In his last days before his disappearance a sort of disappointment came to our Guru Mahārāja. And so he requested us as a body to cooperate. "There are many able persons amongst you, work in cooperation to spread the doctrine of Mahāprabhu." That was his desire.

Generally this is the characteristic of the *ācāryas* before their departure—*mādhavāham kariyānudāsa.* This expression comes from Vidyāpati. *Mādhavāham purināma nivāsa. Nivāsa* means disappointed. About my future I am disappointed.

Bhaktivinoda Ṭhākura also displayed such feelings. "Oh Mahāprabhu, none will receive Your grace, I am quite disappointed, what can I do? Let me chant Your Name, please allow me. No one will accept." That was also the saying of Bhaktivinoda Ṭhākura. We also heard several times this expression come from the lips of Prabhupāda—*mādhavāham purināma nivāsa.* "Oh, Mādhava, about the future I am disappointed." Before leaving this bodily plane, the *ācārya* generally displays such a mood. It comes down in the *ācārya* like that, so that they may not have any affinity for the activities they have begun—that in all connections they withdraw from this plane.

Generally chaos and disorder comes when the *ācārya* leaves and we have to tolerate it and go on—it is a test for us. Just as when the great *ācārya* comes down, that is a boon for the world and his disappearance is a curse for the world. Of course, it leads to many things and ultimately it depends on our chastity, our purity of purpose. We have to make it our own thing. When this is there many things may go on, but when it comes to the final settlement and the realization of that particular thing, then we shall receive more light and we will be able to understand it more clearly.

After departure one may take help from the *sādhu* quarter but the scriptural help is there also, the writings and other things. That is not *sādhu,* but *śāstra-saṅga.* And that depends mostly on our own selves to understand the real meaning from the *śāstra.*

Sastra and Sadhu

Śāstra is passive but *sādhu* is active. *Sādhu* can give active help but *śāstra* helps in a passive way. We have to draw the purport from it, but *sādhu* can distribute its nectar, he can correct me from my erroneous ideas but *śāstra* cannot do so. Only a living thing can do so, we have to take the real meaning according to our capacity. The knowledge of the experts has been collected there in the *śāstra.* Spiritual experts have placed there the results of their experience in spiritual life.

Also, we are told that we must approach the spiritual substance within the books. I remember, perhaps as a result of my previous birth, when I received *gāyatrī.* Without consulting any book explaining the meaning of *gāyatrī,* I appealed to Gāyatrī herself, "Please, please reveal to me what you are in this *mantra.*" She is living, not only in these mundane words, a cluster of mundane words, but she is a living thing, Gāyatrī herself. And if she likes she can express her inner nature to us. With that state I wished to continue the *japam* of *gāyatrī* in my young age. That was also corroborated by the Gauḍīya Maṭha when I joined there, and it is also confirmed in the *śāstra.*

Even in *Bhagavad-gītā* there are so many interpretations. According to ones angle of vision, interpretations may be taken differently. So, *yao bhāgavata pāro vaiṣṇavera sthāne*—we are requested to read *śāstra,* Vedic scripture, to understand from the Vaiṣṇava standpoint. *Ācāryavān puruṣo veda*—only one who has their teacher to teach the *śāstra,* can understand the real meaning. Otherwise if one pretends to know many scriptures without the real meaning from the *śāstra,* they may be deceived. They may not understand the real purpose of *śāstra.* It may be this way. So, *ācāryavān puruṣo veda*—only those who have studied *śāstra* under the direction of a real *ācārya,* can realize the real meaning of the *śāstra.*

Sri Murti

Also, something greater is to be learned in the association of a devotee even more than service to the Deity (*śrī mūrti*) because *mūrti* is passive and devotee is active. The *śāstra* also is passive but more living than *śrī mūrti.* The *śāstra* will give you more than *śrī mūrti* and the *sādhu* will give more than what the scripture can give. This is general. We are to learn everything to its fullest conception from the *sādhu.* When the Lord wills, even a jungle can remind you of the conception of Vṛndāvana and Kṛṣṇa. You may find it anywhere. By His will He can do anything and everything with the devotee. That is a separate thing. It is always under regulation. By His special will He can do anything and everything. This is the ordinary law of the country and then the emergency law from ordinance may be proclaimed. Everything belongs to the state during the war. There is no personal property. This way the autocracy is above all. General law is there for the general public, according to gradation set by state, but special connectivity is reserved to be utilised anywhere and everywhere.

The Living Scripture

Śāstra is written by whom? Some saint. So, we require the association of the *sādhu* and the *śāstra. Sādhu śāstra kṛpāya yadi kṛṣṇa mukha haya*—the *sādhu* is the living scripture, and the scripture is also there in a passive way to advise you. But the *sādhu* actively can approach and passively we may get benefit from the scripture. The association of these two can help us to have our realization in that way.

Sādhu śāstra kṛpāya haya—we advance by the grace of the scripture and the saints, the scripture personified, who are living the life of the scriptural advice, and are more powerful. In their association we can imbibe such higher subtle knowledge and faith, which can lead us, *śraddhā.* All our experiences are futile, just as if we are to connect with the sun and the moon. There, the air, earth, these instruments will fail, but only electricity will help us to have connection with the furthest place. Similarly, *śraddhā* can give us information and the necessary achievement. It is far, far away—beyond the jurisdiction of our experience and the meager, limited experience of the eye, ear, mind, and all these things. This is very meager, very limited, and faith can rise up and pierce through this area, and go far away to the moon or the sun—in this way.

Faith should be developed with the help of the scriptures and the saints. The eternal world is dark to us and we are awake in this mortal world, but the opposite has to be effected. We must be awake there in the eternal world, and this (the mortal world) will be neglected and disregarded, it will be dark to us. *Yā niśā sarva-bhūtānāṁ...*

Proper Shelter Awakens Bhakti

So, we must get help from the *sādhus* who have Kṛṣṇa consciousness within them. Just as from one light another candle may be lit. A candle cannot produce light from within but it is to be lit from another candle. It is something like that. We have to awaken our buried Kṛṣṇa consciousness which is covered by *anyābhilāṣa karma jñāna.* That should be awakened by another light—that should help the sleeping Kṛṣṇa consciousness within us. So it is like that—*sādhu-saṅga. Kṛṣṇa-bhakti-janma mūla haya 'sādhu-saṅga'*—at the same time it is *ahaituki*—causeless! We can get *kṛṣṇa-bhakti,* that which is pleasing Kṛṣṇa, from the *sādhu.*

At the same time we are told that it is causeless.

sa vai puṁsāṁ paro dharmo yato bhaktir adhokṣaje
ahaituky apratihatā yayātmā suprasīdati
(*Bhāg.* 1.2.6)

It is causeless and it cannot be checked. When it is awakened within our hearts we can feel that the heart is feeling wonderfully satisfied. The satisfaction is produced in our hearts—we can feel it. *Ahaituky apratihatā*—it has no cause and cannot be checked. There will be a flow upwards and any opposition will not have any effect there. It is such.

Rememberance of the lotus feet of Kṛṣṇa will bring us closer to the eternal divine realm.

avismṛtiḥ kṛṣṇa-padāravindayoḥ
kṣiṇoty abhadrāṇi ca śaṁ tanoti
sattvasya śuddhiṁ paramātma-bhaktiṁ
jñānaṁ ca vijñāna-virāga-yuktam

Remembrance of Lord Kṛṣṇa's lotus feet destroys everything inauspicious and awards the greatest good fortune. It purifies the heart and bestows devotion for the Supreme Soul, along with knowledge enriched with realization and renunciation. (*Bhāg.* 12.12.55)

Avismṛtiḥ kṛṣṇa-padāravindayoḥ, kṣinoty abhadrāṇi—it will seek and destroy the undesirable *abhadra,* that element that is nasty and impure within us. That will be destroyed by the continuance of Kṛṣṇa consciousness at any stage. In its lower stage, even in the slightest negligent connection, it can destroy the desirability of connecting with things of a lower nature.

Kṣinoty abhadrāṇi ca śam tanoti—and it will promote goodness (*maṅgalam*) within us. *Sattvasya śuddhim*—the substantial character of our existence will be improved. Our sole existence will be purified, our standpoint, our understanding, our aspiration—everything will be purified. *Paramātma-bhaktiṁ*—and we shall attain devotion, attachment towards the Supreme Personality. *Jñānam ca*—and our knowledge and conception about the same will improve. *Virāga-yuktam*—*jñāna* and *vairāgya* are the two formulative charms. And the knowledge, the conception of that will take its proper form and show apathy to this mundane world.

Here, the advice is that we have to try to maintain our Kṛṣṇa consciousness—it is the medicine. There is no other medicine which can produce Kṛṣṇa consciousness, and cure our disease and discover Kṛṣṇa consciousness within us. Kṛṣṇa consciousness is the cause of Kṛṣṇa consciousness—*bhaktyā sañjātayā bhaktyā.*

The Best Medicine

The only medicine for lazy devotion is good association—to associate with those for whom you have some regard. Keep yourself in their association so they can help you from your slothfulness. Association is the most powerful thing to convert from one thing to another. Bad *saṅga,* bad association, takes one in a bad direction. And good association takes one in a good direction. There is no other medicine.

Sādhu is more living and *śāstra* is passive. *Sādhu* is active. So active help is necessary, to put ones own self in the charge of a *sādhu* for whom one has sufficient regard. You won't be able to avoid his request, his order. It is best to live with such a *sādhu*, so that he will take care of you and will try to guide us towards our destination. He is our well-wisher, and will take care of us and out of his affection for us will come to help us on his own accord. We should make arrangements for such company. The environment is drawing our senses towards it for exploitation—sleep and indolence is *tamo-guṇa*. And *raja-guṇa* is the exploiting tendency. These are enemies.

If possible we should engage in some responsible service. Responsibility automatically engages us in activity. So there must be some responsible duty under the direction of one whom we can respect, revere. That is meant to take me up again, to rise up with energy and engage in the service of the unknown divinity which is far off. We can feel the presence of this in the *sādhu*—in their activity, their endeavor, their talk, discussion and everything. We can trace the divinity, the divine presence, only in the contact of the *sādhu*. Otherwise that is far off from us, and we may tend to go away because that seems to be unknown and unknowable. But the living and the earnest activity and the hope, the sacrifice—all these things encourage us to be reinstated in our former expectation and prospect. To associate with the *sādhu* whom you can regard and get some responsible duty from him, will relieve the despair and depression. That can help.

Asat-sanga

Sādhu-saṅga means that it is promoting me towards my goal. The mundane plane is the perverted reflection, but just above that is the real plane which is just the opposite of this. So we must not be maladjusted. *Asat saṅga tyāga ei vaiṣṇava acāra*. The practices of a student of Vaiṣṇavism are only one—to renounce the environment; but that does not mean that the *sādhu* is eliminated also if he is found. *Strī saṅgī-eka asādhu kṛṣṇa bhakta āra.* There are two types of *asat.* One is *strī-saṅgī* or *yoṣit-saṅgī*—those who are attached to sensual pleasures. And the other is *kṛṣṇa-abhakta*—one who has no attraction for Kṛṣṇa but is engaged in other errands. *Bhukti kāmī siddhi kāmī*—those who have other desires such as for liberation or material perfection, should be eliminated. We should be cautious about these two. One may be a scholar, a *yogī*, a *tyāgī* and all these things, but if one is not a devotee of Kṛṣṇa they should be eliminated.

Sukrti Guides Us

In Kurukṣetra, one gentleman of that time came to see our Guru Mahārāja there and put the question, 'How shall we know who is a *sādhu* and who is not?' Then he was told that generally to know a *sādhu*, we have to consult the scriptures. We have to consult scripture with the spirit that it is not an ordinary book that can assert, that can hide itself or can come to my knowledge. Scripture is animate not inanimate. Then the *śāstra* will come to help us about the selection of who is a *sādhu*, in a general way. Of course, the *sukṛti* from our previous lives, that inner guidance, is accepted also.

One gentleman was a good doctor, and when he was dying, the best among junior doctors came to cure him. He was a heart specialist and a genius. The junior doctor told him what was his case. "Yes, yes, I understand this. I am also of the same opinion as you, but who has received the injection and put it into effect, he is absent. The receiver of the injection is absent in me, the vitality." That is the medicine for such disease. But the receiving capacity must be in the body to receive the medicine and utilize it.

So also, the external help may come, but the receiver must be up to the standard to receive and utilize it, to fulfill such purpose. That is the *sukṛti* within. That takes the external help and utilizes it in constructive work. *Ajñāta-sukṛti, jñāta-sukṛti* then *śāstra,* then *śraddhā, sādhu*—in this way we progress. Gradually by *bhajana,* by *sādhana,* it will seem that, "Yes, it is my own. It is my inner wealth," a stage when one can feel, reveal what they are searching for—this heart-pleasing thing. When the inner nature will feel it is there, then one is near the home—sweet, sweet home.

Then, go on with more energy and more speed, in a more confident way, go on. This is what we are in need of, what we are searching for. With this hearty energy make progress—*āpanna.* And *prapanna* also, not only have I tasted, it must be given widely to all. They are also suffering from the same problem that I was suffering from. So it must be spread everywhere widely. That is *prapanna*—well established, without a doubt. I shall not do any mischief to the people—if I spread this thing, then I shall be giving the highest benefit to the world. There is no doubt—*bhidyate hṛdaya granthiś chidyante sarva-saṁśayāḥ*—all doubts are cleared. This is the thing for which not only myself but the whole world is madly searching.

Previous Experience

New persons may be drawn in to some understanding of devotional activities. This is all due to their *sukṛti*—previous connection with the transcendental *nirguṇa* wave. You have all previously had some connection with the transcendental wave, and wherever you are it has kept you floating above, near to thoughts of the Vṛndāvana plane. The underground activity of previous lives is there. You were floating just near where Svāmī Mahārāja began his preaching—that nearness, the capacity of acceptance of his words, that sort of merit already was within you, in a variagated nature. That has taken you to appreciate his preaching, otherwise it is not possible to get that connection with *nirguṇa*.

Gopa-kumāra had some previous acquaintance with the *nirguṇa* world. Otherwise, how was it possible that after the experience of some time in the material world that it did not have any charm for him? After living and passing some time in that plane he felt unsatisfied. Then some connection with the upper agent came and he went there. What does it mean? This means that the background is such that the external is gradually going on, but some healthy backing is there, so that wherever he is led, he's not satisfied. Fulfillment is only possible in the highest position. *Sukṛti*, that background was there. *Adau śraddhā tataḥ sādhu-saṅgo*—from there it began.

How Sraddha is Produced

How is *śraddhā* produced? *Sat-saṅga*—that we meet a proper *sādhu* is not a chance coincidence, but is the result of previous *sukṛti*. What is *sukṛti*? It is our connection with the plane of service and dedication. It is not of this land of exploitation or renunciation. That is called *sukṛti*.

Svāmī Mahārāja has brought you all here and now he has departed. He also spoke about that and we are both connected. This talk is going on—the praise of Rādhārāṇī, which proves the highest attainment. We have the advantage, for we are forced to talk about Rādhārāṇī, about Her greatness and all these things. There may be so many engagements, but by their grace we are engaged in discussing topics of the highest order for our realization.

Mad bhaktiṁ labhate paraṁ; brahma-bhūta indicates they have attained their spiritual position, and are fully placed on the spiritual plane—they have crossed the mundane and obtained identification with the pure conscious unit and are *prasannātmā* (fully joyful). This sort of self-satisfaction is there. *Na śocati na kāṅkṣati*— they are indifferent to mundane loss and gain. *Samaḥ sarveṣu bhūteṣu*— they are neutral towards the worldly persons, and *sarveṣu bhūteṣu*—they are all equal on the soul platform. They are all units of soul, *samaḥ sarveṣu bhūteṣu mad-bhaktiṁ labhate parām*—then one is in a position to come to their affectionate quarter. *Mad bhaktiṁ labhate parām*—my higher devotional service. From this position they are eligible to search or to advance towards the land of Kṛṣṇa and His devotional service—*mad bhaktiṁ labhate parām. Bhakti* is always above the land of renunciation. We must always take it for granted that it is *cinmayī*, never mundane. *Bhakti* means dedication.

Extended Selfishness

Dedication to the country, to the society, to the nation, to the family—this is all extended selfishness. Previously, I joined the Gandhi movement of non-cooperation, and when I came to the Gauḍīya Maṭha, then, in my preaching I had to fight with the same people. Their nature was one of extended selfishness. Extended selfishness is to identify with the country, with the body and bodily comforts, and this is extended to the family, to the village, to the clan, and to the country. Just as there is the clash between the greater units of Hindustan and Pakistan—they fight with one another—the clash is inevitable and is only extended selfishness. Even the philanthropist—all extended selfishness. Nothing less than identification with the infinite will bring us proper relief—no amount of finite can make infinite. So from the beginning, the plane of the infinite should be taken up. We think that, "I shall begin from here by extending the area of my activity and I shall one day reach to the infinite," but that is not possible.

It is impossible because no amount of finite can make infinite—from the beginning that comes from the higher to the lower. *Śrota-panthā*—the method of descent, the deductive method—we are to submit to that. He is trying to reveal Himself and we must connect with Him. We must sell our head there—that is the only way, *śrota-panthā.* And that depends on *ajñāta-sukṛti, jñāta-sukṛti,* then *śraddhā.* If I do my duty towards that wonderful One, my duty is done to the whole and more than that. "Whatever you can conceive, that is but a small fragment of My splendor." No part can be any important part in Him—He always transcends that.

Sometimes, unconsciously we pass over the layers of *māyā* by the help of *sādhu-saṅga, saṅkīrtana,* and all these things—progress is such that unconsciously we pass those very subtle different stratas of *māyā.* A hundred-petals of a lotus may be pierced by a needle all at once. It takes no time unconsciously, only within a very short time they are all penetrated. Similarly, we may pass through different stratas unconsciously. If we walk, our progess is very slow, but in an aeroplane, in no time we may pass through so many provinces. As we inquire about the nature of the Absolute Truth our search may take us many places.

All Dharma Leads to Vaisnava-dharma

Yasmin jñāte sarvaṁ idaṁ—this is the only inquiry of the world. They are moving, unsatisfied and only searching for this sort of satisfaction, nothing of a lower standard. This is the quest. The whole world is moving—moving for *sukham,* for pleasure, for satisfaction, for ecstasy, joy. And this is the substance that everyone is madly searching for.

Athāto brahma-jijñāsa—why have I come with the *brahma-jijñāsa,* inquiry of Brahman in *Vedānta*? *Brahma-jijñāsa* is of general interest. Knowingly or unknowingly, they are all after this *brahma-jijñāsa.* Intuitively, everything is moving to search—for what? That is this Brahman conception. Is that Brahman something like inner substance? No! It is Kṛṣṇa. Mahāprabhu put Kṛṣṇa in the place of Brahman—*Bhāgavatam* states it is not Brahman.

In the farther conception of the highest goal, we will find that there is Kṛṣṇa—the Kṛṣṇa conception, whose halo is Brahman, the halo of the domain of pastimes of Kṛṣṇa is Brahman. So when a ship makes progress there is the lighthouse, then, another lighthouse—in that way. What is Brahman? It is all accommodating and most general. Then the real representation of the most general conception is to be found in Kṛṣṇa consciousness. It is inert. There is no movement in this *brahma-nirviśeṣa.* But in *saviśeṣa,* we find differentiation and specification in the pastimes—everything will be there. Still it will be all accomodating. Even this Brahman also, that is Kṛṣṇa.

In this way our attention is strongly drawn towards Him. This is the most general question in all the world, which none can deny if they are a little sensible in their own disease or want. It cannot but be, even if we have no interest in Kṛṣṇa consciousness.

Once I delivered a lecture in Medinapur, beginning with, 'What is *dharma*?' Then it came to the Brahman conception. And then from Brahman we explained the Vāsudeva conception, and then Lakṣmī-Nārāyaṇa. In this way I went to the Kṛṣṇa conception of Godhead. In a broad and universal way I was marshalling. There was one man who began to cry. "We were so great in our previous times, in our ancient days. But now these philosophies come to entice us that we are far more advanced than in previous times—now in the scientific age of civilization we have advanced so much. But Svāmījī, you have stated that our ancient predecessors were so great, so noble." In this way he began to cry in the meeting.

And there was another scholar who was made president in Poona in some party conference, one Mr. Bosak. He happened to be present there. We did not know him, but he came out of his own accord and asked permission to say something in favor of us. When permitted he rose and began, "For so long we considered *vaiṣṇava-dharma* as a branch of Hindu *dharma*, but I have heard today from Svāmījī, that *vaiṣṇava-dharma* is the highest conception, the highest goal of the whole of Hindu *dharma*. The whole of Hindu *dharma* is trying its utmost to lead us to *vaiṣṇava-dharma*." He also asked that our lectures be arranged amongst the scholars of India in different places. He spoke like this.

Vaiṣṇava-dharma is not only the source of Hindu *dharma*—any *dharma* must lead to *vaiṣṇava-dharma*, otherwise it is a faulty one. Not only *dharma*—*dharmaḥ projjhita kaitavo 'tra paramo nirmatsarāṇāṁ satāṁ*—those that are jealous, have jealousy in any way or rather at the bottom of their heart cannot tolerate this. Everything is lost for them.

Prestige is Our Enemy

Mahāprabhu has taught *tṛṇād api sunīcena taror api sahiṣṇunā amāninā mānadena*. It is very difficult to conquer one's fame or prestige. *Pratiṣṭhā*, one's love for position, is very difficult to give up. It is easier to give up attraction for females or money, but hankering for one's own position is most difficult. Prestige for position is our innermost enemy. So long as that remains we cannot offer ourselves in the service of a Vaiṣṇava. I may accept somewhat hesitatingly the service of God, but to serve a Vaiṣṇava would be like coming to a lower settlement. In fact, to become the servant of a Vaiṣṇava would actually be the be all and end all of my life. But how can I accept that idea? I may accept service under the Supreme Lord, but to become the servant of the servant of the servant—what is this? Where is the fun? Should a man stoop so low as this? Therefore, *pratiṣṭhā*, position, the consciousness of prestige, is the greatest enemy of the conditioned soul.

Rādhā-dāsyam means to become a slave, to embrace the ideal, the hope of becoming a slave. To classify oneself as the slave of Kṛṣṇa is not the end. One must be willing to become the slave of the slave of the slave. Some will think, "This is the most ludicrous thing, I cannot accept this. I am the biggest of the big. *So 'ham, śivo 'ham.* I am the master of *māyā.*" This is the point where the false, separate existence from God begins.

Transcending mortality one comes to the plane of *maṅgala*, auspiciousness, which is good in comparison with the plane of mortality. The first reach beyond the limit of mortality or *mṛtya-loka*, is Mahādeva, Śiva. But from Śiva we have to pass to *sundaram*, the land of beauty. Śiva is only the middle position or *maṅgalam*. But this *maṅgalam* is not differentiated in its fullest characteristics at this point, only it is out of danger. To be out of danger is nothing positive, but it is the highest safe position. However, one must not only be safe, but engaged in the most desireable thing. The safe position is relative Śiva. Above that is Sadāśiva and the plane of positive engagement.

Once we had one godbrother named Kumāra Surendranātha Nārāyaṇa Rāya, an M.A. graduate of Punjab University. He was a rich man whose annual income was three lakhs. He took *hari-nāma* from our Guru Mahārāja. That gentleman went with him to Shillong on one occasion. When Guru Mahārāja was passing in a car, Surendranātha Nārāyaṇa Rāya, who was out for a walk, met him on the wayside and immediately fell flat in the road offering his obeisances in the mud, since at that time it was the rainy season. Then Prabhupāda asked, "What are you doing down in the mud? What are you doing? You have a rich dress but it is all smeared with mud." Then Surendranātha said, "We have only one thing to do in life, to make prostration to the Vaiṣṇava. We can't do anything else. Should I be a miser with this? *Praṇāma* is our only wealth, it is everything. If I am a miser there, then what will be my fate? *Praṇāma*—that is our only aspiration."

Enjoyment Only for Krsna

One gentleman came to our Guru Mahārāja in Calcutta, and said that it is written in *śāstra* that the *kāminī kāma,* the aspect of enjoying women, is not for us, it is only reserved for Kṛṣṇa. Kṛṣṇa is the only enjoyer of the beauty of the women section." That point is mentioned there. "What do you say to this? Then what is our position? Have you written it in the literal sense, that all the enjoyment with women is only meant for Kṛṣṇa and no one else?" "Yes, yes, that is the true naked billing of this—that type of enjoyment is meant only for Kṛṣṇa—all others are trespassing. Now you may ask whether or not Kṛṣṇa was a debauchee."

Kāminī for the Kṛṣṇa conception is to be adjusted, otherwise we are lost. It must be adjusted with Him—any *kāminī* consciousness, lady consciousness, must have connection with Kṛṣṇa.

And *kanaka,* money—the master of money is Nārāyaṇa, Lakṣmī-pati, wealth. And we are all servitors more or less in different ways. And Baladeva is the guru, the master of name and fame—*kanaka, kāminī, pratiṣṭhā.*

Any money conception, wealth conception must have connection with Nārāyaṇa, the subsidiary function. And all the name and fame must be connected with Baladeva. Baladeva Nityānanda here, Baladeva and Rādhikā.

Whomever will be the prime cause of distributing Kṛṣṇa, will receive fame and glory. So much glory can never be expected anywhere else. Can anyone hope to attain a more glorious position? One who can give Kṛṣṇa holds the highest fame—he is the recipient of the highest fame. And all the money should be used for His service—that is Nārāyaṇa, Lakṣmī-pati, the commander of everything. The *kāminī* conception must be connected with Kṛṣṇa—there is no higher recipient.

No Exploiting Sense in Vrndavana

The exploiting sense is absent in Vraja. We may conceive this or we may not conceive this, but still everything there is only actuated by the motive of service. And there is the beauty. *Tat paratvena nirmalam*—the *nirmalata,* the purity, depends only on how much it is for the satisfaction of the center. The criterion of measuring the purity is this—otherwise we will be here in the land of exploitation. There, in that plane, there is no exploitation, but the whole thing is informal. All is full of service, with purity—otherwise there is no entrance in that domain. So we must be very cautious about the real theme of exploitation. What does this mean?

There is no exploitation there—that is divinity. Without dedication, without serving, no divinity is possible—it is not possible to enter into Vṛndāvana, what to speak of Śivaloka or Vaikuṇṭha-loka? *Mādhurya-rasa* is most intensive there.

These are the things which we should know. We should try to keep the conception of such a standard on our head. However far away it may be, we may not make any easy compromise with the very cheap things in this world. Our future will depend on our highest ideal.

Service of Vrajavasi

Vraja-vāsī-gaṇa pracāraka-dhana, pratiṣṭhā-bhikṣuka tā'rā nahe śava—the *pracāraka* (preachers) desire is to attain the service of the *vraja-vāsī*—their aim is not mundane money. Their aim is the grace of a *vraja-vāsī*. That they want. *Dhana* means they hanker after the wealth and qualities of *vraja-vāsīs*. That is their desire, their will.

The foot dust of the *vraja-vāsīs* is the wealth of the genuine preacher. They don't want any admiration from the ordinary mass of this world—no admiration, no attraction do they want from the mass. "Oh, he is a big personality, he is doing very great service"—all these things they do not want. Their only aim is to get the foot dust of the *vraja-vāsīs*, that is their wealth. *Tāṅra se hetu pracāra*—they cannot but do the preaching of *kṛṣṇa-nāma*—the inspiration is coming from within, not from the external world. They cannot stop the flow of their hearts to praise Kṛṣṇa. It is coming from within, not from outside. *Pratiṣṭhāśā hīna*—no admiration, nothing of the kind do they want from the outside ordinary people of the mundane world. His internal self engages him to speak about Kṛṣṇa. There is no reward nor rebuke from the outside world. The cause of his action is the eternal flow.

It is coming from within. *Prāṇa āche tāṅra se hetu pracāra.* His very life is meant for that. *Prāṇa* means life, *prāṇa* means vitality, inner urge, the very internal energy. In other words, it is devotion, *svarūpa-śakti*, not any artificial thing there. *Svarūpa-śakti* is within. Only that should be discovered. That is within, the inner wealth, and only the outer cover has checked the activities of *svarūpa-śakti*—that of distributing this divine message to one and all.

Hari-Katha

According to the preacher's intensity and purity of realization, their preaching of *hari-kathā* may be of many types. The *mahā-bhāgavata, madhyama-bhāgavata, kaniṣṭha-bhāgavata* may talk about

Hari, but there is a great difference in the deepness of their conception and commitment.

The *kaniṣṭha's hari-kathā* is better than nothing but the *avaiṣṇava* (non-devotee) should not be heard at all. The *kaniṣṭha-adhikārī* is lower but not insincere. But one who is insincere, *avaiṣṇava,* his *hari-kathā* is poison. *Hari-kathā* from an *avaiṣṇava* is not *hari-kathā* at all. He says it is *hari-kathā,* but it is not *hari-kathā*—it is *māyā-kathā.* "Kṛṣṇa and other gods are one, they are the same"—with this message he will go on with his '*hari-kathā.*' That is *māyā-kathā,* not *hari-kathā.* In Śaṅkarācārya's conception Hari is *saguṇa, sattva-guṇa*—so that is *māyā* conception. That is not *hari-kathā,* it is *māyā-kathā.*

Everyone is taking the Name of Kṛṣṇa, so why is there the distinction between *śuddha-nāma* and *nāma-aparādha?* Also there are distinctions in *bhāgavata-kathā.* Why? It is the same Name, but one says it is *aparādha,* another says it is *śuddha-nāma.* How is this? Another says *nāmābhāsa,* why? When uttering the Name, there may be a great gulf between the two—one *śuddha-nāma* and the other *nāma-aparādha.*

Bhāgavata-kathā-aparādha is not actually *Bhāgavata* reading—that is making offense to *Bhāgavata.* That is not a real interpretation. He does not know the *Bhāgavata,* but he is speaking for some other lower purpose. He wants money, he wants prestige, or he wants something else—he doesn't want the real Hari. He cannot see properly. *Sītāra ākṛti-māyā harila rāvaṇa*—the demon Rāvaṇa stole Sītā forcibly. Mahāprabhu says he took only *māyā*—Rāvaṇa has no power even to see Sītā. She is all spiritual embodiment.

One non-devotee, Devānanda Paṇḍita, was reading the *Bhāgavata* and explaining. One day Mahāprabhu aspired for *kṛṣṇa-kathā,* "Oh, Devānanda is misinterpreting *Bhāgavatam.* I shall go and tear it up." Then Śrīvāsa Paṇḍita and others said,

"No, no, don't go!" and they took Him away. He wanted to tear the very book of *Bhāgavatam* but He did not do so. He wanted to tear it up, He expressed that, "I want to tear up that book—that book is *māyā*—he is giving misinterpretation." Of course, Mahāprabhu did not do that. But Mahāprabhu only expressed it. Then Devānanda again came to the feet of Mahāprabhu. "I have done wrong, I have offended the *Bhāgavatam*, please forgive me."

Opposing Statements of Bhagavatam

The aim of every letter, the aim and object of every letter of the *Bhāgavatam* is to show and identify Kṛṣṇa. Some statements are direct, and some are indirect—*anvayād itarataś ca.* Though all these statements are not in the positive line, some in the negative line are also showing Kṛṣṇa. You will find that the character of Hiraṇyakaśipu is also playing a part to establish Prahlāda-Hari. The background is necessary. So in an indirect way that is also showing Kṛṣṇa and *kṛṣṇa-līlā*. Such pastimes have something to contribute in *kṛṣṇa-līlā* in different ways, so indirectly they are leading to Kṛṣṇa. *Anvaya gauṇa mukhya vṛtti*—there is an ordinary meaning and a special meaning. *Mukhya gauṇa vṛtti kiṁvā anvaya*—direct or indirect. In every way it is pointing towards Kṛṣṇa.

Why is Hiraṇyakaśipu necessary? He was used to establish the greatness of the devotion in Prahlāda to Kṛṣṇa. So he is necessary. For the structure of a building, bricks and many other things are necessary. So, similarly it has been stated that everything is Kṛṣṇa in the *Bhāgavatam*. Even what is seen to be negative is also necessary because it shows Kṛṣṇa.

Biographies of Mahaprabhu

Vṛndāvana Dāsa is the Vyāsa of *caitanya-līlā*. Just as the original Vyāsadeva wrote in detail about *kṛṣṇa-līlā* in *Bhāgavatam*, especially the *bala-līlā* of Kṛṣṇa—similarly, the early pastimes of Mahāprabhu have been elaborately described by Vṛndāvana Dāsa Ṭhākura in the first half of *Caitanya-bhāgavata.*

Vṛndāvana Dāsa Ṭhākura was the first biographer of Mahāprabhu and the first distributor of *caitanya-līlā.* Kavirāja Gosvāmī has given much respect to Vṛndāvana Dāsa Ṭhākura in his *Caitanya-caritāmṛta.*

ore mūḍha loka, śuna caitanya-maṅgala
caitanya-mahimā yāte jānibe sakala
(*Cc. Ādi* 8.33)

Kavirāja Gosvāmī has said, "Oh you stupid people, somehow or other, hear the *Caitanya-maṅgala* of Vṛndāvana Dāsa. Then you will be able to understand who Śrī Caitanya is." He has recommended in this way. *Caitanya-bhāgavata* was originally named *Caitanya-maṅgala* but a little after, Locana Dāsa Ṭhākura, a disciple of Narahari Sarakāra Ṭhākura of Śrīkhaṇḍa, also wrote a book and named it *Caitanya-maṅgala.* So, Vṛndāvana Dāsa changed the name to *Caitanya-bhāgavata.* We have heard this conclusion from ancient reporters.

Vṛndāvana Dāsa Ṭhākura did not describe the later pastimes of Mahāprabhu as elaborately as His earlier pastimes because that was mainly centered around Purī. He remained here in Gauḍadeśa and could not get much information, therefore he did not want to interfere with that. He only gave a short sketch about those pastimes. He has given a general description of the early life of Mahāprabhu, but the descriptions of the later life of Mahāprabhu and His philosophical teachings are not described so much. *Caitanya-bhāgavata* relates to the activities of the *yuga-avatāra*—preaching and distributing the Holy Name, more than the concept of Mahāprabhu's inner mood as Rādhā-Kṛṣṇa combined.

Of course, Vṛndāvana Dāsa Ṭhākura's conception about Caitanyadeva and His *līlā* has been given in a very emotional way, but as regards the *siddhānta,* the ontological aspect of Śrī Caitanyadevas' teachings are not to be found in great detail there. We find the real *siddhānta* in *Caitanya-caritāmṛta*—the concept of Śrī Caitanyadeva which is more valuable to us. In *Caitanya-bhāgavata, rasa* may be there of some order, but no ontological aspect about Śrī Caitanya has been presented there. Ontology, as well as *rasa,* we find in *Caitanya-caritāmṛta* and *Śrīmad Bhāgavatam.*

The philosophy of Mahāprabhu, especially in His later days, is found in *Caitanya-caritāmṛta* and it is found very authentically. With great authenticity we can rely upon *Caitanya-caritāmṛta* at every point. Every part of *Caitanya-caritāmṛta* represents Mahāprabhu completely, because the source is Rūpa-Sanātana and Raghunātha. They all came in direct contact with Mahāprabhu and were inspired by Him. He empowered Rūpa Gosvāmī to reveal, in a scientific and exhaustive way, the *śāstras* of divine love—the love of Vṛndāvana. We also find that in Purī, Mahāprabhu asked Svarūpa Dāmodara, "I have given My all to him—you also grace him. He is the fittest person to deal with this science of divine love. You can put full confidence in him." First was Rūpa Gosvāmī, and then there was Raghunātha Dāsa Gosvāmī who also had direct contact with Mahāprabhu. Kavirāja Gosvāmī was a disciple of Raghunātha Dāsa Gosvāmī and he came in close association with Rūpa-Sanātana and got their blessings. So, what Kavirāja Gosvāmī has given is unparalleled.

Our Guru Mahārāja once wrote in a letter that every part of *Caitanya-caritāmṛta* can be taken as fully bona-fide, both from the historical and ontological point of view. *Caitanya-caritāmṛta* can be accepted as one hundred percent bona-fide, whereas the position of other *śāstras* may be modified or incomplete. Just as we accept some of the historical elements in *Bhakti-ratnakāra*, but not the ontological aspects. Then there is another book, *Caitanya-maṅgala* which is a little more sentimental, so much so that it leans towards the *gaura-nāgarī* misconception. So, books such as *Caitanya-maṅgala* are not so desirable. *Caitanya-bhāgavata* is reliable and is in *śuddha-bhakti*, but we consider it as of a primary order compared to *Caitanya-caritāmṛta*.

The *Caitanya-caritāmṛta*, the gift of Kavirāja Gosvāmī, is the highest wealth of the *sampradāya*. Whatever we may think, it is our highest capital. So, just as Vṛndāvana Dāsa Ṭhākura is considered to be the Vyāsa of *gaura-līlā*, Kavirāja Gosvāmī is the Śukadeva of *gaura-līlā*.

Krsna-lila is Aprakrta

According to my estimation, the best theistic book in the whole universe is *Caitanya-caritāmṛta*. The scholarship which has been shown by Kavirāja Gosvāmī is unique. It is *cid-vilāsa*. After reading *Caitanya-caritāmṛta* even the ordinary man of little scholarly abilities, can understand that *kṛṣṇa-līlā* is *aprākṛta* (divine).

This standard is shown when you read the description by Kavirāja Gosvāmī where he is describing the *jala-krīḍa*—how Kṛṣṇa and the *gopīs* are playing in the water. So beautifully it has been dealt with, that none can think that this has any connection with mundane lust. In such a way it has been described. So in *Gaura-gaṇoddeśa-dīpikā*, Kavirāja Gosvāmī is said to be the incarnation of Śukadeva—*śuka-mukhāmṛtam*. Kavirāja Gosvāmī's words are percolated by the principle of pure consciousness—that pure love has been transmitted to this world. It is very safe for the ordinary beings also. Take that path, there is guidance everywhere, it is *cid-vilāsa*. It is from the other side, not this side of the world. The mundane touch has been exhaustively eliminated in these descriptions.

Just as in *Bhāgavatam,* Śukadeva Gosvāmī is dealing with the pastimes, so many fine and sentimental things have been dealt with by Kavirāja Gosvāmī, but still it is *aprākṛta,* not *prākṛta.* In Kavirāja Gosvāmī's writing that characteristic is fully maintained—it is untouched by this world, it is something divine. The very nature of the description is self-evident—that it is love-divine, not mundane. That is the peculiarity in his style of writing. There is no possibility of misunderstanding. Mistakes have been exhaustively eliminated there. It is divine. The divine character of *kṛṣṇa-līlā* has been fully maintained there. That is the peculiar style of Kavirāja Gosvāmī.

If we can think that the teachings of Śrī Caitanyadeva are the highest, full-fledged theism as told by Prabhupāda several times and that *Bhāgavata* is the highest development, then that has reality, that is true, that cannot but be true.

That the revealed truth means that thousands and thousands of years back it was revealed by some *ṛṣi* and that the revelation cannot come at present—I don't think like that. Any time the revelation may come—to support this highest form of theism, whatever the revelation. Some consider that Bhaktivinoda's *Jaiva-dharma* is fictitious, but I think that these things actually must have been true—and may be found somewhere in the creation. When it has come in the consciousness of Bhaktivinoda Ṭhākura, it is not contradictory. It is floating, sometimes appearing and sometimes disappearing. It is all eternal truth.

Sambandha, Abhidheya, and Prayojana

Full fledged theism is divided into three aspects—*sambandha, abhidheya* and *prayojana.* Sanātana Gosvāmī is the *sambandha-ācārya.* He has given us a graphic description of the environment and who we are. He asked Mahāprabhu, "*ke āmi kene āmāya, jāre tāpa traya*—who am I and why do I suffer." Mahāprabhu replied with a description of everything in detail. Who are you? *Jīvera svarūpa haya, kṛṣṇera nitya-dāsa*—in a nutshell, you are the slave to Kṛṣṇa, slave of the Lord.

When these European style people accused Gauḍīya Maṭha of being preachers of slavery, Prabhupāda came to Dacca University and a lecture was arranged. Prabhupāda selected the subject, "The Gauḍīya Maṭha stands for the dignity of the human race, not for slavery." It is not a very easy thing to get the service of Kṛṣṇa. So, *jīvera svarūpa haya. Nitya-dāsa* means 'born slave, born servant.' That was the clarion call in a high voice which was declared first. "*Jīvera svarūpa haya.*" With such great magnanimous pride, the *jīva* soul has such a dignified position. Now in the garb of a master he is a slave of *māyā*, a slave of *ajñāna*, ignorance. But the souls real innate position is that he is constitutionally in such a high position that Kṛṣṇa holds autocratic power over him.

The souls are so fortunate to have such an innate close connection with Kṛṣṇa.

jīvera svarūpa haya kṛṣṇera nitya-dāsa
kṛṣṇera taṭastha śakti bhedābheda prakāśa
(*Cc. Madhya* 20.108)

But this close connection with the Lord is not visible at this time. His prospect is such, but coming from the line of demarcation, the marginal potency, his entrance into *māyā* has been possible. Otherwise, it would not have happened. *Kṛṣṇera taṭastha śakti bhedābheda prakāśa*—adaptability of both sides is within him—to be with Kṛṣṇa or to be in *māyā*.

In this way, Mahāprabhu began to explain these topics as Sanātana Gosvāmī asked question after question. Mahāprabhu explained the proper conception of the environment, the position of the *jīva,* and Bhagavān—who is who. This knowledge is called *sambandha.*

Rūpa Gosvāmī generally deals with the *abhidheya,* the means to the end. How can we attain our desired position? That is called *abhidheya. Abhidha* means *abhidhana*—'the natural meaning.' This is the dictionary meaning—what comes naturally from the *Veda,* from the *śrauta,* what flows naturally. *Veda* explains what we must do. That is *abhidheya. Abhidhana* and *abhidheya.* The natural implication of the *śruti* has been extended to us by Kṛṣṇa—"Do this and come to Me"—that is *abhidheya.* So Rūpa Gosvāmī is the *abhidheya-ācārya,* revealing the means to the end—which is *sādhana.*

Rūpa Gosvāmī has elaborately given the way and described how one progresses, step by step:

ādau śraddhā tataḥ sādhu-saṅgo 'tha bhajana-kriyā
anartha-nivṛttiḥ syāt tato niṣṭhā rucis tataḥ
athaśaktis tato bhāvas tataḥ premābhyudañcati
(*Brs.* 1.4.15)

This describes the gradual process by which we may enter into our natural position, which we are missing for a long time. The way has been graphically described in detail by Rūpa Gosvāmī. *Prema, sneha, māna, praṇaya, rāga, anurāga, bhāva, mahā-bhāva*—in this plane do this, and then the next step is this, and then the next step is this, and in this way, you can come to the highest. That has been given by Rūpa—the means to the end, how to come to the desired goal.

And *prayojana-tattva* has been given by Raghunātha Dāsa Gosvāmī, because he has clearly and boldly asserted that our necessity is not so much with Kṛṣṇa, as with His highest servitor, Śrīmatī Rādhārāṇī. Generally, because we are coming from *taṭastha-śakti,* our prospect is limited. Even so, this limited prospect when taken to its highest degree, takes us to the highest servitor, the eternal servitor in *mādhurya-rasa*—to Rādhārāṇī. That is the general case. And in other *rasas,* we may be taken to the highest order of that service. So Dāsa Gosvāmī declared boldly, "Oh Kṛṣṇa, I do not want You if I do not find Rādhārāṇī there. I only want Rādhārāṇī."

Two phases of meaning are found here. "I really do not have the capacity to give You the highest quality of service. So, what is the necessity of my coming in the front rank? I was wandering in the street just the other day, and now I have such audacity to come so near to You and venture to render service to You. There are permanent servitors there and how great they are—such high quality service they are rendering. I must admit this—if I am really liberated and really I am graced, then I must understand my real position—I must not cross over the original and higher servitors. That will be a fault in me, and that will be suicidal. That will defeat its own object."

"My highest goal will be to help the real and eternal servitors who are taking that grave charge of serving You in a high way." That is the thing.

Also, our necessity is that we are to be a part of the serving group. So, we must accommodate our natural group leader. "I am not hankering after Your direct service but that of the serving leader—I must try to earn the confidence of her or him who is the leader. Then I am seeking, I am searching for Your proper service, otherwise it would be self-seeking."

You Want the Infinite in Your Fist

Rūpa, Sanātana and Dāsa Gosvāmīs have expressed the highest theistic understanding of *sambandha, abhidheya* and *prayojana.* Then, Jīva Gosvāmī has given us protection from the public and the scholarly side, to create some adjustment, and shown how the scripture, step by step takes us there. First, Rūpa Gosvāmī announced the highest thing and how the *śāstra* supports that. To the scholarly people Jīva Gosvāmī has given so many explanations, both logical and *śāstrika*—he supplied the support for this Gauḍīya *siddhānta*—first Jīva Gosvāmī and afterwards Baladeva Vidyābhūṣaṇa. Baladeva was the *vedānta-ācārya*, the author of *Govinda-bhāṣya* on *Brahma-sūtra.*

Parakīyā-rasa has been dealt with mostly by both Rūpa Gosvāmī and Sanātana Gosvāmī. The *viddhi* or scriptural law-abiding devotion, as well as a tinge of *anurāga* (free love), has been given by Sanātana Gosvāmī—and the path of pure free love as the way to attain the Absolute in its highest position, has been put forward and proven by Rūpa Gosvāmī. *Vaikunṭḥa janito vara madhu-purī*. He has shown to us the development of *rasa* in consideration with the environment.

In Christianity we see the fatherhood of Godhead, but here we are given not only sonhood of Godhead but His fullness in consorthood of Godhead. Sonhood of Godhead is greater than fatherhood of Godhead. We have to realize that, because parents are also servants. This particular kind of service in filial affection is really a service which we can't ignore and we have no necessity to ignore it either—the Lord must be in the center, not in the circumference. He is the creater, He is the father, He is above all, He is always in the center.

He is really in a state, which here in this world is translated as lust. The center of all our being is love and affection—not knowledge, nor energy. So He must have His central position in the domain of love. From there He will control everything. The controlling office of the whole must be the domain of love—we are to realize that. If we can realize that then we'll understand what Gauḍīya Maṭha, what Mahāprabhu, what *Bhāgavatam* has given us—what sort of wealth has been given to us.

We must understand that this *jñāna* and *karma*—the energy and knowledge, are of lower importance. They are rather covers of real life, not a part of real life. That is rather a cover and love is our real life—these two will be subservient to love and beauty. This is the situation of the world in reality. When we understand this, then we'll understand what is devotion, what is *bhakti*. Otherwise we will become Sahajiyā—imitationist. We shall go on with a fashion, wearing *tilaka,* the garb and all these things but if at heart we can really realize what is the position of real love then we will understand that this faculty of trying to know everything is a luxury, a fashion which is impossible.

Finite can never measure Infinite—*jñāna* is sheer folly. And *karma* is an enemy—any *karma* is digging your own grave. The energy by which you want to thrive here, that is digging your grave if it is not connected with the Absolute. And *jñāna* is a ludicrous thing. As the finite, you want to get the Infinite in your fist—this is a ludicrous attempt. Only the method of love, through which the Infinite will be inclined to come to you by *śaraṇāgati,* is the sole realistic attempt of our development. All else is absurd and injurious, a madman's gesticulation.

Part Three

Divine Manifestation

Divine Manifestation

Viṣṇupriyā-devī and Lakṣmīpriyā-devī are the wedded consorts of Śrī Caitanya Mahāprabhu when He is in the Vaikuṇṭha mood of Gaura-Nārāyaṇa. Śrī, Bhū and Līlā are considered in the case of Gaura-Nārāyaṇa. Śrī is Lakṣmīpriyā, Bhū-śakti is Viṣṇupriyā and Līlā-śakti is the *dhāma*. In this way they are serving Gaura-Nārāyaṇa. *Sandhinī, saṁvit, and hlādinī*—we find in the *Upaniṣads* the phrase *jñāna bala kriyā ca*. Thinking, feeling and willing—we generally find three potencies in the relativity of the infinite existence. The three phases are *sat, cit, ānanda* or *satyam, śivam, sundaram*—the basis or foundation, the enjoyer and the enjoyed. The predominating and predominated moiety, the negative and positive; predominated, predominating and in the background is Baladeva. In this way everything is analyzed.

When we want to see by analysis, then we come to analyze Him in three aspects. Thinking, feeling and willing—*jñāna bala kriyā ca*—*sat, cit, ānanda*. All are conscious—the Enjoyer who wants to enjoy, what is to be enjoyed, and what He is searching for (enjoyment or *rasa*)—these are the three aspects of the one Absolute Whole. We find the first division in three ways, three forms to understand—Śrī, Bhū and Līlā. Bhū-śakti is represented by Viṣṇupriyā—the ground on which the pastimes are manifested. The Lord's paraphernalia then comes from Līlā—the environment.

They are assisting Viṣṇupriyā, or Bhū-śakti—the assistants help directly in the propaganda. By separation, by accepting the show of the pangs of separation, Viṣṇupriyā helped a great deal with the propaganda—her attitude, her ideal, her penances helped a great deal. It melted the hearts of many and did away with the jealousy or antagonistic feelings about Śrī Caitanyadeva, especially in this locality in Bengal (Navadvīpa). And thereby she facilitated the preaching of Nityānanda Prabhu. Her penances and attitude contributed greatly to propagate Mahāprabhu's mission. As a *sannyāsī,* Śrī Caitanya, wandered the length and breadth of India and she stayed in one place and intensely engaged herself in the worship of Hari, Mahāprabhu. That also was a very valuable contribution—especially to the locality which was full of searchers of Śrī Caitanya Mahāprabhu. In the whole country the most furious type of devotion was invoked here in this locality.

Gaura is Not a Nagara

Viṣṇupriyā and Lakṣmīpriyā are considered to be the consorts of Gaura-Nārāyaṇa in the mood of Vaikuṇṭha *rasa.* That is externally connected with the *yuga-avatāra,* not with Rādhā-Kṛṣṇa. Gaura-Nārāyaṇa is the *yuga-avatāra,* but with a connection to the higher plane. So, in *navadvīpa-līlā,* the only consorthood that we find connected with Mahāprabhu is with Viṣṇupriyā and Lakṣmīpriyā.

The practice of *gaura-nāgara* is not accepted by the bona-fide school of Śrī Caitanyadeva's followers. The *gaura-nāgara* advocates improperly think that Gaurāṅga is an enjoyer, just as the Kṛṣṇa of *Bhāgavatam.* But the bona-fide school of Śrī

Caitanyadeva's followers do not accept that the practice of *gaura-nāgara* is proper. There is a conflict of *rasa*. Our *ācāryas*, Vṛndāvana Dāsa Ṭhākura, Kavirāja Gosvāmī, the Gosvāmīs and others, have rejected this idea of *gaura-nāgara*. Vṛndāvana Dāsa has rejected it wholesale in his *Caitanya-bhāgavata*:

ei mata cāpalya karen sabā sane
sabe strī mātra nā dekhena dṛṣṭikāṇe
'strī' hena nā prabhu ei avatāre
śravaṇe o nā karilā-vidita saṁsāre
ataeva yata mahā-mahimā sakale
'gaurāṅga-nāgara' hena stava nāhi bale
(*Cb. Ādi* 15.28-30)

Vṛndāvana Dāsa says, "Mahāprabhu never cast a glance towards girls in this life. He is not a *nāgara* because He came from a *brāhmaṇa* and *ācārya* family—Kṛṣṇa came from a milk-man's clan. Mahāprabhu has come to show the position of an *ācārya*, and an *ācārya* may not have such misconduct. Otherwise, who will care for Him? Who will take Him as an *ācārya* if He shows such slack character mixing amongst the girls? So, He never showed that sort of conduct. He was very particular about that, very careful. He never, even through the corner of His eye, cast any glance towards any girls. He maintained very strict morality throughout His life."

We see that in *gaura-līlā* there are three different sections. One section is more attached to *gaura-līlā*, the magnanimous side. Then there are the devotees like Narahari Sarakāra Ṭhākura who are more attracted to *kṛṣṇa-līlā*. A third section keeps the balance.

The followers of Narahari Ṭhākura could not tolerate that Kṛṣṇa would come in the role of a *sannyāsī*. "We don't like this—we don't want to see You as a *sannyāsī*. You are our Kṛṣṇa. Why have You come in this role? Are You not the hunter of the *gopīs?* Why have You come in the dress of a sage? All this is a sham! It is cheating! But we won't be cheated—we have recognized who You are. We don't like Your *sannyāsī-veśa* and our camp won't admit that You are a *sannyāsī*."

But those who are in favor of *gaura-līlā* say, "Who would care for your Kṛṣṇa if our Gaurāṅga did not preach about Him? It is only Gaurāṅga who has made your Kṛṣṇa popular. Kṛṣṇa is a debauchee, a thief, a liar and whatnot—who would recognize Him if Gaurāṅga did not stand and preach for your Master on His behalf. He has brought your Kṛṣṇa to the public."

Only Krsna No Other

Afterwards, the followers of Narahari Sarakāra Ṭhākura had some misconception of *gaura-nāgarī-līlā* and could not conceive the true spirit of Narahari Ṭhākura, but began to preach that, "As Gaurāṅga, He also mixed with so many ladies—He was also a *nāgara* like Kṛṣṇa (*gaura-nāgarī*)."

These two things cannot go together—the *ācārya* and the enjoyer. One in the position of an *ācārya* may advocate the enjoyment of Kṛṣṇa, and explain how this is the highest conception, and at what stage that is possible. Mahāprabhu came to do the work of a preceptor, a preacher—so He is not a *nāgara*, not an exploiter of the girls as we find in Vṛndāvana. It cannot be—there is a conflict. It is incorrect to think that Mahāprabhu can take the position of an *ācārya*, and at the same time appear as a debauchee. This conflict of *rasa* is not possible. Entering the temple to worship the Deity, one may take his wife to help in the worship. But she must not make jokes with her husband while in the temple. That will be *rasābhāsa*. A particular sober tone is necessary. In this way, Mahāprabhu has come in a serious mood to distribute the Holy Name of the Lord and divine love to the world. He is spreading Kṛṣṇa consciousness as a preacher. Such a reverent position cannot coexist with the enjoying mood of *gaura-nāgara.*

So, no one should consider that Gaurāṅga was a frivolous boy who mixed with the girls in a loose way. This is explained by Vṛndāvana Dāsa Ṭhākura in his *Caitanya-bhāgavata,* the original book written on the life of Śrī Caitanyadeva. But later, Locana Dāsa wrote *Caitanya-maṅgala* where we find some contamination of *nāgarī-bhāva.* So, we are not fully in agreement with Locana Dāsa in this regard. And there is also *Bhakti-ratnākara,* which was written two hundred years after Śrī Caitanyadeva—there also we find a tinge of *gaura-nāgarī-bhāva.* Our Guru Mahārāja mentioned that we may take some aspects of geography and history from *Bhakti-ratnākara* but not the *tattva,* the ontological side. Even then, some of the history found in that book has been spoilt with ontological misconceptions. So, we are not to take everything from that book completely.

Rūpa Gosvāmī, Sanātana Gosvāmī, Dāsa Gosvāmī, Kavirāja Gosvāmī, Vṛndāvana Dāsa Ṭhākura, and so many others have given descriptions about Mahāprabhu, but no one mentioned Him as a *nāgara.*

Only Kṛṣṇa can show that *līlā,* no other! Even Nārāyaṇa and other incarnations of Kṛṣṇa, never did so. Kṛṣṇa is the only exception. So this is all imaginary—a foolish tendency to make *kṛṣṇa-līlā* and *gaura-līlā* seem more similar. In order to prove that Gaurāṅga and Kṛṣṇa are one and the same, this sort of imagination has been resorted to.

Nobility of Gaura-lila

If Lord Gaura had not appeared as the *yuga-avatāra* in this age of Kali, then what would have become of us? How could we have tolerated living? Who in this universe would have ever learned about the topmost limits of loving mellows that comprise the glory of Śrī Rādhā?

yadi gaura nā ha'ta, tabe ki haita
kemane dharitāma de
rādhāra mahimā, prema-rasa-sīmā
jagate jānāta ke
(Vāsu Ghoṣa)

Vāsu Ghoṣa says, "Without this, how could I live? Through Gaurāṅga I have received the taste of such a high type of nectar. If Gaurāṅga did not come, we would not have any taste of this highest thing. Then how would it be possible for me to live? It is so life-sustaining, such nectar. Such a high degree of sustenance I find from this nectar brought by Gaurāṅga, that I can't imagine if He did not come, how I could live without my highest prospect of life. I could not know my own fulfillment. I was just a foreigner to my own self. He came and showed me how beautiful I am, how high I am. So much dignity of mind He has shown to me. I was devoid of that, I was bereft for so long. He has given me the key of my own home, my sweet home. So much wealth I have received. How much indebtedness I have to Gaurāṅga. I take it to be the secret of my life, the secret of success of my life."

"But what sort of gratitude can I show? He has given so much but I have nothing to give Him in return—I cannot show my proper thankfulness. O creator, what stony heart have you given to me that I cannot show my appropriate respect to Gaurāṅga—who has given me so much, that I cannot overestimate." These are the feelings of the devotees of Gaurāṅga. They are impressed with the land of Gaurāṅga.

Who except Kavirāja Gosvāmī could reveal the nobility and greatness of *gaura-līlā?* Kavirāja Gosvāmī has most successfully established the *cid-vilāsa.* And also our Vṛndāvana Dāsa Ṭhākura has given a graphic description of *gaura-līlā,* especially that of *Ādi-līlā.* In his teachings we have the conception of Gaurāṅga mostly. *Tāṅre kṣīroda-śāyī kahi, ki tāṅra mahimā*—Kavirāja Gosvāmī has pointed out the great difference between the Kṛṣṇa conception of Godhead and Kṣīrodakaśāyī Viṣṇu. Kavirāja Gosvāmī has harmonized these two points in this way—that in *svayam-bhagavān* Kṛṣṇa, of course Kṣīrodakaśāyī is there. If anyone says that He is Kṣīrodakaśāyī, it is not false. It is also real.

Svayam-bhagavan Mahaprabhu

But there is of course a great difference between Kṣīrodakaśāyī-Gaurāṅga, and *Svayam-bhagavān* Gaurāṅga. Kṣīrodakaśāyī-Gaurāṅga is the *yuga-avātara* giving *hari-nāma.* But *svayam-bhagavān* Kṛṣṇa—*rādhā-govinda milita tanu*—this form was seen when Mahāprabhu granted His *darśana* to Rāya Rāmānanda. And the Gosvāmīs have finally given us their highest conception of that.

When Mahāprabhu is performing *saṅkīrtana,* in general, He is not *svayam-bhagavān.* That is the duty of the *yuga-avatāra*—this is sometimes Kṣīrodakaśāyī. But in one day of Brahmā, *aṣṭāviṁśa,* the twenty-eighth day of Brahmā, *svayam-bhagavān* Kṛṣṇa Himself comes as Mahāprabhu. He gives us the mentality of the highest degree of separation—*svayam-bhagavān* Kṛṣṇa in His separation from Rādhārāṇī—He comes to teach that. He does not appear in each Kali-yuga, but only in the twenty-eighth Kali-yuga. In other ages of Kali, the *yuga-avatāra* generally comes to inaugurate *nāma-saṅkīrtana.*

Gaurāṅga is both Rādhā and Kṛṣṇa combined. He is Kṛṣṇa Himself, but in the mood of Rādhikā—He has accepted Her nature. He is Kṛṣṇa, when He is searching after Himself, trying to taste what ecstasy is within Himself. Self-searching Kṛṣṇa is Gaurāṅga. Self-introspection, self-searcher, trying to understand Himself, His own wealth.

We find the *siddhānta* in Kavirāja Gosvāmī, which Mahāprabhu's direct disciples, Rūpa and Sanātana, have imparted to us. Mahāprabhu wanted to teach us about *kṛṣṇa-līlā* and about Himself and He transmitted it to Rūpa-Sanātana. That which Rūpa-Sanātana thought and percolated by their opinion, was delivered by Kavirāja Gosvāmī. Who is Nityānanda? Who is Gauracandra? What is His gift? All this we can get rightly from *Caitanya-caritāmṛta* by Kavirāja Gosvāmī.

We are indebted to Kavirāja Gosvāmī in an immeasurable way—indebted to him for what he has given. In *Bhāgavatam,* we find so many narrations which are meant to attract many. A great number of these narrations are non-essential, but they are there nevertheless. Here though, we find wholesale Gaura-Nityānanda, nothing else. The substance of the substance, that is *Caitanya-caritāmṛta.*

I heard from Guru Mahārāja, "If all the religious scriptures vanished and only *Bhāgavata* remained, then everything would be fully represented there. So also, if *Caitanya-caritāmṛta* remains and all other theological books disappear, then there is no loss." The *aṅgī* is there. From this *bīja* (seed), the very gist is there. The *aṅgī* (whole) is there, and *aṅga* (part) will spring up from that principle, from Kavirāja Gosvāmī's *Caitanya-caritāmṛta.*

Śrī Caitanyadeva is the highest principle in theology—*rādhā-govinda milita tanu*—so the *Caitanya-caritāmṛta* also holds that position—Caitanyadeva is Rādhā-Govinda combined. His position and the corresponding *śāstrika* position we find in *Caitanya-caritāmṛta*—it is also eternally there.

Sweet Distribution of Krsna-lila

Gaurāṅga has taken the mood of His devotee, Śrīmatī Rādhārāṇī, and is trying to understand Himself and distribute this to others. He is showing the public how He should be served, by serving Himself. And then He Himself is giving this to others. He is showing how Kṛṣṇa is guru. When Kṛṣṇa Himself is guru, then He is Gaurāṅga.

krsna-līlāmṛta-sāra, tāra śata śata dhāra'
daśa-dike vahe yāhā haite
se caitanya-līlā haya, sarovara akṣaya
mano-haṁsa carāha' tāhāte

Caitanya-līlā is the infinite sweetness of Caitanya—whatever is within and whatever is coming from Him, that is all the high nectar of *kṛṣṇa-līlā* and nothing else. *Caitanya-līlā* means the center from which *kṛṣṇa-līlā* flows in different forms, flowing from all sides and even from every pore. There is nothing but *rādhā-kṛṣṇa-līlā* embodied in Him, and He is distributing it in order to help the public. The voluntary distribution of the different nectarine tastes of *kṛṣṇa-līlā*—that is Śrī Caitanya Mahāprabhu.

He has no separate existence from the *nāma, guṇa, rūpa,* and *līlā* of Rādhā-Kṛṣṇa—this includes Yaśodā and all others within the relativity of Kṛṣṇa. If one is there then all others must necessarily be there—*kṛṣṇa-līlā* means Kṛṣṇa with His group. Also Vṛndāvana—the water, the forest, the animals, the birds, all are included in *kṛṣṇa-līlā.* This is all coming from Śrī Caitanya, Who is Rādhā-Kṛṣṇa in a self-distributing mood. Whatever comes from Him, that is all Kṛṣṇa. Even in Śrī Caitanya's childhood, when one could not trace anything of Kṛṣṇa, it was there—in different ways He was preparing the background for distributing *kṛṣṇa-līlā* to others.

kṛṣṇa-nāma dhare kata bala
(*Śrī Nāma-māhātmya*—Śrīla Bhaktivinoda Ṭhākura)

What is the value of this sound 'Kṛṣṇa?' Śrīla Rūpa Gosvāmī has explained that Kṛṣṇa has four unique special qualities. Every *jīva* has fifty innate qualities. Certain *devatās* have fifty-five, and five additional qualities are partially manifest in them. Śrī Nārāyaṇa has sixty qualities in full, and Kṛṣṇa has four more qualities not found even in Nārāyaṇa. Those four qualities are: *rūpa-mādhurya* (sweet form), *veṇu-mādhurya* (sweet flute), *līlā-mādhurya* (sweet pastimes), and *parikara-mādhurya* (sweet associates). Śrīla Rūpa Gosvāmī has established the speciality of *kṛṣṇa-līlā* in this way. And this is only found in Vṛndāvana. Vāsudeva-Kṛṣṇa has no flute, and it has been mentioned that even Dvārakeśa-Kṛṣṇa is charmed to search for the *rūpa-mādhurya* of Vṛndāvana-Kṛṣṇa, the sweet Lord of Vraja, Reality the Beautiful.

Mukhya-rasa

Mahāprabhu came mainly to distribute *mādhurya-rasa* and automatically other *rasas,* because they are depending on *mādhurya-rasa. Mādhurya-rasa* is the *mukhya-rasa* or the *ādi-rasa.* In both these important ways *mādhurya-rasa* has been described. It is the first original *rasa* and it is the combination of all *rasas.* All others are like satellites, *vātsalya, sakhya,* etc. They are depending on this transaction—*vilāsa.*

Mahāprabhu came to give the original, principle *rasa,* and all others automatically followed. Rūpa Gosvāmī is exclusively in *mādhurya-rasa,* so his *sampradāya* is known as *rūpānuga.* Explicitly we profess that we are in *mādhurya-rasa.* There may be some exceptional cases, but mainly it is *rūpānuga.*

Because it is *rūpānuga,* our *ācārya guru-paramparā* is *mādhurya-rasa.* Even Nityānanda Prabhu is in *vātsalya-rasa* and is not in the list of *guru-paramparā*. Svarūpa Dāmodara, Rūpa, Sanātana, and Raghunātha are all *mādhurya-rasa-ācāryas*. Mainly our *sampradāya* is that of *mādhurya-rasa* tending to *rādhā-dāsyam*. But *rādhā-dāsyam* presupposes all other *rasas*. There must also be *vātsalya-rasa* and there must be *sakhya-rasa*. This means that Kṛṣṇa is always with such a group, never alone. He must have His paraphernalia, mother, father, and all these things. But even though *mādhurya-rasa* may be covered, it is the main current there, and all other *rasas* are subsidiary—helping His *līlā* with *mādhurya-rasa*. They also cannot be eliminated. They also must be there, but they are subsisting on *mādhurya-rasa*. The principle thing is *mādhurya-rasa* and to help its transaction, all other *rasas* are necessary.

Mahaprabhu Distributes His Inner Wealth

Is Kṛṣṇa serving Mahāprabhu? Yes, we can think that Kṛṣṇa is charmed by His own parallel existence as Gaurāṅga, because Gaurāṅga means Rādhā-Kṛṣṇa. And Gaurāṅga is prepared to distribute *kṛṣṇa-prema* to one and all—to extend the market for distribution of divine love. He is Kṛṣṇa in the mood of magnaminity. When Kṛṣṇa is in the mood of Rādhā, both combine to distribute their inner wealth to one and all for the public's benefit. That is Kṛṣṇa in the mood of Rādhā.

For us, Kṛṣṇa is more valuable when He is Gaurāṅga because we get our heart's satisfaction. In that way Gaurāṅga is higher than Kṛṣṇa. One combined, one divided. The whole into One becomes Gaurāṅga, not Brahman according to the *jñānīs*—they say it is non-differentiated Brahman. But to us that becomes Gaurāṅga searching Himself. When the Potency and the Owner of that Potency combine together in one whole Absolute, then He is searching and feeling Himself and in that way He is distributing Himself to others.

In the *Prema-dhāma-deva Stotram* it is written: Mahāprabhu is dancing because He is overjoyed in His own inner satisfaction. The dancing attitude is to show that He is full in Himself and the *kīrtana* is distributing Himself to others. That we find in Gaurāṅga. This is self-evident and this is the sign of the fullest substance, the highest Absolute.

Svarūpa Dāmodara says, "Who is Rādhārāṇī? She is the love of Kṛṣṇa in a particular form, the object of love of Kṛṣṇa." So They are one in the same. She is the affection of Kṛṣṇa in a particular form—so it is one. But for the pastimes in Dvāpara-yuga they divided in *vṛndāvana-līlā* into two parties—one Predominating, the other the Predominated Moiety. They parted with Their own paraphernalia and began Their pastimes in a different way. Again, They combined together to become Gaurāṅga and He began to distribute Himself to the public. "Come, take Me. I am yours also." He has appeared in the mood of Rādhārāṇī and it is Their own common treasure. They began to allow Themselves to be looted by the public. So Gaurāṅga is our greatest shelter.

Gauranga Admits Us to Radha-Krsna-lila

For one who hankers after the grace of Mahāprabhu, Nityānanda Prabhu will give admittance. The visa issuing officer is Nityānanda—*hena nitāi bine bhāi, rādhā kṛṣṇa paite nāi, dṛdha kari dhara nitāi pāya.* First, hold firmly the feet of Nityānanda Prabhu to get entrance into the domain of Gaurāṅga. And once you have secured your admission card from Gaurāṅga, you'll find that automatically you are present in the harem of Kṛṣṇa.

yathā yathā gaura-padāravinde
vindeta bhaktiṁ kṛta-puṇya-rāśiḥ
tathā tathotsarpati hṛdy-akasmād
rādhā-padāmbhoja-sudhāmbu-rāśiḥ

> As devotion unto the lotus feet of Śrī Gaurasundara is attained by a greatly pious person, inevitably the ocean of nectar which is the service of the lotus feet of Śrī Rādhā is accordingly born within his heart. (*Śrī Caitanya-candrāmṛta* 88)

You are in the group of Rādhārāṇī—the admission card is issued from here if you are expected in the confidential circle of service there. So Nityānanda Prabhu tried His best, "Somehow, anyhow connect yourself with Gaurāṅga, my fallen souls, my friends—connect yourself with Gaurāṅga in any way. It is very easy for you fallen souls to make connection with Him. Automatically everything will come unexpectedly to you for your inner heart's satisfaction." From door to door He canvassed, with tears in His eyes, rolling on the ground with His golden body, "Accept Gaurāṅga!" Try to get the grace of Nityānanda. He can give Gaurāṅga. If you've got Gaurāṅga, you've got everything—both the parties, Rādhā-Kṛṣṇa.

So we received caution often—don't try to force your way, for it will come automatically. Go on with the program that is given by *śāstra* and guru. If you have such a possibility of fortune, then it will come to you. It is not a matter of experience, that it can be given to this one and that one. It is not to be tackled in such a way—*yathā yathā gaura-padāravinde*—engage your full attention in *gaura-līlā* and that will come automatically within you. Indirectly it will come to you. From the higher domain, when it so desires, it will come down for some time to give you that experience and you will simply be astonished, "What is this?" And then, when it withdraws, you will only lament. It is a living thing. We cannot make such a higher thing the object of our experience. Even an ordinary man's conduct with his intimate friends is very hard to access, what to speak of the secret *līlā* of the Supreme Lord. How can we dare to enter! Especially publicly, that is not possible. Externally we can try to give some description of the outer possibilities, but not the actual thing. We won't venture to enter.

We have to try to follow not only the sound of the syllables, but the meaning underlining them. What is meant by these sounds? We are not to consider this from the external side, but to consider the substance within—we are to try to search for that.

The Search for Krsna

Brahma-jijñāsa: Search for Kṛṣṇa, Reality the Beautiful. Dive deep. Die to live. What is its real meaning? Search not only here on the surface of your sensual sense experience—you are to dive deep into reality. So many superficial covers, so many stages of our mental covers we are to pass through and then we are to come into touch with reality. Die to live—our progress and speed will be such that we will have to pass through all these covers and enter into the substantial world.

First there is *śraddhā* (faith) and then *sādhu-saṅga* (association) and then *bhajana-kriyā* (discharge of our duties) then *anartha-nivṛtti* (ulterior demands will disappear) then *niṣṭhā* (continuous aspiration for Kṛṣṇa). Then *ruci* (taste) and then that will continue to increase into *asakti* (attachment), then *bhāva* (connection with reality) then *prema* (divine love). Then the positive participation into reality will create so many things in us. The process is there—it is not imagination but it is a process of elimination and acceptance.

Then that which is real to us at present, the world of our sense experience, will evaporate and we shall find ourselves in the midst of the inner world. We should not approach like a *yogī,* like a scientific scholar engaged in research, trying to understand the world. A much deeper interest we will find here—we will forget these external things. At present we are living on the surface of the world but that which is the inner substance, we do not care to know. We must let that go—it is a cover floating on our consciousness. Leaving the cover, we shall try to enter into a deeper consciousness.

Outer consciousness is a part of the whole consciousness, so we are to tackle the extensive consciousness and we are a part of that. We should not be a party to subjective exploitation—we are not part of the world of stone, fossil, earth or water. No, we will have to enter into subjective consciousness—the causal truth, the source of knowledge. We are to enter into the fountain from where the water is emanating. We are to enter into that fountain to understand what type of water it is. So we enter into the source of knowledge to find out where it comes from. We are to move against the current. And what is the product of that current? It is just floating on our senses, and it is transient, and it is reactionary, and it is temporary. So we are to enter into the source, and we are to have proper exploitation with the help of the agents there—*ātma,* Paramātma, and then the Bhagavān conception.

Ultimately we shall find that we are to serve the wonderful substance of ecstasy, and if we can become a slave unto that part, we shall find our fortune is fulfilled. Such high, high kind of pleasure is there—satisfaction is there. Somehow, if we get any kind of meager connection there, we shall see all our fulfillment. We will obtain our final fulfillment—a slight connection with that treasure, which is the source of all knowledge and the source of all ecstacy.

Not Previously Available

Mādhurya-rasa was the gracious gift of Mahāprabhu—*anarpita carīṁ cirāt*—that which was not possible to distribute before Mahāprabhu appeared. It is called '*anarpita carīṁ*,' because it was not previously available to the ordinary person. And what is it? It is the complete surrender to Kṛṣṇa in consorthood, where ones entire existence is embraced.

Bhakti to the highest degree is found in *mādhurya-rasa*. In *vātsalya-rasa* a little less is found, in *sakhya-rasa* a little less, in this way it is distributed—*pūrṇa-rasa* or full-*rasa* is *mādhurya-rasa*.

kintu yāṅra yei rasa sei sarvottama
taṭastha haña vicārile, āche tara-tama

Each servitor in their own department thinks that they are holding the highest position. But in the absolute consideration, if the comparison is drawn, then we see that *dāsya* is superior to *śānta*, then *vātsalya* is superior and the supermost is *mādhurya*. But the very origin is Rādhārāṇī. She and Her extensions are distributing all these various gradations of *rasa* to the fullest extent.

Sweetness and Magnanimity

Audārya-līlā means mostly to distribute the *līlā* pastimes within the Rādhā-Kṛṣṇa camp to the public in a gradual way. *Audārya* is in Navadvīpa. *Udāra* means generous or magnanimous. And here, we must distribute it to others in a scientific way. That is the difference between *mādhurya* and *audārya*. Sweetness and sweetness mixed with magnanimity.

In Jagannātha Purī we mainly find the Dvārakā mood with some modification—to accept the most fallen, especially through *prasādam*. *Patita-pāvana jagannātha sarveśvara, vṛndāvana-candra sarva-rasera ākara*. In this way Bhaktivinoda Ṭhākura is writing the 108 names of Kṛṣṇa.

Dvārakā-līlā is adjusted to recruit the most fallen—and afterwards they may be members in Vṛndāvana. Both are mixed, the *dvārakā-līlā* and *navadvīpa-līlā* are mixed. We find the Lord's aspect as *patita-pāvana* (savior of the most fallen) here in Navadvīpa and in Purī. There are two sections—there is Vṛndāvana and Navadvīpa, and there is Dvārakā and Navadvīpa—there Vṛndāvana is suppressed. When Jagannātha comes to the Guṇḍicā temple in Purī the connection with Vṛndāvana expresses itself. Otherwise, in the Jagannātha temple, that is in the mood of Dvārakā.

Rasa-lila in Dvaraka

When Dvārakā and Vṛndāvana mix, that is Jagannātha. He is mainly in Dvārakā, but the posing of Vṛndāvana is there. He has infinite forms of *līlā,* so what can we trace or know with our finite capacity? In *Dvārakā-saṁhitā* we find that there was an arrangement of *rasa-līlā* in Dvārakā also. The queens had heard that in Vṛndāvana there was the *rasa-līlā* and that it was most wonderful. So, on one occasion when the whole Vṛndāvana party was invited to Dvārakā, the queens privately approached Kṛṣṇa and petitioned Him, "The *gopīs* have come, and for a long time it is our hearts' desire that You will show Your *rasa-līlā* to us. "Will You request them?"

Kṛṣṇa replied, "If they will give their consent, then I have no objection." The queens made their request to the *gopīs* and the *rasa-līlā* was arranged. When it was complete, all that saw it were astonished, and the queens went to the camp of the *gopīs* to express their wonder. "What we have seen is the most wonderful thing, it is impossible to conceive even—we cannot properly express such a thing." And Śrīmatī Rādhārāṇī made this statement in reply, "What have you seen? That was nothing, an almost dead representation. Where is the Yamunā? Where is the *kadamba* tree, the peacock, the deer, and all these things? There in Vṛndāvana that was a natural stage, and that was performed there in our youth. What you saw, that is nothing, a sham, a mere mockery."

Then the queens began to reflect, "If what we saw is of such lower order, then what type of superior quality *līlā* must be found in the original? It is totally inconceivable." So the psychology of Vṛndāvana is all-important.

The Form of Lord Jagannatha

The conception came amongst the queens of Dvārakā that, "Although we have Kṛṣṇa as our Husband, we feel that somehow He is not Kṛṣṇa in His fullness. He always seems absent-minded, as if His heart is not wholly with us." Pondering the cause of this, the queens came to know that previously Kṛṣṇa had some very sweet connection with Vṛndāvana and the *gopīs* there. Thinking this to be the key to Kṛṣṇa's absent-minded mood, they began searching for an opportunity to find out how Kṛṣṇa lived in Vṛndāvana.

They wanted to know about His pastimes there with the *gopīs,* and to hear the descriptions of His childhood. Balarāma's mother Rohiṇī lived in Vṛndāvana during Kṛṣṇa's childhood, and although she is situated in *vātsalya-rasa,* she had heard many things about Kṛṣṇa's *līlā* with the *gopīs.* So meeting her privately the queens requested her, "Please describe Kṛṣṇa's *mādhurya-līlā* in Vṛndāvana to us." Rohiṇī was unable to avoid the queens' sincere request, and so posting Kṛṣṇa's sister Subhadrā to keep watch, she began to narrate His *līlā* with the milkmaids of Vraja.

It so happened that at that same time, Kṛṣṇa and Balarāma were taking rest in a nearby room, and as Rohiṇī was describing the *vṛndāvana-līlā,* They became aware of what was taking place. Coming to the door where Subhadrā was standing guard, Kṛṣṇa and Balarāma could hear the talk of Rohiṇī, and remembering Vṛndāvana, the *gopīs* and all these things, a great intensity of feeling came over Them. A great change came over Kṛṣṇa and Balarāma, a feeling so great that Their bodies also began to change—just as Mahāprabhu had shown when He fell at the gate of the Jagannātha Mandira and His arms and legs entered into His body.

Such a change in the body is possible according to some particular feeling of ecstasy, and feeling the ecstasy of Vṛndāvana, Kṛṣṇa and Balarāma were undergoing such a transformation. And Subhadrā, although she had not lived in Vṛndāvana, seeing her Brothers in this way, also experienced some sort of sympathetic transformation. Internally that feeling came to her and externally she was also transformed. The cause of Their transformation was the Vṛndāvana statements of Rohiṇī. Remembering that *vṛndāvana-līlā,* these changes came in Their bodies. Suddenly the queens and Rohiṇī understood that Kṛṣṇa and Balarāma were there listening to their talk, and so immediately they stopped.

Vraja-rasa in Dvaraka

With the *līlā-kathā* thus suspended, the transformed figure of Kṛṣṇa remained, and He fell into a trance. Nothing could be done to reverse the situation, and so, in desperation Kṛṣṇa was taken to Nava-Vṛndāvana—a replica of Vṛndāvana that had been created in Dvārakā by Brahmā for Kṛṣṇa's pleasure. Although Kṛṣṇa was awake, He could not come out of that trance until He was taken to that Nava-Vṛndāvana. There, in His trance, He could only see Baladeva—all others present were eliminated from His vision. Seeing Baladeva, Kṛṣṇa was happy that He was in Vṛndāvana.

Then He saw Rohiṇī, "Oh yes, it is Vṛndāvana." Mannequins of all the other residents of Vṛndāvana were also arranged there, and the queens were following from a distance to see what would happen. After seeing Baladeva, Kṛṣṇa saw that His cowherd friends Śrīdāmā and Sudāmā were also there. In one place, the *gopīs* were there, and in another Śrīmatī Rādhārāṇī was standing. Seeing Her mannequin Kṛṣṇa ran and embraced Her, and when Satyabhāmā saw this, some transformation also appeared in Her body. While Kṛṣṇa was in this temperament, Baladeva was able to go to Him and gradually bring Kṛṣṇa back to the consciousness of Dvārakā. The attraction for that *vṛndāvana-līlā* is such that when it was suddenly stopped, the result was a great change in the physical plane.

Of course it is not physical, but for the purpose of explanation we can say physical. That check caused the transformation of the external plane. It is something like that which occurs when there is an earthquake. The internal movement of the Earth disfigures the surface, so the internal disturbance that was created by the recollection of *vṛndāvana-līlā*, caused a great transformation in the superficial appearance of Kṛṣṇa. And when that internal *līlā* rememberance was suddenly checked, that external appearance remained. That has been shown in Jagannāthadeva. When the higher prospect is suddenly checked, then the reaction comes.

A Mixture of Vrndavana and Dvaraka

So, Jagannātha is a reactionary stage between Vṛndāvana and Dvārakā—the conflict between the emotion of *svayam-bhagavān* and the *vaibhava-vilāsa* of Kṛṣṇa. It is something like *rasābhāsa*. In higher ecstasy also, *rasābhāsa* is possible—the clash of two different waves of *rasa*. The train may be proceeding in a particular motion and the carriage along with it. But if suddenly the train should brake, then the contents inside the carriage will be thrown into a great disorder. It is something like that.

ado yad dāru 'plavate sindhoḥ pāre apūruṣam
(*Ṛg Veda* 10.155.3)

This verse says that the Jagannātha *mūrti* has been there from the very conception, from the most ancient times. Every *līlā* of the Lord is eternal—every part of the infinite is eternal. In the beginning of *Mahābhārata* we find *Dhṛtarāṣṭra-vilāpa,* where Dhṛtarāṣṭra is naming the main incidents of *Mahābhārata* and lamenting that, "Because of this incident and that incident I know that my party must be defeated." But at this stage of *Mahābhārata* none of these incidents had taken place. So how can Dhṛtarāṣṭra speak of these incidents at the beginning of the book?

It is because it is *nitya,* eternal. The beginning of the *līlā* and the end of the *līlā* cannot be differentiated. It is in a cyclic order and it is eternal. That is a very difficult thing to understand—to adjust to the eternal—everywhere beginning, everywhere end. Everywhere there is center and nowhere is there circumference. This is the meaning of infinite. This is *nitya-līlā*—everywhere beginning, everywhere end, and all coexistent at the same time. Kṛṣṇa Dāsa Kavirāja Gosvāmī has represented this in a particular way. He has given the example that the sunrise is to be found always in one place or another. Not that it is here, and then somewhere else.

So like the sun, *kṛṣṇa-līlā* is moving—His birth, His childhood, etc. is being shown here and then continues in another *brahmāṇḍa,* another universe. That is the aspect of *bhauma-līlā.* And in another aspect, in Goloka, we find that every *līlā* is also *nitya.* It is reflected here in this world and the reflection is revolving like the sun. It may be traced here, then somewhere else—it is a question of space. But in Goloka, in the central place, it is all there simultaneously. It is also no less in the heart of the devotees. When a devotee remembers a *līlā*, it may first be *vraja-līlā*, and then *dvārakā-līlā*, but what is reflected in the heart of a devotee is also real. So in this way it is coexistent and it is continuing always. Every *līlā* and every part of *līlā* is always present, coexistent—succession and coexistence are both harmonized.

Just as the Lord's *līlās* are eternal and unlimited, similarly His forms are also unlimited. Rāmānuja has classified the expression of the Supreme Entity in five forms: *para, vyūha, vaibhava, antaryāmī,* and *arcā.*

Para—the central conception of the highest entity. *Vyūha*—His extended self in different functions, in different figures. *Vaibhava*—His appearance in this mundane plane as *avatāras* like Matsya, Kūrma, and Varāha. *Antaryāmī*—His presence in every heart and every soul, every conscious unit, and *arcā*—His appearance in the plane of our physical perception as the Deity. In His form as the Deity, I can touch Him, I can see Him, and I can serve Him. In a concrete form He has come to help our understanding.

Salagrama Worship and Sacred Thread

In the Gauḍīya temples we find *śālagrāma-śīla* worship, even though Mahāprabhu preferred Govardhana. Just as the sacred thread is not necessary, also *śālagrāma-śīla* worship is not necessary for a Gauḍīya Vaiṣṇava devotee to make progress in his path to the goal. But it was arranged only for two purposes, positive and negative.

Firstly, the positive side is that one should not think that Kṛṣṇa worship is lower than that of Nārāyaṇa worship. Goloka is on the upper position of Vaikuṇṭha, so we are to go there. We have to pass through Vaikuṇṭha first—we have to pass through many stages, otherwise one will become a Sahajiyā. *Svayam-bhagavān* Kṛṣṇa is above all. To promote such faith in the devotee it is necessary that they will think that they must pass through Vaikuṇṭha and rise above that to service in the mood of love.

Secondly, on the negative site, the so-called blood *brāhmaṇas* think that the Vaiṣṇava has no right to come to Vaikuṇṭha. They are also worshiping Kṛṣṇa, the cowboy. Actually, their position is lower than ours, because they commit offenses against the Vaiṣṇavas.

So, it is necessary to save the blood *brāhmaṇas* from their offenses to the Vaiṣṇavas and to make the Vaiṣṇavas aware that their demand crosses Brahmaloka and Vaikuṇṭha and brings them to Goloka. So one must be very careful in this valuable campaign.

For these two purposes *śālagrāma* (Nārāyaṇa) worship has been introduced, along with the sacred thread. Otherwise, neither the sacred thread nor the worship of Śālagrāma-Nārāyaṇa is necessary. But these intermediate steps were supplied upon finding that there is a misconception about the social status of the Vaiṣṇava—that the Vaiṣṇava is lower than a caste *brāhmaṇa,* they have no right to worship *śālagrāma,* etc. In this way their value is minimized and their position comes in a lower conception.

In order to remove these misconceptions in the Vaiṣṇava society as well as the society of the so-called *brāhmaṇas,* this method has been especially introduced by our Guru Mahārāja, Bhaktisiddhānta Sarasvatī Ṭhākura, and we are also following in his footsteps.

Govardhana Worship

Govardhana-śīla was given by Mahāprabhu to Raghunātha Dāsa Gosvāmī. As *śālagrāma* is considered with respect amongst the *brāhmaṇas,* similarly amongst the Vaiṣṇavas, the *govardhana-śīla* is worshiped. *Śālagrāma* is called *gaṇḍakī-śīla.* Naturally we know by revelation that *gaṇḍakī-śīla* is found in the river Gaṇḍakī, where we find the natural existence of Lord Nārāyaṇa in different ways. It is revealed. And so one who has faith in that revelation, accepts the path of worshiping Nārāyaṇa in *gaṇḍakī-śīla* or *śālagrāma.*

Also Kṛṣṇa expresses Himself in *Bhāgavatam* and other places. There we find that, "I am in Govardhana. Govardhana and Myself are inseparably connected. Anyone who worships Govardhana, worships Me." This is the conception that Mahāprabhu gave with *govardhana-śīla* to Dāsa Gosvāmī Prabhu. That worship of *govardhana-śīla* is continuing in the Gauḍīya Vaiṣṇava school. This type of worship gives entrance into the *rāga-mārga*—the line of divine love towards Kṛṣṇa. The worship of *śālagrāma* is *vidhi-mārga.* The worship of Nārāyaṇa in *vidhi-mārga* is very hard and very strict.

Rāga-marga is more liberal. It is from the heart and does not require much formality. So the Gauḍīya Vaiṣṇavas, who want to attain their position in the land of divinity, worship *govardhana-śīla.* That is very advantageous, encouraging, and fruitful for them.

In a nutshell, the worship of *govardhana-śīla* helps us to enter into the domain of divine love. Lawful devotion, following rules and regulations according to the order of the *śāstra,* may damage our prospect. Mahāprabhu wanted us to avoid that path. Our faith is somewhere above this land's law. So the worship of *govardhana-śīla* will be safer and more fruitful for our purpose—we want to have service in the Vṛndāvana area, the domain of love divine. This is the purport and the utility of having our *dīkṣā* initiation in the line of worshiping *govardhana-śīla.*

Govardhana worship is very simple. Mahāprabhu advised that a little water and *tulasī* is the minimum that should be offered. And generally whatever food we take, in a simple way with no splendor or grandeur, we must offer to Govardhana. If possible, bedding and a flower, *tulasī,* and then some food in a bowl may be offered. And anything else may be done as we normally do for the *vigraha* of Kṛṣṇa. Govardhana is easily self-satisfied with a simple and short way of worshiping Him. But, we have found that He is satisfied by simply offering water and *tulasī.* According to your circumstances, offer whatever you can.

Serve in Kirtana

It is not necessary to have Deities while traveling and preaching. *Kīrtana* is of a higher type. *Arcana* is less powerful. If we are asked by a superior to take up the service of *arcana,* that is alright. Otherwise, in the general case, *kīrtana* is more powerful, and more fruitful. Serve in *kīrtana*—the preaching department. The important thing is, whose guidance we are working under. My energy will be transformed and led to the higher quarter. By devoting my energy, I shall receive some remuneration, and that will be in the charge of whom I shall obey—*sādhu-anugatya.* That is the all-important thing.

On one side, I will be relieved from my mental tendencies which are forcing me to undergo the different stages of this material world. And on the positive side, my soul will be lead to the plane from which the order is coming to me. In that quarter I shall be paid. His qualities will come down to help me and my lower energy will diminish and disappear. And I will find myself in the plane of whom I am working for. That is all-important in *nava-vidha bhakti.*

And the worship of the Deity may be included in that. It depends on the quality. At whose disposal I am doing the work. Hanumānjī killed so many, but that was done in pure devotion. At the same time, there is so much money being spent to construct temples and Deities are also being installed according to the *śāstrika* order and in a grand way there is arrangement for the worshiping. That may be *karma-kāṇḍa* if there is any begging purpose in mind. *Kiṁ karma kim akarmeti kavayo'py atra mohitāḥ*—higher scholars cannot understand what is *karma*, what is *akarma*, what is the cause. The object is all-important, for which I am working.

Hatvāpi sa imāl lokān na hanti na nibadhyate. If one is standing on that plane, he can pass so many *brahmāṇḍas*. He does not do anything. This is a revolutionary thought. Passing through so many solar systems, one may not be entangled in any activities, good or bad. Such a plane is there. The universal wave—that is moving and if I can dance in tune to that wave, I am free. No reaction will have any effect on me. That is called *nirguṇa*. No local interest is there. Absolutely irresistible. And *bhakti* proper, means to adjust ourselves with the dance of that plane. Local interest, provincial interest—they clash with one another. That may be very small and that doesn't matter. That is *saguṇa*. *Bhayaṁ dvitiyābhiniveśataḥ syād*—consideration of secondary interest. But in a higher case also, it is apparent that there is no local interest or personal interest. The only consideration is the absolute interest.

Gradations of Arcana

Arcana is especially meant for Vaikuṇṭha, not Goloka. In the Rāmānuja *sampradāya*, *arcana* holds an important position, but in the Gauḍīya *sampradāya*, *sevā* and *bhajana* are more important. *Arcana* has been explained to be of a lower status.

arcayam eva haraye pūjām yaḥ śraddhāyehate
na tad-bhakteṣu cānyeṣu, sa bhaktaḥ prākṛtaḥ smṛtaḥ

A devotee who faithfully worships the Deity, but does not properly respect the Vaiṣṇavas or the people in general is called a materialistic devotee, and is considered to be in the lowest position of devotional service. (*Bhāg.* 11.2.47)

Arcana means trial. Before the actual fight there is sometimes a mock fight—an air-show, when the planes of the air-force show some posing of fighting. So *arcana* is something like that—in preparation for the real service, we engage ourselves in similar things. On the external plane, with the external senses, we make attempts for some service. But because we are not fully matured in devotion, we cannot see the Lord in the Deity—we do not see Him fully there. It is a mere appearance. *Arcana* is practice for when we come in connection with the real thing. It will be helpful for us. This is for the *kaniṣṭha-adhikārī*.

The *kaniṣṭha* devotee has more reverence for the Deity and not so much for the Vaiṣṇava because he thinks, "He is a only a man and he may have some devotion, but that is also in me—I am also worshiping the Deity." The *kaniṣṭha* is not so particular about the devotees (*na tad-bhakteṣu*), he is more accustomed to deal with the material aspect of things (*sa bhaktaḥ prākṛtaḥ smṛtaḥ*). But the *madhyama-adhikārī* makes friendship with the devotee:

īśvare tad adhīnesu bālīśeṣu dviṣatsu ca
prema maitrī-kṛpopekṣa yaḥ karoti sa madhyamaḥ

> A *madhyama-adhikārī* is one who loves the Supreme Lord, is friendly towards His devotees, shows mercy towards those who are ignorant of the process of devotion and rejects those who are envious of the Lord and His devotees. (*Bhāg.* 11.2.46)

He will show kindness to the ordinary masses by talking about the Lord, and he will be indifferent to those who are unfriendly to Him. He has particular care for the devotee, where there is the living presence of the Lord. His attention is not so acute for the Deity, but he finds more valuable representation in the heart of a devotee. When one is able to appreciate that, he will come to the middle class stage.

But in the higher conception one will leave *arcana* and serve a devotee. The presence of the Lord is more real in the heart of a devotee—He is in a more conscious form. For those that cannot understand and are bound by sense experience, the Lord takes the form of the Deity for them. But for those who can catch His spiritual existence, it will be more beneficial to serve a devotee than to serve the Deity.

Position of the Devotee

There is one incident mentioned in *Bhāgavatam* about Gajendra. There was a king in South India, who was engaged in worshiping his family Deity. At that time the great devotee Mahārṣi Agastya, came to his palace as a guest. The king was informed by a servant, but the king thought, "I am busy serving my Deity, I should not leave this and go and receive Agastya." Agastya was a devotee and a *yogī* of the highest type, and if he became displeased then he could do much mischief to the kingdom. Knowing this, the king made a show that he had not heard and after finishing the worship, he came and enquired and made arrangements for the *ṛṣi*. But because he had pretended not to hear about the arrival of a Vaiṣṇava as he was so deeply engaged in worship, he committed an offense against Agastya and in his next life took birth as an elephant. An elephant by nature is very slow at reacting. This is called *stabdhī-buddhi*. So because the king took his time to take care of the sage, he received the body of an elephant.

When there was a fight between that elephant and a crocodile, the elephant became tired and couldn't fight and took the Name of Kṛṣṇa. "Lord, save me!" That temperament came because he was a devotee internally and so he was saved. His birth as an elephant came only due to his offence of disregarding the devotee on the plea of his own engagement to the Deity. He took the Vaiṣṇava as an ordinary man and the Deity as God Himself—he should have left the worship of the Deity and received the devotee. The dictation of the *śāstra* is that if we are engaged in worshiping the Deity and we hear that Gurudeva or a Vaiṣṇava of a higher order has come, we should take permission of the Deity and go and attend the devotee. Then we should come later and finish the worship. We must make some arrangement. This is not a man who has come—there is also the expression of the Lord in him. The Lord is present in the Deity, but the Lord is also present in the heart of the devotee—that is a higher conception. God's existence in his heart is more important than in the Deity. We have to respect that first.

When I first came to Gauḍīya Maṭha in Calcutta, I saw that in that rented house the Deity of Mahāprabhu was installed in a room facing the street on the ground floor, and Guru Mahārāja was living in a room on the first floor. First, I asked one *brahmacārī*, "Is the Deity of Mahāprabhu made from wood or something else?" He got excited and told, "What are you saying? He is *sākṣāt* Mahāprabhu—He is Mahāprabhu

Himself. Don't take the Deity to be made from wood, earth or any mundane element. Mahāprabhu Himself is there."

Then I put another question: "All right," I said, "Who is considered greater—Mahāprabhu or your Gurudeva? If your Gurudeva is considered to be the greatest devotee, why is he not staying by the side of Mahāprabhu, Who is directly here. He is staying on the first floor in another room and Mahāprabhu is left here on the ground floor near the road? The Deity is on the ground floor, and the guru is above in a safe position. What is the reason?"

Hearing this naughty question, that *brahmacārī* was a little calm and tried to make me understand that Guru Mahārāja was also close to Mahāprabhu there. "In his heart, there is Mahāprabhu. Here also, in the temple is the Deity of Mahāprabhu, and there also, in his room, Guru Mahārāja is living close to Mahāprabhu. But the Mahāprabhu within his heart is superior to the Mahāprabhu here in the temple—that is the highest expression. " I could not understand so much, but still I thought that, "Yes, there must be some reality in his argument." I was silent.

Afterwards I came to understand that Mahāprabhu is in the heart of the devotee and also in the Deity, but the higher expression is found in the heart of a devotee than in the Deity. So He is active in the devotee and passive in the Deity.

tomāra hṛdaya sadā govinda viśrāma
govinda kahena – mora vaiṣṇava parāṇa

Your heart is always the resting place of Govinda and Govinda says, 'The devotees are always in My heart.' (*Prārthanā,* Narottama Dāsa Ṭhākura)

Arcana and Bhajana

Prabhupāda told us that we cannot accept that *arcana* is *bhajana*. *Arcana* is a medium and the worship is through *mantra*. *Bhajana* means direct service—soul to Supersoul. Through the process of *arcana*, one day we hope to come to the direct position of service. *Bhajana* is not performed through the medium of any mental system to purify ones own mind.

Mahāprabhu did not give so much stress to *arcana* but to *nāma-bhajana*. So a question may arise as to why the Gosvāmīs installed the Deities of Govinda, Gopīnātha and Madana-mohana in Vṛndāvana when the Holy Name was sufficient. Our Guru Mahārāja once answered that we should understand the difference between *arcana* and *bhajana*. The Gosvāmīs were engaged in *bhajana* not in *arcana*. They did not see the Deity representation of Kṛṣṇa—they were directly in contact with Him. There was no barrier between this plane and that plane—it was all on the same plane.

Once Madana-mohana told Sanātana Gosvāmī, "I can't eat what you offer without some salt!"

"Oh, You want me to give You some salt only? Alright, I will add some salt."

"No no, Sanātana, I can't eat this without a little *ghee*."

"Then why have You come to a beggar? You can eat nicely elsewhere. Why have You come here to trouble me? Where shall I get *ghee* and all these things?" In this way, their transaction went on.

So, the Gosvāmīs have recommended *arcana* for others, but they themselves engaged in direct service. That is *bhajana*. They were taking the Holy Name but they encouraged *arcana* which is generally found in the Rāmānuja section. Rūpa, Sanātana and other *mahājanas* installed Deities and their service to the Deities was *bhajana* cent-percent. But general *arcana* is of a lower class. The *arcana* of the *mahājanas* holds more importance to us. The *arcana* performed by liberated souls, (*svarūpa-siddhas*), should not be considered as ordinary *arcana*. That is *bhajana*—direct service.

So, *arcana* is of different gradations—there is a difference in quality. There is the worship of a *kaniṣṭha-adhikārī*, the worship of a *madhyama-adhikārī*, and also the worship of an *uttama-adhikārī*. But one is direct communion, while the other is according to *śāstra*.

Gradations of Prasadam

Sometimes the question is asked whether the ordinary masses benefit from *prasāda* distribution. So much purity will be transmitted to those that will take *prasādam*, but the question of degree is there. There is *prasādam* from the *mahā-bhāgavata*, *prasādam* from the *madhyama-bhāgavata*, and *prasādam* from the *kaniṣṭha-bhāgavata*. It all depends upon who is responsible for the *prasādam* and what is his connection with divinity. The current must be there, just as it is with an electrical box—you may connect all the wiring, but if there is no current then what is its value? *Vaikuṇṭha nāma grahaṇe*—the transcendental connection must be there. Otherwise form is simply form and it is useless. The spirit must be within the form. Form is also necessary—wiring is necessary in order to utilize the electric current, but mere wiring has no utility. So *prasāda* distribution should have a real connection with divinity otherwise it is all trade, an external exhibition. An ulterior motive may be there and it will become a business. Just as the *jāti-gosvāmīs* make a trade of taking money by reading the *Bhāgavatam*. But if the man behind the *prasāda* distribution has a sincere connection with the Lord, and the connection comes and pervades everything, then that is *prasādam*. Otherwise it is imitation.

Also, it may not always be that if some ordinary person takes *kṛṣṇa-prasādam,* he will take a human birth in his next life. They may attain a human form after four or five births also. But wherever they may go, the connection will be there. It is all recorded on a higher plane and it won't be lost.

The Standard for Nama Sankirtana

A connection with divinity must always be there. Bhaktivinoda Ṭhākura has said that the leader of the congregational *saṅkīrtana* party must be a *śuddha-bhakta* (pure devotee)—the *kīrtana* party must be guided by such a person. Otherwise it will be dancing and jumping on the mundane plane. A divine connection must be there. If the congregational chanting is not under the guidance of a man of a higher plane, then it should be discarded. We should not mix with that. Bhaktivinoda Ṭhākura has written—*śuddha-bhakta anugati, kīrtana haile sekhana yāya.* If it is under the guidance of a *śuddha-bhakta,* then we may attend that function, otherwise not. There will be *nāma-aparādha*—offences committed against the Holy Name. We should not participate there. It will be *nāmākara*—only the sound of the Name will be there, but the inner realization is missing and that is the main thing. What sort of vibration is being created? That is all-important. We do not care for the sweet tone nor the expertise in the pronunciation. We must try to improve the quality. So there must be a connection with the divine, a connection with a descending agent. One who has the eye can percieve that connection. *Oṁ ajñāna timirāndhasya jñānāñjana śalākayā.* Our own realization will be the guarantee, our own knowledge. That perception is given by Gurudeva. He removes the cataract of ignorance and gives *divya-darśana*—the divine eye. *Divya-cakṣu dīkṣā*—*dīkṣā* means that he imparts transcendental knowledge. As much as one has that knowledge they will impart it to the disciple. Guru will teach the disciple how to exclusively connect with Kṛṣṇa—exclusive identification with the interest of Kṛṣṇa. And Kṛṣṇa is not seen, therefore the connection is through guru or Vaiṣṇava. In this way, we must develope self-abnegation to the extreme and according to our degree of surrender, we will be benefited.

Offer Everything to Krsna

Once something is dedicated for the service of Kṛṣṇa, it is an all-conscious unit. Everything here is exclusively meant for Kṛṣṇa and no other god. It is all meant for Kṛṣṇa consciousness—not for Subrahmaṇya consciousness or any other consciousness—only for Him. Everything is conscious and fresh, and no consciousness is allowed except full dedication to the Lord.

Every flower born here is meant only to satisfy Kṛṣṇa. Rādhārāṇī will curse us if we try to utilize them for the service of others. They are all meant for Kṛṣṇa's service. So here also at our *maṭha*, trespassers may pluck flowers, or for medicinal purposes they will take some, but it pains my heart—they are all meant for the service of Kṛṣṇa. For medicinal purposes, these people want to take the roots of plants on the *maṭha* property, so I tell them, "Go to Mahāprabhu, take His permission, then take them away." If it is necessary and it cannot be avoided then I tell them, "Go get His permission first."

I heard that once, at Yogapīṭha, the appearance place of Mahāprabhu, there was one *kadamba* tree. As Prabhupāda was coming out of the *maṭha* to go to Calcutta, one devotee said, "A new flower has come on the *kadamba* tree, and it has not been given to Prabhupāda." So he took the flower and ran towards Prabhupāda's car.

Prabhupāda asked, "What is this?"

"A new flower from the tree at Yogapīṭha."

"A new flower?"

"We have come to show you, Prabhupāda, and we shall give it to Mahāprabhu."

"Then go and show it to Mahāprabhu first. Take His permission and then bring it to me. I am going away now. If I was staying, you could put it in my hand and I could show Him myself. But I am going away, so go and show Him first and then bring it to me. You must take His permission—that is *prasāda.* To show it to Him is to dedicate it to Him. Then we can take the *prasāda.*" The Lord is our shelter—*tena tyaktena bhuñjītā mā gṛdhaḥ kasya svid dhanam.* This is the key to our life—*tena tyaktena*—after offering to Him, then you may use it.

yajña-śiṣṭāśinaḥ santo
mucyante sarva-kilbiṣaiḥ
bhuñjate te tv aghaṁ pāpā
ye pacanty ātma-kāraṇāt
(*Gītā* 3.13)

Whenever you dedicate anything to your own self, you create sin—you create disharmony in the environment. But if you offer it to Kṛṣṇa, and then you use it, the harmony is maintained. Everything is created to serve Kṛṣṇa, everything is for Him. So, first you must dedicate anything and everything to Him, and then you can take the remaining *prasāda. Īśāvāsyam idaṁ sarvaṁ*—everywhere, everything is in the possession of the Supreme Entity, everything belongs to Him. *Tena tyaktena bhuñjītā*—whatever you need, after offering, when sanctioned above by Him, then you can take.

There should be no disturbance to the law and order—the law and order of the whole should be kept intact. You must live here as a loyal subject—not illegally, either physically or mentally.

Through word and deed you must be a loyal subject in this kingdom of the Lord. That is what is required from us, then there is peace and harmony and no reaction. Otherwise there will be reaction and you will have to suffer for that.

Sacrifice and Self-forgetfulness

The conception of the highest Absolute has been found in the Kṛṣṇa conception of Godhead—the beauty, the harmony, the ecstasy, the sweetness, and the charm. Charm attracts and that attraction is service, that is surrender. Anything that surrenders to beauty gives charm. He becomes conscious of his own charm. Sacrifice means that. We are worshipers of beauty—*sundaram. Satyam śivam sundaram*—that harmony is beautiful. Harmony means *samānya*—proper adjustment. Proper adjustment is beauty. There is no complaint, everyone's demands are met there. They are unconscious of their own selves, charmed by the beauty. We find self-forgetfulness in beauty.

Sacrifice and self-forgetfulness is said to be a higher conception. Self-forgetfulness, with its subtle independence, is considered as higher than self-sacrifice. In sacrifice one is conscious of themself and is giving something, they are conscious that, "I am giving something for some cause." And in forgetfulness in the plenary movement, one is giving something, but has been fully captured by the interest of the whole. The *gopīs* say:

deha smṛti nāhi yāra, saṁsāra-kūpa khāhāṅ tāra
tāhā haite nā cāhe uddhāra

> We do not care for ourselves, we have no separate interest. If Kṛṣṇa is satisfied we do not care whatever be our condition. We are not conscious of our own existence. (*Cc. Madhya* 13.142)

For one who has no conception of their own body (*deha smṛti nāhi yāra, saṁsāra-kūpa khāhāṅ tāra*)—the ditch of this material world, Hell, and all these things, are nothing for him. They are not conscious of their own body. What will Hell do to them? All are fully in Kṛṣṇa consciousness, self-forgetfulness. So no pain can approach them. If there is self-consciousness then pleasure and pain will come into effect. So Kṛṣṇa's interest is first.

Such a degree of love divine. Self-forgetfulness for the cause, for the center. So much consciousness of the Benefactor. They do not care for society, nor for scripture, nor for any religious conception—Kṛṣṇa is all in all. Wholesale attraction and slavery to the Lord.

Religion Means Proper Adjustment

Of course, no one wants slavery, everyone hates slavery. But slavery to Kṛṣṇa is the highest attainment according to the Vaiṣṇava. It is most valuable—according to the degree of slavery, we get a dignified position. Slavery to that highest Entity is not so cheap. Slavery means unconditional surrender—wholesale surrender. It requires the greatest surrender to be so much self-abnegated. Selfishness means aggression, exploitation. To dissolve the so-called selfishness of our aggressive nature is necessary. The whole is represented in this call and that call is love divine, to have direct connection with Him.

Hanumān had his unchangeable heart in the service of *dāsya-rasa*. Wherever the consideration of *dāsya-rasa* comes in, then Hanumān is represented as the ideal servant. Of course, his particular service is so famous that sometimes his superiority is supported by some special consideration which cannot be accommodated in the ordinary science of devotion. Garuḍa is considered to be the servant of Kṛṣṇa and Kṛṣṇa is considered to hold a higher position than Rāmacandra. So Garuḍa must be considered higher in *dāsya-rasa*—but it is seen that Garuḍa is defeated at the hands of Hanumān several times.

Once, Garuḍa had the advantage over Hanumān when Rāma and Lakṣmaṇa were at war with Rāvaṇa. Rāma and Lakṣmaṇa were both tied up with snakes. Then Brahmā intimated to them to think about Garuḍa. Garuḍa came, and as he approached, all the snakes fled away. Rāmacandra was satisfied, propitiated by Garuḍa's service, and asked him to ask for a benediction. Garuḍa asked, "I know that You are my Master, Kṛṣṇa, Nārāyaṇa, but You are now in another form, where Hanumān is Your exclusive servant. But if You are satisfied with my service in the least, I pray that You please show the figure of my own beloved Lord Kṛṣṇa."

Then Rāmacandra said, "Hanumān is there and won't be able to tolerate such a thing." Garuḍa said, "That does not matter, I shall manage." So, Garuḍa, with his wings, created a temporary shelter and there Rāmacandra showed His form of Kṛṣṇa to Garuḍa. Of course, Hanumān could understand what was happening, and he promised, "I shall take revenge when my Lord Rāma comes as Kṛṣṇa."

Later, in Dvāpara-yuga, Garuḍa was asked by Kṛṣṇa to collect one hundred and eight blue lotuses, and Garuḍa went to collect them from a lake which is close to Hanumān's residence. Hanumān knew that Garuḍa was coming, so he sat there on the path like an old small monkey. Garuḍa wanted to pass, but it is not good etiquette to step over another living being, so Garuḍa asked the monkey, "Get out of my path. I don't want to jump over you. Please move off the path."

But Hanumān had a motive and said, "I am an old monkey. I have no power to move my limbs. Please take some other path or move me from this path. I can't move. I am too old and I don't feel well."

Then Garuḍa again requested with some urgency, "No, no, you don't know who I am. Move! Clear the way, otherwise I shall have to teach you a lesson."

"What can I do? I am infirm, I can't move my limbs. So, don't be angry with me, what can I do?" Then Garuḍa threatened him again, but the same answer came.

"What am I to do with him?" He thought. "I shall have to move him from the path."

"Yes," said Hanumān, "You may do so if you wish."

Garuḍa said, "I won't touch you. By the fluttering of my wings I shall move you far away."

"Yes," said Hanumān, "You may do so if you like."

Then Garuḍa began to flap his wings with the kind of jet power that the British used to attack the Falkland Islands. Garuḍa began to flutter his wings and saw, "What is this? The fluttering of my wings can remove so many trees, but this small monkey can't be moved. What's the matter?" And then he saw, that what to speak of moving his body, not even the hairs on his body were moving. Then with all his force he caught Hanumān with his beak, but that also failed.

Then Garuḍa could do no more, and Hanumān rose and caught hold of him and put him under his armpit.

"No, no, I have come to collect blue lotuses for my Lord. Who are you? Why are you disturbing me in this way?"

Hanumān said, "Don't worry about the blue lotuses. I can manage." Keeping Garuḍa under his armpit, Hanumān took the blue lotuses and began to head towards Dvārakā.

Kṛṣṇa knows everything. He knew these things would happen. He was staying in Dvārakā at the time, and Rukmiṇī and Satyabhāmā were present with Him. As Hanumān approached the gates of Dvārakā, Kṛṣṇa began discussing Hanumān's devotion to Rāma with Rukmiṇī and Satyabhāmā.

When Hanumān reached Dvārakā, he found the Sudarśana *cakra* guarding the gate. Hanumān approached the gate chanting, "*Jaya rāma, jaya rāma, sītā-rāma, jaya rāma.*" In the meantime, Kṛṣṇa told Satyabhāmā, "My devotee Hanumān is approaching. Since he worships Sītā and Rāma, I will take the form of Rāmacandra and you take the form of Sītā." Satyabhāmā could not take the role of any other consort, so, Kṛṣṇa said, "If you can't do it, then I shall ask Rukmiṇī." Then Rukmiṇī came forward and took the form of Sītā. Then they considered, "Hanumān is almost here! What about Satyabhāmā?" Kṛṣṇa turned to Satyabhāmā and said, "You go and hide under the throne."

The Sudarśana *cakra* was revolving near the gate as a watchman. Hanumān was chanting, "*Jaya rāma, jaya rāma.*" The Sudarśana *cakra* told him, "There is no Rāma here! Where are you going, monkey?" Hanumān said, "No, no, my Rāma is here, you do not understand." Sudarśana said, "No! I cannot allow you to enter." Then Hanumān just extended his finger within the center of the Sudarsana *cakra* and suddenly made it so big that the *cakra* lost its twirling movement and became a tight ring on the finger of Hanumān.

And so Hanumān entered Dvārakā, with Garuḍa under his armpit, the blue lotuses in his hand, and the Sudarśana *cakra* on his finger. When he entered the palace where Kṛṣṇa was, he saw Rukmiṇī as Sītā and Kṛṣṇa as Rāma. Hanumān thought, "My Lord is here!" He began to offer those blue lotuses to the holy feet of Rāmacandra, while chanting "*Sītā-Rāma, Sīta-Rāma!*" Then after that, he began asking, "My Lord, who is that moving under the throne? What is this?"

"No, no," said Kṛṣṇa. "You need not mind that."

Garuḍa, the Sudarśana *cakra,* and Satyabhāmā had some conceit, some sort of pride in their mind in their respective zones, and it was the will of Kṛṣṇa to give some check to these three.

And in this way, with the help of Hanumān, Kṛṣṇa managed to check their pride. Kṛṣṇa has a higher position than Rāmacandra, but His attendants met some dishonor at the hands of Hanumān. So Hanumān's *dāsya-rasa,* his mellow of servitude, is very intensified and famous.

This is the *līlā* of the Lord. Everything is there but the standpoint is just the opposite. That is *līlā,* all surrender is to the center. Here, it is a perverted reflection and that is the original movement. So it is all similar—only the standpoint is just the opposite.

One is full sacrifice and one is the full aggrandizing principle. It is only a question of internal adjustment. Our Guru Mahārāja, every now and then used the phrase, "Religion means proper adjustment." Adjusting the whole. And the concentration of the whole also varies according to different stages of understanding. The highest adjustment is adjustment with love. There can be no complaint there. If there is something else, then that can be corrected with adjustment. Poison becomes medicine and medicine becomes poison.

What is medicine of the Māyāvadī, that is poison to the devotee—the question of non-differentiated liberation, is their highest goal. That is their nectar—that is their highest form of medicine, but that is poison to a Vaiṣṇava.

Renunciation Means All For Krsna

One can utilize poison as nectar in medicine, otherwise it will kill the person, just like the *viṣayī* who is trying to enjoy that which is meant for Kṛṣṇa. Energy also comes with poison. *Sampati* means the energy which carries the mentality of the owner.

Enchanted by money one begins to make trade, then their soul becomes dead and the activity of the worldly man begins. By amassing money, the real principle is lost. If the *adhikārī* is not a genuine one, one may be carried away by money towards the exploiting world—*kāmanī kañcana.*

Mahāprabhu did not wish to meet Pratāparudra because he was a *viṣayī. Sandarśanaṁ viṣayiṇām atha yoṣitāṁ ca hā hanta hanta viṣa bhakṣaṇato 'py asādhu*—for a *sannyāsī* it is worse than swallowing poison to meet a king who is the embodiment of monetary wealth. He is in the center of the management of the material prosperity. *Yoṣi* means that his tendency is towards enjoyment, and Mahāprabhu says that to come in connection with these two is like swallowing poison—so one must be careful.

Those who are in the company of devotees (*sādhu-saṅga*) and are following the instructions of a higher *sādhu* are rightly situated—that is all that is needed.

Once Vana Mahārāja, during the month of August, went to collect donations for Kṛṣṇa-janmāṣṭamī. For one month the festival was observed in Calcutta. At that time all the preachers were brought back to Calcutta and they would go from door to door for collecting *bhikṣā.* Vana Mahārāja was in a party with one or two *brahmacārīs,* and he went to a part of Calcutta for collection. Generally one member of the party would approach any gentleman and request that, "We have come from Gauḍīya Maṭha. Dear sir, please help, we want to make some collection, you are the devoted persons of this locality."

Vana Mahārāja asked one gentleman, "Please give me the address of a few good benevolent gentlemen to whom we can approach and get some money for our purpose." That gentleman replied, "Just go to that house—there you will find some one." But that was the house of a prostitute. Vana Mahārāja went in good faith and knocked on the door. The door opened, and a lady came, "Oh, you are a *sādhu,* what do you want from me?" That gentleman who asked Mahārāja to go to that house was laughing there with his friends. Vana Mahārāja gave the lady an invitation and said, "We are having a festival, and would like some contribution from you." Whether the lady gave something or not I don't know.

Vana Mahārāja returned, and these people were laughing at him very much. Vana Mahārāja came back to the *maṭha,* and said to Prabhupāda, "I won't go for any more collection."

"Why?"

"These rogues guided me to a prostitute's house. I won't go anymore for collecting."

Then Prabhupāda delivered a lecture. "There are many of you who have left your own property, but still I send you out for collection. Do you think that I am wrong to do so? No. The *viṣayī* always wants to entrap us in their snare. Everything should be utilized—we must learn to utilize everything and anything for the service of Kṛṣṇa—then only are we saved. Otherwise if we leave it, then when it has a chance, it will come back to bite us."

"So we must use whatever comes to us, everything—we should deal with it in such a way. Anywhere I shall come across anything that will give some impression about or rememberance of Kṛṣṇa, I must utilize it in His service. If we leave it, it will become our enemy. But we should make them our friends. This will help us in the service of Kṛṣṇa. We must make such adjustments in this world, and leave nothing aside.

anāsaktasya viṣayān yathārham upayuñjataḥ
nirbandhaḥ kṛṣṇa-sambandhe yuktaṁ vairāgyam ucyate
prāpañcikatayā buddhyā hari-sambandhi-vastunaḥ
mumukṣubhiḥ parityāgo vairāgyaṁ phalgu kathyate
(*Bhakti-rasāmṛta-sindhu* 2.255-256)

Parityājya vairāgyam—to leave everything that is non-Kṛṣṇa—that is bogus and artificial renunciation. Rather, it is proper renunciation to see everything in the service of Kṛṣṇa—*nirbandhaḥ kṛṣṇa sambandhe.*

Purusottama Month

Renunciation is meant to provide us with a more favorable opportunity for *kṛṣṇa-sevā.* Every so many years there is an extra month, Puruṣottama month, which is particularly auspicious for the fortunate *jīvas.* Puruṣottama month has all good qualities, just like Bhagavān Puruṣottama Himself, and is considered the crown of all months. Even the most holy months such as Vaiśākha month, cannot be compared with this Puruṣottama month—Bhagavān, the Lord Himself, has mercifully accepted this month and given it all His power. This is described in the *Śrī Bṛhan-nāradīya Purāṇa.*

The materialistic *smārta-sampradāya,* by their *karmika* standard of judgment, avoid performing any rituals during this month and avoid anything considered materially auspicious. By their calculation this extra month is materially barren or gloomy.

In *Śrīmad Bhagavad-gītā* 4.33 the Lord says that if we do *karma* properly then we gain some capacity to enter within *jñāna.*

sarvam karmākhilaṁ partha
jñāne parisamāpyate

By doing holy activities we may be able to attain heaven, but after finishing that good reaction, we return to this world known as *martya-loka,* the plane of death. In this way, those who aspire for material things have to undergo reactions to their actions.

The devotees of Kṛṣṇa, however, are worshipers of '*kīrtanīyaḥ sadā hariḥ.*' Their process of worshiping is given in *Śrī Caitanya-caritāmṛta*:

nijābhīṣṭa kṛṣṇa-preṣṭha pācheta' lāgiyā
nirantara sevā kare antarmanā hañā
(Cc. Madhya 22.159)

They are twenty-four hours per day engaged in the service of the Lord, for they do not have a moment for their own sense enjoyment. They cannot tolerate those who are against doing *sevā*, especially those who want some result in this world. When they see these types of *jīvas* they dislike them more than hell—we can see many scriptural examples of this.

Similarly, the worshipers of *saguṇa*, the plane within the modes of nature, always show their objection to those who are worshipers of the *nirguṇa*—the realm above the modes of nature. There is no lack of scriptural examples here also.

The *smārtas*, those under the rules of mundane nature—their material duties are already scheduled within the regular twelve months—so they dismiss this extra month. Those who desire material results from fruitive activity consider this month to be barren, to be materially unhealthy. Because such persons neglect this month, this extra month feels rejected and feels the necessity to surrender to its Master.

However, those who continually spend their time in worship and service of the Lord give much attention to this month. They know that fruitive activity is a cause of material bondage.

The Lord always gives much protection to the surrendered, so He gives all His own wealth and property to this month and in this way it takes on His properties and becomes like Him. Therefore the Lord gave His own Name, Puruṣottama, making this extra month the king of all months. He Himself glorified this month and gave it to His most dear devotees, whom He loves as Himself. The devotees serve the Lord Goloka-vihārī Puruṣottama very happily in this Puruṣottama month and are very happy to engage in extra austerities during this time—the month when the materialists are very silent in their activities.

The Appearance of Ekadasi

Just as the month of Puruṣottama is dear to Kṛṣṇa, Ekādaśī is considered to be the favorite day of Kṛṣṇa, when devotees refrain from material activities. Ekādaśī is *aprākṛta. Aprākṛta* means, which is like *prākṛta* but is supramundane. We are warned that Ekādaśī is not mundane, though it seems to be. Because it is influenced by the moon, Ekādaśī seems to be mundane. The heat of the world, and the watery portion in the body increases due to the influence of the moon just as the high tide and low tide of the ocean are also effected by the moon. As we approach the full moon and the new moon, the watery portion of our bodies is enhanced, and thereby the enjoying spirit is also developed. My Guru Mahārāja mentioned these things in a lecture at Kurukṣetra in 1927—the scientific basis is that by the movement of the Earth, the moon planet and the sun, the heat becomes less, and the exciting *rasa* (the water in our body) is enhanced, and thereby it increases the tendency of enjoyment.

So, fasting is necessary to meet with that external movement of nature. Fasting can save us from that peculiar reaction. Fasting has been recommended, and especially, if one can't fast at all, then one may take some process of diet that will give less cause for excitement, therefore one may take *anukalpa* (non-grains). We fast to check the senses, because the senses by the natural flow, become more intense at that time. The result is, that one will be excited and want to enjoy—to encroach on the environment. So this unfair encroachment of one's own self is to be controlled, therefore this fasting has been recommended—this is one way.

We take some types of food, and not others, because they are considered to be less injurious, and less exciting to the body.

Also, it is mentioned in *Hari-bhakti-vilāsa,* that some particular sins are fond of taking shelter in those foods that we reject. *Pāpa* means a type of sin that is very fond of taking shelter in grains and those places which we surely want to avoid. First-class fasting means without even taking water (*nirjala*). Those who cannot do without food, may take fruit, roots and milk.

Also, from the spiritual perspective, Kṛṣṇa Himself also feels more necessity for enjoyment, and when Kṛṣṇa feels more necessity, the devotees have a greater chance to offer service. The time is more valuable for them, because Kṛṣṇa wants to enjoy, and at that time, devotees should be busy to supply the things for His enjoyment—so much so that they won't have any time for their own necessities. The devotees always remain by the side of Kṛṣṇa, supplying whatever He wants, even forgetting to take their own food or any other thing. They want to be busily engaged in the service of Kṛṣṇa and in that time of need this will fetch more remuneration—that is affinity towards Kṛṣṇa, and it brings more grace. So, the first reason is to please Kṛṣṇa and the secondary reason is, that by fasting, we can make our body dry and so our enjoying spirit will be lessened. This is the general explanation.

There are so many other things also. Everything is conscious, everything is personal, and Ekādaśī has her own personal character, and she devotes herself with all her company in the service of Kṛṣṇa. She does not take any food or anything else, and also does not allow others in her group to take food or waste time, but is always engaged in the service of Kṛṣṇa.

The Importance of Dvadasi

We are told that Ekādaśī and Dvādaśī are favored by Hari—the underlying cause is already explained. Hari will be pleased with any small service performed on these days. So, Dvādaśī and

Ekādaśī are both considered the favorite days of Kṛṣṇa. Ekādaśī observance is compulsory—though Dvādaśī is also honored as the favorite of Hari, still Ekādaśī has preference. Dvādaśī has preference over Ekādaśī only in eight cases, determined by the combination of *nakṣatra, tithi,* etc—when we observe Mahā-Dvādaśī and not Ekādaśī.

On Ekādaśī and Dvādaśī, even a little service gives some greater remuneration. Remuneration means that our serving attitude and our earnestness, will be enhanced at that particular time. In a deeper sense, this means that Hari, at that time, wants to accept more service. That is the fortune of the servitors, that Hari demands more of the servitors, so the importance for the servitors increases at that time during Ekādaśī and Dvādaśī. Also on Dvādaśī, we do not pick the leaves of *tulasī* because it is considered that Tulasī-devī has observed fasting on Ekādaśī.

Service Better than Idle Fasting

It is also noted that service is the first consideration. If I fast and do not take any water, then I may have to lie down and not be able to do any service to the Lord. That is not desirable. So, to take *anukalpa* and do service to the Lord is better.

Service is better than sitting idly. So, if *prasāda-sevā* is taken as service, this is best. But at the same time, the individual position of a devotee should be considered. The Sahajiyās do not observe Ekādaśī fasting at all. They say, "Oh, we are in Vṛndāvana—no fasting here!" But Śrīla Prabhupāda did not like this—the Sahajiyā, in the name of *kṛṣṇa-bhakti,* goes on feeding the senses. But when necessary for the service of Kṛṣṇa, to keep up the body, we take *prasādam*—we don't like that by fasting the loss of energy may occur. In this way we honor Ekādaśī. If fasting does not hamper our service, we may go on fasting.

Once on Janmāṣṭamī day, Hayagrīva Brahmacārī (Bhakti Dayita Mādhava Mahārāja) had to arrange for Prabhupāda to go to Mathurā, in order to observe the Puruṣottama-māsa. Hayagrīva was sent one day earlier to hire a suitable house and that day happened to be Janmāṣṭamī. Prabhupāda asked his own cook to feed Hayagrīva rice on Janmāṣṭamī day. "He will have to take a tedious journey and his energy will be wasted—he has an important duty to arrange that house there." That was his order. But Hayagrīva hesitated and the cook also hesitated. Anyhow, he did not take rice on Janmāṣṭamī—instead he took *sābhu* (tapioca), plantain and curd.

However, if Professor Sanyal had been in such a position, he would have certainly taken rice—he was so much adherent and extremely submissive to Prabhupāda's order. He would have said, "Oh Prabhupāda has asked me to take rice—I must take rice!" That was his line of thought. But Hayagrīva hesitated, "No, no, it is not necessary, I am strong enough. I can do my duty." Also, when Prabhupāda wanted to eat something on fasting days, he would take *anukalpa*.

My Guru Mahārāja felt that you will get the maximum energy if you take good food and you do good service. That was his maxim. Kṛṣṇa is not a liquidated party. Take full *prasādam* and do full service. Whatever is necessary, take it for the cause of Kṛṣṇa—not for your own cause. You are Kṛṣṇa's, so if you grow weak and your service is hampered, then you will be the loser. "Better that my soldiers are well fed and working well." That was my Guru Mahārāja's principle. Napoleon also told, "One fully-fed soldier is equal to ten half-fed soldiers."

By Your Will

One *sannyāsī* came here by Toofan Mail on the day of Ekādaśī. He reached here during the evening and took bath in the Ganges, then did *kīrtana,* dancing, circumambulation, and all these things. Later I asked him if he would take any *anukalpa.* He said, "Generally I don't, but if you like then of course I must take some *anukalpa.* Your will is greater than fasting." That was his decision.

It is necessary to understand that whatever action I shall take in response to my own ego will create a material atmosphere. I must place myself at the disposal of a higher devotee—I want to kill the subtle hankering of my inner body. If I obey its order, it will thrive. If I stop the ration it will die.

The whole mental system may die without food. No insinuation from my ego within. I am doing the service that my guru has asked me to do. I am involved with Vaikuṇṭha, the transcendental world. I want to dissolve my ego, and get out of the world produced by my ego. I am living in my own imaginary world and that world must go away. Then, another world will come to me—the world of my Guru. I want to live in that way.

Once one *sannyāsī,* leaving the engagement given to him by our Guru Mahārāja, went to visit Badarikāśrama and other holy places. Then he was punished, "Why have you left the responsibility of your service and gone on pilgrimage?" At that time I was a new man and was in charge of the Kurukṣetra *maṭha,* when I was sent a letter which said, "If that *sannyāsī* comes to the *maṭha* don't allow him to enter." He was a senior *sannyāsī* and I was a newcomer, so I felt great pressure from this. "What is this? A *sannyāsī* has gone to visit Badarikāśrama, the place of Vyāsadeva and Śukadeva—what is the fault there? It is so great a fault that he has been forbidden entrance to the *maṭha!*"

It was a great shock for me. That *sannyāsī* came a day or two later. Previously, I had shown so much respect to him so how could I say that, "You can't enter this *maṭha?*" This was very difficult for me. When he came, I read the letter to him, "This is the order of the central *maṭha.*" First he became excited and began to abuse the higher authorities. Finally I said to him, "Mahārāja, I feel much apprehension in my mind and I am very much afraid."

He inquired, "Why you are afraid?"

I replied, "After fifteen years of service, if you have come to such a level that you are to be ousted from the mission, then what hope do I have? I am just a beginner."

Then he came out in another color, "No, no, no—you need not be afraid. A boy may not pass a B.A. degree or M.A. degree, but it does not mean that a primary student like you will also fail." Then he accepted that, "It is not injustice, rather it is justice as I have done something wrong." He finally came to that conclusion.

Anyhow, that *sannyāsī* returned to the Calcutta *maṭha* and he was punished for some time—his *daṇḍa* was taken from him and his name was changed, but after a year or so he was reinstated. He was an old devotee of Guru Mahārāja and he told me himself that he went to Prabhupāda and said to him, "You have taken my *daṇḍa* and changed my name, so here is your shoe and here is my head—why don't you just give me a good beating with your shoe?" Prabhupāda answered, "Do you think that I am very happy punishing you?" Then that *sannyāsī* told me, "At that point all my frustration evaporated and I came back."

This whole incident left a great impression on my mind. Disengagement—leaving the service of guru to go to a holy place, is a punishable offence? What is this?

But in reality this service is our higher connection. God's will is coming through His agent, and to be engaged in His service is very, very valuable. Conversely, to choose from our lower position what is good and what is bad, and to go to a holy place is some sort of religious luxury. Divine service is above the independence of an ordinary soul.

"I am doing the right thing by visiting holy places"—the origin of this is from my false-ego and a far higher ego is giving the instruction, "Do this! God wants this from you!" This is from another world. This realization came to me gradually, that to obey the orders of a Vaiṣṇava means to serve Divinity, and this will lead us to the supreme destination.

Renunciation More Dangerous

Near Italy in the Mediterranean, there is a place called Scylla. It is a hidden rock and nearby is Charybdis a whirlpool, so when a ship goes between them, either it will strike against the rock and be doomed or if it nears Charybdis, it will come under the course of the whirlpool and it will go down. So it is very difficult to pass through Scylla and Charybdis.

So, on one side is *bhoga* and on the other is *tyāga*—exploitation and renunciation. Both are dangerous. Renunciation is more dangerous than exploitation—it is a more powerful enemy. The tendency of renunciation is a more powerful enemy to devotion to Kṛṣṇa than the enemy of exploitation. And the Māyāvādīs are fond of renunciation.

For the purpose of capturing those in the rank of *sannyāsa,* Caitanya Mahāprabhu took *sannyāsa.* He even took Māyāvāda *sannyāsa* to capture the Māyāvādīs, because they had the power in their hand. At that time the society was under the control of the Māyāvādīs mostly, so He took the garb of a Māyāvādī *sannyāsī,* and entered within their camp. He preached that, "What you are doing is all anti-devotional and that is mad. With your Buddhistic principles, you are trying to enter into the Vedic doctrine, and are doing great disservice to the society. *Veda nā māniyā bauddha haila nāstika*—you are delivering the goods of the Buddhistic school disguised in a Vedic fashion. That is more dangerous, and it is doing great harm to society."

Varṇāśrama of the *Vedas* always leads towards Kṛṣṇa—*kṛṣṇa-bhakti* is a positive thing, not negative Brahman.

What sort of strictness should I observe as a *sannyāsī*? I should devote my maximum energy to Kṛṣṇa and whatever will be favorable to that I'll accept. Whatever is more favorable to the service of Kṛṣṇa, I shall do that, and whatever is not, I shall reject.

Raghunatha Dasa Gosvami

Raghunātha Dāsa was known for his renunciation. Mahāprabhu blessed him, and told the devotees that, "He has the opulence of Indra the king of heaven, and his wife is like the beautiful heavenly girls, but that can't attract his mind. We should all bless him, that he may be successful in his life." Raghunātha, after going back home, kept himself quite indifferent in household affairs. Ten persons were engaged to protect him always, twenty-four hours a day so that he may not run away, but still he fled from there and went to Purī.

Mahāprabhu put him in the charge of Svarūpa Dāmodara, who is the double of Mahāprabhu—*sākṣād mahāprabhu svarūpa*. Svarūpa Dāmodara is Lalitā-devī in *kṛṣṇa-līlā*. Mahāprabhu told Raghunātha, "What I do not know, Svarūpa Dāmodara knows all, so, I put you under him. Whenever you feel any necessity, you ask him."

Raghunātha again came to Mahāprabhu and was told, "I have already given you to Svarūpa Dāmodara, still if you want to hear something from My lips, then follow these instructions:

grāmya-kathā nā śunibe grāmya-vārtā nā kahibe
bhāla nā khāibe āra bhāla na paribe
amānī mānada hañā kṛṣṇa-nāma sadā la'be
vraje rādhā-kṛṣṇa-sevā mānase karibe

> On the negative side, don't eat palatable dishes, nor indulge in worldly talks and on the positive side, always try to take the Name of Kṛṣṇa, and in your mind, try to connect with the service of Rādhā-Govinda in Vṛndāvana. *(Cc. Antya 6.236)*

These four instructions were given to Raghunātha Dāsa directly by Mahāprabhu, and for his whole life, he followed them. Mahāprabhu gave him *govardhana-śīla* and a *guñja-mālā* from Vṛndāvana. Raghunātha thought of the *govardhana-śīla* as Kṛṣṇa, and the *guñja-mālā* as Rādhikā. So, with this mood, he used to offer *tulasī* and water to Them. For sixteen years he lived in this way in Purī. Because Orissa was a Hindu state, and Bengal was under Mohammedan rule, no influence from Bengal could work in Orissa. So his father could not influence the government and could only make arrangements for a cook, a servant, and some money for him. They were told to hire a good house, and prepare food for Raghunātha and try to help him in his daily life. But Raghunātha did not accept it for himself, only he requested Mahāprabhu to take *prasādam* there twice in a month so that they will be blessed.

Then after some time he left that idea, feeling that Mahāprabhu was not pleased to take this *prasādam,* since it was from worldly-minded persons, and some poison may enter. Mahāprabhu was thereby pleased with Raghunātha Dāsa.

The *vairāgya* of Raghunātha was above the standard of our thinking—sometimes begging from the temple, sometimes having regular food, and some time later he began to collect the rotten *prasādam* of Jagannātha, which even Jagannātha's cows would not eat because of its bad smell. Raghunātha collected that *prasādam,* and by washing the rotten portion he collected the inner part and took it with some salt.

When Mahāprabhu found out that Raghunātha was living on such *prasādam*, He suddenly came, "Oh, what nice *prasādam* you take! Such sweet *prasāda* you take every day, and you don't offer it to Me?" Then Mahāprabhu took that *prasādam*. After the third time, Svarūpa Dāmodarā stopped Him, "No, no, this is not for You, my Lord." Such was the intense degree of self-abnegation of Raghunātha Dāsa.

After Mahāprabhu's departure from this world, Raghunātha went to Vṛndāvana with a mind that after taking *darśana* of Vṛndāvana, he would leave his body—"By climbing up on Govardhana, I shall cast myself down and pass away." With this idea, Raghunātha went to Vṛndāvana.

There he found Rūpa and Sanātana, and what is more wonderful, he found Mahāprabhu in them. "Oh, Mahāprabhu is here!" Mahāprabhu is working through them. Mahāprabhu is in the literature of Rūpa and Sanātana, in their deeds, in their movement"—he found them fully possessed by Mahāprabhu. "Mahāprabhu is here, I can't die." So, he came in closer and closer connection with Rūpa and Sanātana, and we see extreme indifference and self-abnegation in his life. He has gone through the literature, especially that of Rūpa, the *rāga-marga* and perhaps he was the greatest student of the *rūpānuga* school—so much so that he has developed even more, he has clearly given us more than Rūpa—that we should aspire exclusively after the service of Rādhārāṇī, and not of Kṛṣṇa without Her.

In his last days in Vṛndāvana, Raghunātha Dāsa would pass each day taking only a small pot of buttermilk. This is not possible for an ordinary man of flesh and blood. Great souls like the Gosvāmīs are really personalities who have come down from the other world, and so it was possible for them to show the ideal of abnegation. It is not possible for ordinary humans of flesh and blood to observe such a degree of abnegation without dying, but the Gosvāmīs created the standard and ideal by such *vairāgya*. Each day, a thousand times, Raghunātha Dāsa gave his obeisances to different Vaiṣṇavas and chanted one *lakh* of the Holy Name. He repeated the names of about two *lakhs* of Vaiṣṇavas, meditating on them. He showed his respect to two-thousand Vaiṣṇavas daily in this way, as well as offering a thousand *daṇḍavats*. Such was the abnegation of Raghunātha Dāsa Gosvāmī.

Precedence for Tridandi Sannyasa

It is said that the renounced order (*sannyāsa*) is forbidden in Kali-yuga—*aśvamedham gavālambaṁ sannyāsaṁ pala paitṛkam.* However, this refers to *karma-sannyāsa. Karma-sannyāsa* means that you leave everything—and that type of *sannyāsa* is not possible in Kali-yuga. It is described in the *śāstras* that in Satya-yuga, as long as a man's bones exist, that is how long he would live—along with the longevity of the bones, the life will be there. In Treta-yuga, life may be maintained in the nervous system. In ages other then Kali, people could tolerate great penances because their bodies were not completely dependent on food. However, it is stated that in Kali-yuga, *kalav annagataḥ prāṇaḥ*—one's longevity depends on food. It is not possible to live without food.

All penances have been especially adjusted for Kali-yuga, and the only continuous fast allowed in Kali-yuga is for twenty-four hours, not more than that. In other ages, at least twelve days fasting was generally done—if a person had done anything wrong, then according to the *smṛti-śāstra*, twelve days fasting was the standard punishment for any sins. But in Kali-yuga, twenty-four hour fasting is the maximum, because without food a man cannot survive. If he were to take *karma-sannyāsa* while being so extremely dependent on material giving and taking, then he wouldn't be able to maintain his existence. So *karma-sannyāsa*—which means to stop totally all activity with this material world—is useless because with complete non-cooperation with the material world, one cannot live in Kali-yuga, what to speak of preach. But the life of a Vaiṣṇava *tridaṇḍi-sannyāsī* is not very extreme. Take *prasādam* and do service—this is a sort of modified form based on *yuktāhāra vihārasya*—one living according to this principle can take *sannyāsa*.

We find *tridaṇḍi-sannyāsa* in the *śāstra*. Rāvaṇa, when he came to steal away Sītā-devī, came as a *tridaṇḍi*. Arjuna, when he met Subhadrā in disguise, took *tridaṇḍi-veśa*. *Tridaṇḍi-sannyāsa* is in the *Bhāgavata*—the Avanti *brāhmaṇa* took *tridaṇḍi-veśa* and Kṛṣṇa relates the story to Uddhava. *Tridaṇḍi-sannyāsīs* were well-respected in the society at that time. There are many types of *sannyāsīs*, but *tridaṇḍi* seems to hold the highest position of all *sannyāsīs*. The *ekadaṇḍi* we find in the Śaṅkara school, and in the Rāmānuja *sampradāya* we find *tridaṇḍi-sannyāsa*.

Prabodhananda and Prakasananda

Our Guru Mahārāja reasoned that Prabodhānanda Sarasvatī was a *tridaṇḍi-sannyāsī* of the Rāmānuja *sampradāya*. Prabodhānanda came from the south and was the uncle and Gurudeva of Gopāla Bhaṭṭa Gosvāmī. He wrote many books such as *Rādhā-rasa-sudhā-nidhi*, *Vṛndāvana-śataka* and *Navadvīpa-śataka*. Prabodhānanda generally used to live at Kāmyavana in Vṛndāvana.

When Kavirāja Gosvāmī was ordered to produce the *Caitanya-caritāmṛta*, he went to the senior Vaiṣṇavas to get their mercy. He went to Prabodhānanda also who said, "Yes, I have every sympathy for this book. It will be very much adored, but I have one request—don't mention my name." So we do not find his name in *Caitanya-caritāmṛta*, but he is mentioned in *Bhakti-ratnākara*. He did not want any admiration, so he requested,

"Don't mention my name, but I give my blessings that your book will be of a very high order."

Sishir Kumara Ghosh, the founder of the newspaper *Ananda Bazaar Patrika,* mistakenly thought that the Māyāvādī Prakāśānanda Sarasvatī converted into Prabodhānanda Sarasvatī—he wrote this, but it is not true. Prabodhānanda is considered to be Tuṅgavidyā, one of the eight intimate friends of Rādhārāṇī in Vṛndāvana, so Prabodhānanda cannot be a Māyāvādī. Vṛndāvana Dāsa Ṭhākura writes in *Caitanya-bhāgavata,*

kāśīte paḍāya beṭā prakāśānanda
sei beṭā mora aṅga kare khaṇḍa khaṇḍa
(*Cb. Madhya* 3.37)

Mahāprabhu said that, "In Benares there is a Māyāvādī and a great offender called Prakāśānanda. He does not recognize My form and cuts to pieces My spiritual body." In this way, Prakāśānanda of Benares has been mentioned. Thus, Prabodhānanda cannot be a Māyāvādī—these two are separate persons.

Prakāśānanda was converted to Vaiṣṇavism and he may have also gone to Vṛndāvana, but he did not get much recognition in the Vaiṣṇava society. He was rejected both from this side, and he also did not attain much respect from the impersonalist side; it seems that he almost went to an unknown quarter. So, Tuṅgavidyā became Prabodhānanda in *gaura-līlā* and his writings are very sweet, grand and most appealing—hitting the mark. And our Guru Mahārāja reasoned that he was of the *tridaṇḍi* order in the line of Rāmānuja. Also here and there, some other *tridaṇḍi-sannyāsīs* we see, but we find it extensively in the Rāmānuja *sampradāya.*

In the Vallabha *sampradāya* there is no *sannyāsa*. But in the Viṣṇu-svāmī *sampradāya,* we find Śrīdhara Svāmī, who was a *sannyāsī.* Our Guru Mahārāja inaugurated *tridaṇḍi-sannyāsa* extensively in our *sampradāya.* He filled up the gap by awarding the *brāhmaṇa's* thread and the *daṇḍa.*

Varṇāśrama-dharma is but a step to *Vaiṣṇava-dharma. Brāhmaṇa-dharma* vanishes, and above this *Vaiṣṇava-dharma* begins. To show that, to preach that position to the society, and to the Vaiṣṇava, he supplied the *sannyāsa* order to fill up the gap.

Prabhupada's Sannyasa

Bhaktisiddhānta Sarasvatī Prabhupāda took *sannyāsa* from his own guru—who was a *bābājī,* which is above *sannyāsa.* He introduced it from the Rāmānuja *sampradāya,* who took it from the *Bhāgavatam.* Following the example of Rāmānuja, he took *sannyāsa* from the picture of his Gurudeva, who was a *bābājī.* So *sannyāsa* is included there in the genuine *bābājī* order. We do not care for the pseudo-*bābājī* order.

At that, time he did not find any suitable Vaiṣṇava guru, so he had to take from a photo of his Gurudeva. He wandered through Vṛndāvana and struck his forehead with his palm. "I came to such a holy place, but I could not find a true Vaiṣṇava here." That was his impression there. That came from his mouth. He could not find a true Vaiṣṇava in the whole of Vṛndāvana and Navadvīpa. He had such a high standard of Vaiṣṇavism in his mind—only Bhaktivinoda Ṭhākura and Gaura-kiśora Dāsa Bābājī.

In *jyotiṣa* (astrology) we find that where the planet of Bṛhaspati (Jupiter), has a greater influence, one may take *tridaṇḍa-sannyāsa*—Bṛhaspati is the *deva-guru. Ekadaṇḍa-sannyāsa* is influenced by Budha-graha (Mercury). Maṅgala (Mars) is very influencial with the *kāpālikas,* who are Tāntrikas. When Śani

(Saturn) is very influential it is favorable for Jain *sannyāsa*. In this way it has been mentioned. Bṛhaspati is *deva-guru*—his influence is in favor of the *tridaṇḍa* order.

Tridaṇḍis have much confidence in the society. So in the disguise of *tridaṇḍis*, Rāvaṇa and Arjuna went to fulfill their purpose, and Nityānanda Prabhu broke the *ekadaṇḍa* of Mahāprabhu into three pieces, and Prabhupāda also got some inspiration from there, to give the *tridaṇḍa* to his followers; in contrast with the *ekadaṇḍa* which was current in Bengal.

Our *daṇḍa* has four *daṇḍas*—one representing ones own self, the *jīva-daṇḍa*, and the *prāsa*, which is the the emblem of cutting the *anarthas* of those we preach to, as well as those of the disciple.

The *sannyāsī* also takes a vow of dedicating three things. They must use their words only for the service of the Lord, they shall not think in an ordinary way, but in the cause of Mahāprabhu and guru, and they will preserve and dedicate their body in the service of the Lord, not otherwise.

If they fail to do that, then there may be some deviation. We are to pray for that dedication, to invoke grace, and be forgiven in every case. When we slip and fall down on the ground, with the help of that same ground, we can again get up. Following this principle we are to try.

Sannyasa-vesa For Preaching

Prabhupāda took the red cloth of *sannyāsa*. Though Mahāprabhu and His colleagues wore red cloth, still Sanātana Gosvāmī in the presence of Mahāprabhu, took the white dress—the dress of a *niṣkiñcana*. *Bābājīs* are the gurus of the *sannyāsīs*—the dictators of the preachers, by giving instructions in the form of *śāstra*—the code and the code-keeper. So they are engaged in preparing the spiritual code, and the *bābājīs* are in white cloth. They do not advertise themselves as preachers. The *sannyāsīs* are not engaged for their own benefit, but for helping the public as much as they can. Generally, the function of the *sannyāsīs* is to wander here and there and preach.

So Prabhupāda created another batch of *sannyāsīs* under the *bābājīs*, who have given the directions in the *śāstra*. To carry these instructions out and translate them into action, the next lower batch, the *sannyāsīs* were necessary. The *bābājīs* are *turīya*, beyond *varṇāśrama*, and within *varṇāśrama* the highest section is *sannyāsa*. They're expected to travel through the length and breadth of the country, and to preach the religious doctrine to the people. And that was created by Prabhupāda under the direction of those *śāstra* makers, the *gosvāmīs*, for whom this religious preachers uniform was not necessary. They're *niṣkiñcana*, they did not want anything but they only prepared the religious code.

Our Guru Mahārāja wore this dress till the very end of his life. Almost everyone to whom he gave the red dress kept it, up to their last breath. Only Kṛṣṇa Dāsa Bābājī, who was a *brahmacārī*, and who did not consider himself as a preacher, took *bābājī*, after the departure of Guru Mahārāja. One *sannyāsī*, whimsically, took up *bābājī-veśa* for some time, then rejected it and again took the red robe.

One *maṭha* introduced that white cloth, including their last *ācārya*. Crossing Prabhupāda, they preferred to accept the idea of Rūpa and Sanātana. They thought Prabhupāda's idea was a temporary one for the time being, and the dress that Rūpa and Sanātana accepted in the presence of Mahāprabhu was the real dress of the Gauḍīya Vaiṣṇavas. But Mahāprabhu maintained that red cloth up to the last point of His *līlā* as did His associates, such as Paramānanda Purī, Īśvara Purī, and all the godbrothers of the guru of Mahāprabhu who were in friendly connection with Mahāprabhu—they were all red cloth *sannyāsīs*.

Also, generally it is not the custom for the *sannyāsī* or the *bābājī* to keep a beard and long hair. But for a particular purpose, for preaching, it may be alright. When Sanātana Gosvāmī approached Mahāprabhu, he had a full beard and He ordered, "Take him to a barber and remove it." Both *sannyāsī* and *bābājī* do not keep such things. So, we do not like to keep beards, but during *Cāturmāsya-vrata,* it is mentioned in the *śāstra,* that we may keep hair and beard. Otherwise, generally not. But still, it is not that if one keeps long hair and long beard he cannot be a Vaiṣṇava.

There was one Vaṁsī Dāsa Bābājī, who was an independent Vaiṣṇava. Our Guru Mahārāja also gave respect to him as a Vaiṣṇava, but he had a big beard and did not shave at all. He was very negligent not as a fashion, but he did not allow any barber to shave him, yet he was a respectable Vaiṣṇava. Even our Guru Mahārāja had respect for him. If you keep a beard in order to preach (For example, in a Muslim country) for the purpose of your service for your Gurudeva, then that is alright.

Nowadays, the Christian preachers are abandoning the gown and just wearing western dress, and the nuns who used to dress themselves very discretely, now dress like ordinary women. They're giving up their special dress, because they do not like to advertise that they are religious preachers—they do not like to show that they are a special group.

Adaptability has manifested in this extreme position, so the dress is nothing, but everything is in the creed. What is the principle underlying all these changes in the system of the preachers? The creed is everything and the garment is nothing.

Spirit Must Be Kept Intact

Form may be readjusted, but the spirit must be kept intact. It is also good to maintain the form—because the form may be of a spiritual shape and not from this mundane world.

We have noted that in a drama in Germany, they put the figure of God as a bearded old man high on a balcony and from there he was giving directions. They have no knowledge of the formal aspect of God—some voiçe, some indefinite things, some sound, etc—this is all they show. But in Vṛndāvana, in *aprākṛta-līlā,* the form is also there, and it is all spiritual. Form cannot be eliminated from the spirit, because the spirit has its form. Here we only have the corresponding form. The form is also there—it is not abstract and it can be conceived by one who is on the spiritual platform. Otherwise it will be like Māyāvāda—it is a spiritual, non-differentiated, abstract truth without form.

But our conception is not like that—everything is there in the fullest way, but it has its spiritual meaning. Similarly, we use objects of apparent material form in spiritual service, such as the *mṛdaṅga* (drum) and *karatālas* (cymbals).

Golokera prema-dana—that which was used by Mahāprabhu, is most conducive to that sort of spiritual atmosphere. Form we cannot sacrifice—but we need to understand how that form is indispensably necessary with that spiritual truth. Why is Kṛṣṇa blue, or black, not white? Why is Kṛṣṇa *tribhaṅga*? Why are His eyes tinged with red?

All these things have their meaning, it is not by coincidence, nor does it differ in the hearts of the different devotees in their meditation. The standard is there, and we are to come to that standard. A description is given of the *rūpa, guṇa, līlā*—everything, and we are to understand also that the form has its eternal aspect—the spirit and form, both are to be retained.

Adjustment for Preaching

I heard from Sakhī-caraṇa Bābu that when Prabhupāda took *sannyāsa* he went to Vṛndāvana with two of his followers,

Paramānanda and Kuñja Bābu. Prabhupāda's dress was that of a red cloth *sannyāsī*, but the *bābājīs* did not like this, and they said, *rakta-vastra vaiṣṇavera parite nā yuyāya.* There it is mentioned in *Caitanya-caritāmṛta* that a Vaiṣṇava should not wear red cloth because that represents Māyāvadī or Tāntrika. So, they will always take white cloth, but Prabhupāda took red cloth, and his dress was a *sannyāsī.*

When he went to Vṛndāvana, Paramānanda and Kuñja Bābu were clad in European dress. Sakhī Bābu said that it created a commotion amongst the Sahajiyās. "What is this? He is coming to Vṛndāvana in red cloth, and his *brahmacārīs* are wearing European dress." Generally, we use Indian dress, but he entered Vṛndāvana with revolutionary dress. So, they began to criticize him from all sides, for what Prabhupāda showed—"We see that you people don't appreciate what Mahāprabhu has given for us."

Prabhupāda's reply was that, "All your attention is drawn by the glamour of the European culture. So, Europeans should be approached, and then it will be possible for us to accept them into Mahāprabhu's creed. After the Europeans have accepted this, then you will come and accept."

"You are followers of the glamour of the European civilization. You have become slaves to European civilization—all your attention is towards that, so first the Europeans should be taken in. I am couching myself in such a way so that I can approach the present scientific culture, because the attention is on the Europeans. India is charmed by the European civilization, but European civilization must be crushed! The west is attracting all the stalwarts of this world—that must come under our feet and then these foolish Indians will automatically come."

So, his attitude was to prepare himself as a general and attack the present European civilization. "These fools are simply blind followers of that culture." That was his attitude. We shall search more for the spirit, and not so much for the form. Whether it is a cloth, a pen or a coat—all these have some value. It is not that they have no value, but that the spirit within is all-important.

If necessary for ones service, one may wear the dress of a *gṛhastha*. Even in our Prabhupāda's time, the suit was sometimes used by his disciples, and some were clad in white dress, although they were high level Vaiṣṇavas. They had to approach so many officers and higher ranking people—so that dress was suitable.

To fulfill the orders of our Gurudeva suitably, we may take any dress. It is the question of purity of purpose—a question of the heart.

Sannyasa Names

For *sannyāsa* names, Prabhupāda used first Bhakti and then a three syllable word, and then one of the one-hundred and eight names from the *Sattvata-saṁhitā*. This type of *sannyāsa* name was not in vogue before Prabhupāda. He always gave the names Bhakti and Dāsa, and he did not use the name Ānanda for *sannyāsīs*—generally this was used by Vivekānanda and the Śaṅkara section. Ānanda is generally added in the *brahmācarī-āśrama*—Svarūpa, Ānanda, Caitanya and Prakāśa—these are generally recommended for the *brahmācarī*. We find that in the Ramakrishna Mission and the Śaṅkara *sampradāya* also, in their *sannyāsa* names they use Prakāśānanda, Prabodhānanda etc, but Prabhupāda used them according to scripture only—Ānanda, Prakāśa, Svarūpa and Caitanya as *brahmacārī* names, and not in the name of the *sannyāsīs*.

Nityananda Not a Sannyasi

Nityānanda was not a *sannyāsī*, he was a *brahmacārī*. There are some who say that he was a *sannyāsī*, but he had no special garment of a *sannyāsī* or a *brahmacārī*—He was a very independent spirit.

Nityānanda Prabhu was known as an exalted *avadhūta* absorbed in the esoteric mellows of devotion. *Avadhūta* indicates one who is not very particular of his external activities—it does not indicate that he is a *sannyāsī*. When a higher level person engages in practices of a lower nature, although they are actually above these activities, they are considered an *avadhūta*.

It is not a proven fact that Nityānanda was a *sannyāsī*. This Ānanda in the name Nityānanda indicates the suffix normally added to *brahmacārī* names—Ānanda, Svarūpa and Prakāśa are different *brahmacārī* names. The *dīkṣā-guru* of Nityānanda is known to be Mādhavendra Purī but we do not find the *sannyāsa* guru of Nityānanda mentioned anywhere.

The meeting of Lord Nityānanda with His consort Śrīmatī Jāhnavā-devī is described in the *Bhakti-ratnākara*. Lord Nityānanda and Jāhnavā-devī are eternal associates and their marriage is part of Their eternal *līlā*. Some, so-called *sannyāsīs*, use the marriage of Nityānanda as an excuse to marry and give up their vows of celibacy.

Paramahamsa Babaji

After attaining the qualities of a *brāhmaṇa* and a *sannyāsī*, then one can aspire for the position of *bābājī* (*paramahaṁsa-veśa*)—the dress of the guru of the *sannyāsīs*—*pañcama-āśrama* (the fifth order). Those *bābājīs* who have not surpassed the stage of *sannyāsa* are not accepted as *bābājīs* proper—they have deviated. They are only wearing the external dress, but they cannot maintain the position of a *bābājī*.

Only imitating the dress cannot give one the position of a real *bābājī*. Before you take the dress of a general, you have to learn what is battle, what it is to fight, and how to handle so many weapons—only the dress of a soldier does not make one a soldier. Similarly, you must acquire the inner attributes of a *bābājī*—only the mere dress cannot make you a *bābājī*. So many *bābājīs* are in Vṛndāvana and in Navadvīpa, but our Guru Mahārāja did not recognize any of them. He put his hand to his forehead and exclaimed, "I came to such a sacred land, but it was my own misfortune that I did not see a single Vaiṣṇava here." That was his disappointment. That was his statement in Vṛndāvana. So Vaiṣṇavas cannot be judged by their garments.

One is judged to be a Vaiṣṇava by his internal realization—those who have the real eye to see the internal realization, won't care for any external dress. If a man takes only the dress of a *vidvān*, a *paṇḍita*, that does not make him a *paṇḍita*. *Tavāc ca śobhate mūrkho yāvat kiñcin na bhāṣate*—a well-dressed fool goes unrecognised until he speaks. But only the dress of a *paṇḍita* will not make him a *paṇḍita*—when we have a talk with a real *paṇḍita*, we will detect whether he is a scholar or not.

So, a Vaiṣṇava can only be measured by a Vaiṣṇava. A Vaiṣṇava can see who is a Vaiṣṇava. He has that eye, to see what is the criterion of a Vaiṣṇava—he has the *divya-dṛṣṭi* by which he can feel that, "This is a Vaiṣṇava, here is Vaiṣṇavism." Otherwise, there is only the external form of a Vaiṣṇava, the outer show—*tilaka, mālā* and dress cannot make anyone a Vaiṣṇava.

Babaji-vesa

The position of *bābājī* was given by Mahāprabhu—*bābājī-veśa* was first taken by Sanātana Gosvāmī in Benares in the presence of Mahāprabhu. Mahāprabhu must have given His consent. That *paramahaṁsa-veśa* is considered to be above *sannyāsa*.

nāhaṁ vipro na ca nara-patir nāpi vaiśyo na śūdro
nāhaṁ varṇī na ca gṛha-patir no vana-stho yatir vā
kintu prodyan-nikhila-paramānanda-pūrṇāmṛtābdher
gopī-bhartuḥ pada-kamalayor dāsa-dāsanudāsaḥ

"I am not a priest, a king, a merchant, or a laborer (*brāhmaṇa, kṣatriya, vaiśya, śūdra*); nor am I a student, a householder, a retired householder, or a mendicant (*brahmacārī, gṛhastha, vānaprastha, sannyāsī*). I identify myself only as the servant of the servant of the servant of the lotus feet of Śrī Kṛṣṇa, the Lord of the *gopīs*, who is the personification of the eternally self-revealing nectarean ocean that brims with the totality of divine ecstasy." (*Cc. Madhya* 13.80)

Nāhaṁ varṇī—brahmacārī, na ca gṛha-patir—gṛhastha, no vāna-stho—vānaprastha, yatir va—sannyāsa. These are the four stages in *āśrama-dharma.* Even a *sannyāsī* has some sort of position—he is also to follow some regulations in his life.

But *bābājīs* are considered to be above any sort of law—they have no position in society. The *sannyāsīs* have some position as general guides for society. But *bābājīs* do not care for anything—they have cut off all connection with society. They have given themselves wholesale towards *vṛndāvana-sevā,* and they are engaged in *parakīya-bhajana.*

Our Guru Mahārāja saw that the imitationists were accepting the dress of *bābājīs,* but they did not come up to the standard required. So the *bābājī* dress was being misused by the Sahajīyas, and in the name of that dress they were going on with adulteration. That degraded *bābājī* section produced many deviations.

It is impossible for them to catch the real spirit of that life. So they become degraded and create so many disturbances in the society—creating a bad name for Rūpa, Sanātana, Mahāprabhu, and the Gauḍīya *sampradāya* at large.

So Prabhupāda gave stress to this *sannyāsa* order. "First prepare yourself as the head of society. Then when such a time comes, you may take the position of *bābājī*, if you find it necessary. That does not depend on external dress—that thing depends on internal improvement of ones heart or ones realization. It does not depend on the external dress." So in this way Prabhupāda came and created this *tridaṇḍa sannyāsa* order, and preached that the *bābājīs* are our *gurus.*

He said of them, "We do not recognize anyone taking the dress of *bābājī*. No, you are not *bābājīs*. Simply the external dress does not give you the honor of the post of a *bābājī*. You are all hypocrites, and you are dis-serving the society and the real Vaiṣṇavas. You should not venture to pollute the dress of Rūpa and Sanātana."

This is the warning of our Guru Mahārāja. Prabhupāda also introduced the sacred thread—become a *brāhmaṇa* first. First one must come to Brahmaloka, then *virajā*, then Paravyoma, the Vaiṣṇavas place. First become a *brāhmaṇa, daiva-brāhmaṇa*—try to acquire the quality of a *brāhmaṇa,* and take the sacred thread. Then above this is the Vaiṣṇava.

The *bābājī* class uses the *kaupīna,* but they are afraid of using the *brāhmaṇa* thread. Our Guru Mahārāja told us that the *kaupīna* is higher—*kaupīna* means to stop all mundane sensual inclination to the utmost, so they should not venture to take *kaupīna* as Rūpa and Sanātana did.

Before that you should try to come to the position of a *brāhmaṇa*—take the sacred thread if you have courage and real sincerity to go towards the spiritual world, then come forward and take the red cloth of a *sannyāsī*. Make some substantial progress in the spiritual line—then you will find yourself quite safe—not only that, but you will be established in *kṛṣṇa-līlā* in Vṛndāvana. Then you will give honor to that dress of Rūpa and Sanātana—otherwise you will dishonor them. That was the temperament of our Guru Mahārāja, and he inaugurated this *tridaṇḍī-sannyāsa* order into the Gauḍīya Vaiṣṇava school.

There was one Rāmakṛṣṇa Dāsa Bābājī, who was considered by all the *vraja-vāsīs* in general as a *siddha-mahātma*—only Prabhupāda disregarded him. One *bābājī* disciple of Rāmakṛṣṇa Dāsa Bābājī came to Prabhupāda at Rādhā-kuṇḍa, telling him that the *bhajana-kuṭīra* of Lokanātha Gosvāmī Prabhu was in ruins and requested him to reconstruct it. Prabhupāda agreed to rebuild it, but departed in the mean time. Some time later, Sakhī Bābu reminded me that the man in charge of the *bhajana-kuṭīra* of Lokanātha Gosvāmī, had come to Prabhupāda and Prabhupāda gave his consent to rebuild that *kuṭīra.*

"If you arrange for this work," Sakhī Bābu told me, "I will give you the money." I consented and went there and reconstructed the building and put also a marble plaque in the name of Śrī Caitanya Sārasvata Maṭha—mentioning the name of Sakhī Bābu, who supplied the money. That place, at that time was under some direct disciple of Rāmakṛṣṇa Dāsa Bābājī, whose name was Rāmeśa Dāsa Bābājī.

The *bhajana-kuṭīra* of Lokanātha Gosvāmī was in Maimansingh, Bangladesh. This Rāmeśa Dāsa Bābājī was perhaps a B.S.C. He was a good scholar with variegated capacity, who could capture men by talking. He had so many qualifications.

Rāmeśa Dāsa Bābājī was engaged in *bhajana* there when I came to reconstruct that *kuṭīra.* These *bābājīs* are generally apathetic to us—because we wear red cloth, they are reluctant to accept us amongst them and we also do not care for them, because they are imitationists. Anyhow, the reconstruction of the *bhajana-kuṭīra* had to be done, so we went on with that work.

One day I told him that we take the red cloth of the *varṇāśrama sannyāsī* to prove that *bābājī* is higher than *sannyāsa.* First we must become a *sannyāsī,* and then we may be promoted to the position of *bābājī.* He was highly satisfied with this explanation. I told him that our Guru Mahārāja filled the gap—we won't venture from any position to accept the position of a *bābājī.* He was highly pleased with this statement. Then I told him that we do not consider that the present imitationists are holding the proper position of *bābājīs*—they are false, all hypocrites.

He could not tolerate that we were *sannyāsīs,* that considered the *bābājīs* to be our gurus, but at the same time we did not consider them to be worthy of that position. He was infuriated, and proclaimed, "You are an atheist!" We replied, "Yes, we may be considered so-called atheists by you, because we reject the false *bābājīs* in Vṛndāvana." After finishing the work I left, then I heard from Kṛṣṇa Dāsa Bābājī Mahārāja, who was staying in Nandagrāma, that this gentleman used to keep one sweeper's daughter of a very young age, who used to help him wash his cloth, etc. Outwardly he showed that their relationship was that of father and daughter. Finally, that gentleman was caught there with that girl, then, he had to leave the place. He gave up his *bābājī-veśa* and went straight to Mathurā and being an educated man, he began teaching students as a private tutor.

Kaupina Higher Than Brahmana Thread

I am told that at that time, when this former *bābājī* took up teaching in Mathurā, he met Bhakti Prajñāna Keśava Mahārāja and the same question arose. Keśava Mahārāja told him that, "You complain that we give this sacred thread to anyone and everyone." That was their complaint. That anyone and everyone will come and the Gauḍīya Maṭha will confer the sacred thread on them, as well as the red cloth. Then Keśava Mahārāja put a question to him, whether the sacred thread is superior or the *kaupīna* is superior. Whoever comes to the *bābājī* section is given *kaupīna,* and they make them a *bābājī.* So Keśava Mahārāja put this question, "We admit that we are lavishly giving this sacred thread to anyone and everyone, but you give *kaupīna* to anyone and everyone, without much consideration. Which is superior, the *kaupīna* or sacred thread?" He could not but say that the *kaupīna* was superior to the sacred thread. He was compelled to admit that. "We give the sacred thread to anyone and everyone lavishly, that is of inferior quality—but you give that higher thing, that *kaupīna,* to anyone and everyone. Then, who does greater wrong to the society?" He could not say anything.

We consider the *kaupīna* to be higher—what Śrīman Mahāprabhu gave to Sanātana Gosvāmī is the highest thing. Anyone venturing to take this garb, must first become a *brāhmaṇa,* they must acquire the qualifications of a *brāhmaṇa.* Then, in the higher position, they will get exclusive remembrance of Rādhā-Govinda. That is the highest thing—the *gopīs* are only for that form of life, and the preliminary thing is, that spirit is above matter.

First accustom yourself to think like that—the importance of spirit is always above that of matter. Come to this stage, consolidating your position there, and from that position try to go up in the highest position of spiritual conception. Omitting this, it will be imitation—they will mistake the material things as spiritual—that means to imitate. You are smearing mud on your body and saying that it is nectar—that we can't admit! It is wholesale forgery. On this path we have to consciously cross many steps. From here, you are dreaming of that thing and thinking you are a *siddha-mahātma*—we hate it. You are blasphemous—you are all blasphemous to Mahāprabhu and His *sampradāya*—it is *kalaṅka* (contamination).

Śrīla Bhaktisiddhānta gave *bābājī-veśa* to some, but that was considered something like *vānaprastha*. Those who were bonafide in their life of renunciation, but not very fit to preach, received *bābājī-veśa*. Some stayed in Vṛndāvana, and had no bad tendencies. They were of good character and were very earnest for chanting the Holy Name, but were not fit to preach. Such persons got *bābājī-veśa* from him in their old age.

Vaisnava-dharma

So, *sannyāsa* is the highest order in the *varṇāśrama* system, and *varṇāśrama* is a step towards *vaiṣṇava-dharma*. It is utilized as a favorable step. We may begin from *varṇāśrama-dharma*, but we are to leave that when we enter the domain of *nirguṇa*. *Varṇāśrama* is concerned with *sattva-guṇa*.

Because of our *karma*, our activities, our attention is there. *Jñāna* means our acquisition—when one lives true to their own creed, and surrenders unto a complete dedicated life, then it becomes Vaiṣṇavism—one has to leave their past life. If all *karma* is done only for the satisfaction of Kṛṣṇa, then it is all well and good—that is Vaiṣṇavism. When all inquiry (*jñāna*) is serious and surrendered to the sweet will of Kṛṣṇa—one enters the realm of Vaiṣṇavism. And when *yoga*, the direction of our energy, stops seeking any other achievement and is concentrated wholly for the satisfaction of Kṛṣṇa, then it enters the area of Vaiṣṇavism.

Bhakti-mukha-nirīkṣaka karma-yoga-jñāna—without *bhakti*, *karma*, *jñāna*, and *yoga* cannot succeed. They promise results without the help of *bhakti*—without the support of the aid of the universal wave or force. If God withdraws all His energy from them to support, then they are nowhere—they are powerless and can only give their suggestions, just like so many companies.

In different companies, such as an insurance company, a banking company, etc., if the government does not withdraw its support from them, they can work. But if the government withdraws, they cannot exist. They can thrive, they can work well with the passive support of the government. But if the government withdrawns, they are nowhere.

So if the potency of Kṛṣṇa, His sympathy is withdrawn, then *karma, yoga,* and *jñāna* are nowhere. But on the basis of the supposed support of the government, the support of Kṛṣṇa's will, they can continue independently, and give their own result.

Bhakti-mukha-nirīkṣaka karma-yoga-jñāna—*karma* and *jñāna* are always looking at the face of *bhakti,* service to Kṛṣṇa. *Ei saba sādhanera ati tuccha bala*—what they give is a very negligible thing.

Our *bhakti,* our service, does not depend on anything else—it can go independently from any point. From any point of our life—only with the connection of a bona-fide agent can we link with *bhakti*—we can go on independently without taking any help from the energy. Everything may be rejected, and only through service, through a *sādhu,* can one go on safely towards *bhakti.* So *varṇāśrama* or *sanatana-dharma* generally means the *varnaśrama* orders of *brāhmaṇa, kṣatriya, vaiśya,* and *śūdra.*

The qualification of the *brāhmaṇa,* the highest section, is that they seek something which is not mundane, which is conscious. Generally, they do not have any clear conception of the conscious world, and only some vague conception of the spiritual world. So, *brāhmaṇāṁ sahasrebhyaḥ satrayāji viśiṣyate,* refers to one who is engaged in sacrifice—meaning the model, the standard that everything should be done to satisfy Him, the central Truth, Kṛṣṇa. *Satrayāji sahasrebhyaḥ sarva-vedānta-pāragaḥ.* Then it may come to the stage of an inquirer, *Vedānta,* who loves to deal with consciousness, with fine things—*sarva-vedānta-vit-koṭyā viṣṇu-bhakto viśiṣyate.* There the *yogī* and the *jñānī* are like the *karmī*—they are not dealing with gross things, but they are busy in their dealings with the very subtle things of consciousness.

But mere consciousness does not mean God-consciousness. There is consciousness of the self, consciousness of the cause of this material world, and consciousness of so many things. So *brāhmaṇas,* who are the head of *varṇāśrama-dharma,* are more addicted to spirit than matter. But they have not understood the complete ideal of the spiritual world—the purely spiritual world of Vaikuṇṭha or Goloka. In regard to the *jñānīs:*

bahūnāṁ janmanāṁ ante jñānavān māṁ prapadyate
(Gītā 7.19)

When the *jñānīs* surrender to the feet of Vāsudeva, then they become Vaiṣṇavas. And the *karmīs:*

yajñārthāt karmaṇo n'yatra, loko'yaṁ karma-bandhanaḥ
(Gītā 3.9)

When the *karmīs* can come to understand that any work which is not for Viṣṇu, will bind them with the matter, reaction—then they become Vaiṣṇavas. And the *yogīs:*

yoginām api sarveśāṁ mad-gatenāntar ātmanaḥ
(Gītā 6.47)

They are following so many mystical tactics in body or mind, and trying to raise their consciousness into the higher subtle sphere of the world. But when leaving all those things, they come into contact with the devotees, and begin their *bhajana,* then they become Vaiṣṇavas.

So *varṇāśrama* has been accepted in so many steps—the *śūdra* mentality, *vaiśya* mentality, *kṣatriya* mentality, and *brāhmāṇa* mentality, then Vaiṣṇava mentality. When they accept the Vaiṣṇava mentality—that Viṣṇu is all-in-all, and that our real position is that of a servant of Him, and they begin that life, dismissing all their ambitions in this mundane world whether gross or subtle, then they become Vaiṣṇavas.

You are a *vaiśya* if you earn money, but spend at least a greater portion for the service of Kṛṣṇa, for the propaganda of His Name. If you organize protection and try to help Vaiṣṇavism, the service of Kṛṣṇa, we give recognition to you as a *kṣatriya*—the organizing capacity, the fighting capacity will be utilized for Him. The *brāhmaṇas* explain the Vedic scriptures and *Purāṇas*, etc. But connection with Kṛṣṇa is all-in-all, no other gods are equal or more than Him. So in that way they connect, so we shall accept them. And the *śūdras* can try to utilize their energy for the service of Kṛṣṇa.

Whoever you are, if you come to utilize yourself in the service of Kṛṣṇa, we are in your favor, we have recognition for you.

cari varṇāśramī yadi kṛṣṇa nāhi bhaje
svakarma karite se raurave paḍi maje
(*Cc. Madhya* 22.26)

But if you do not connect with the service of Kṛṣṇa, then in doing your own respective duty you will be the prey of a difficult reaction, that is to go down. Up and down, up and down—you can't get out of this vicious circle. Only with the connection of Kṛṣṇa, the Autocrat, the great repository of love and beauty, can you get out. Connect with Him and you are saved—otherwise in whatever position you are, if you are apathetic to that, you will get a bad reaction. That is our position.

Ramananda Samvada

In the beginning, *varṇāśrama* will give the fundamental conception of divinity. When the talk between Śrī Caitanya Mahāprabhu and Rāmānanda Rāya began, and Mahāprabhu asked the first question, Rāmānanda answered with *varṇāśrama.* The general basis is there—that is the foundation. We should not stay there, but we should make progress also. In the *Gītā* 18.46 it is explained:

yataḥ pravṛttir bhūtānāṁ yena sarvam idaṁ tatam
sva-karmaṇā tam abhyarcya siddhiṁ vindati mānavaḥ

> By worship of the Lord, who is the source of all beings and who is all-pervading, a man can attain perfection through performing his own work.

Yataḥ pravṛttir bhūtānāṁ—we must stick to the position that we have acquired by our previous activities, but, we may utilize this as the basis for our improvement. *Varṇāśramācāravatā puruṣeṇa parā pumān*—Rāmānanda began from there.

Accepting the practice generally recommended in *varṇāśrama,* one should go on with exclusive devotion to Viṣṇu—that is real *dharma.* Then Mahāprabhu said, *eho bāhya, āge kaha āra*—"Go deeper." And Rāmānanda began, "The real purpose of *varṇāśrama* is to realize that the Kṛṣṇa conception is the highest ideal for which *varṇāśrama* has been designed." *Yat karoṣi yad aśnāsi*—the result must be connected with Kṛṣṇa, and *varṇāśrama* has been designed for that purpose. Otherwise *varṇāśrama* defeats it's own object.

So, having ones position in *varṇāśrama,* one must be conscious that Kṛṣṇa or Nārāyaṇa, is all in all. Other gods are subsidiary—they have come to help somewhat with the training of our worship. But the real worship is that of Nārāyaṇa. Mahāprabhu said, "This is also superficial—go further."

Then Rāmānanda said, *sarva dharmān parityajya mām ekaṁ śaraṇaṁ vraja*—"Neglecting all the duties that are mentioned in *varṇāśrama*, exclusively devote yourself to the service of Kṛṣṇa"—this is the gist of all the scriptures. "This is also superficial, go deeper." Then Rāmānanda said:

brahma-bhūtaḥ prasannātmā na śocati na kāṅkṣati
samaḥ sarveṣu bhūteṣu mad-bhaktiṁ labhate parām
(*Gītā* 18.54)

When one has attained such a position that they have nothing to do with matter, and realize they are spirit, then they are qualified to get real contact with devotion. Mahāprabhu said, "This is also superficial, and devotion does not begin here." *Mad-bhaktiṁ labhate parām*—he will attain *bhakti* afterwards, but this is not the position of devotion. Only he has his identification that he is spirit and he has nothing to do with matter. He has come to the marginal position, but he has no conception of the positive side. On the positive side, he will acquire devotion—*mad bhaktiṁ labhate*—he is on the verge of *māyā* and reality.

Then Rāmānanda said, *jñāne prayāsam udapāsya*—leaving his desire for knowledge, one should take the path of *śaraṇāgati* or surrender. And the real wealth is here—this is the vision, the concept of a real agent of Vaikuṇṭha. *Satāṁ prasaṅgam mama vīrya saṁvido*—he knows the agent of Vaikuṇṭha. That is the real wealth and he has to give up the vanity that he will be able to know everything and hold it within his fist. Discarding his vanity, he must get connection with the real agent of Vaikuṇṭha. Here, the real life of devotion begins—all else is external. Now we have come to that point—we must trace the development within the realm of devotion, and how he makes progress—Mahāprabhu requested him to please relate that.

Then, he explained *śānta, dāsya,* and *sakhya.* When *sakhya* came, Mahāprabhu said, "This is good. Go further. Go further!"

Vātsalya-prema. "This is good, go further!"

Mādhurya-prema. "Yes, this is it! Is there anything more?"

Rāmānanda replied, "Yes. *Rādhā-dāsyam. Rādhā-dāsyam* is exclusively the highest."

Then He said, "This is the end of all realization. Can you think of anything more?"

"I have something in my mind, but I do not know if there is anyone who has any evidence for that. But since you ask, I can't quote any scripture from the *śāstra,* but I have one song, composed by myself." This song leads to Kṛṣṇa, and it gives a hint of the *avatāra* of Mahāprabhu.

"The *sambhoga* in Vṛndāvana and the *vipralambha* in Navadvīpa, with Kṛṣṇa Himself combined with Rādhārāṇī—comes to give admission to the public. That is considered to be the highest attainment, and this is in my heart, I don't know whether You can appreciate it."

"No, no, no, don't express this!" Mahāprabhu put his hand over Rāmānanda's mouth, "Go no further!"

Then Rāmānanda said, "Prabhu, You have come to grace me, but You are hiding Yourself. You should not do that. I am Your maidservant. I saw You first as a *sannyāsī,* but now I see there is Śyāma-gopāla, and there is a golden idol of a lady with a dress of Vṛndāvana. Who are You? Speak out plainly! Don't deceive me. I am Your lowest servant."

Then Mahāprabhu said, "Yes, what you have seen, I am such, but I have come in disguise. It is mentioned in the scriptures also, that this descent of Mine will be in disguise. You have seen it." After seeing the special form exhibited by the Lord,

Rāmānanda lost his senses and fell down. Then Mahāprabhu awakened him, and Rāmānanda saw the *sannyāsī* sitting, and saying, "Now, I am satisfied. I am going away, Rāmānanda." He was dumbstruck. Mahāprabhu went away and Rāmānanda came to his senses.

It is also mentioned in their talk—*sakhī līlā vistāriyā, sakhī āsvādaya*—if one wants to enter into this *vraja-rasa,* then it is required that he should go to a *sakhī* in the *mādhurya-rasa.* They are the masters of the situation. The whole storehouse of this *mādhurya-līlā* is in the hands of the *sakhīs.* They can give it to others. So, *guru-rūpa-sakhī*—in *mādhurya-rasa,* the guru is in the form and in the spirit of a *sakhī* of Rādhārāṇī.

Part Four

Divine Revelation

Divine Revelation

Some people say, "Kṛṣṇa is a particular form with a human figure. How can that be a universal representation of the Absolute truth? Kṛṣṇa consciousness is also a local, narrow type of belief. You say that Kṛṣṇa is the Absolute, but He has a particular figure—we don't say that the Absolute is limited to a particular figure. He is beyond the range of our eye and ear experience, our mental and intellectual experience—He is all-comprehensive and all-permeating."

This is the Brahman conception of the Absolute—Brahman means all-comprehensive—everything is contained within that. Brahman means the broadest knowledge, which can complement all possible parts of knowledge. Above that is the Paramātma conception. Paramātma means the all-pervading, smallest of the small. Beyond the atom is the proton and the electron, and the smallest of the small—Paramātma. Paramātma means the smallest of the small, and Brahman is the biggest of the big.

Bhagavān is of a different type—Bhagavān, or the Supreme Lord Kṛṣṇa, is He who attracts the attention of everyone. He is neither the biggest nor the smallest, but He who can attract all attention. That aspect of the Lord in its most extreme form is

Kṛṣṇa, and He is so sweet that He can attract everything. There may be so many atoms both big and small, but gravity attracts them, gives them some form and they become the cosmos. In the highest sense, attraction means not only physical attraction but wholesale attraction in body, mind and soul.

The center of the highest attraction is Kṛṣṇa. Kṛṣṇa means, 'One who can attract everything and give the highest satisfaction in return.' Although He may come within our visualized experience, that experience has no connection with this world—He is transcendental. Kṛṣṇa can play in the *rasa* dance, and appear simultaneously at the side of every *gopī*, by expanding Himself into innumerable doubles, so that, by the side of each *gopī* there is one Kṛṣṇa. Brahmā stole Kṛṣṇa's calves and cowboys, but by His will everything was kept up—there was no loss to Kṛṣṇa, so infinite is He in character. But because we are finite, He approaches us in an easily comprehensible way, in a way that we can visualize Him. Otherwise, our eyes are useless in trying to perceive the infinite.

If something is very dazzling we cannot see it. Our eyes have their limits. If a light is very intense we cannot see it, or if a light is very dim we cannot perceive it. We can only perceive the middle part of the spectrum. Similarly, if a sound is very loud our ear cannot grasp it, and if a sound is very soft also, our ear cannot catch it. Our ear can function only within the limitation of a certain sound range. Everything which is above or below our sense perception is of no use to us, and so Kṛṣṇa appears to us in the middle, in so many ways.

He appears to us in a certain color, a certain figure. He appears for the eye experience as the Deity; for the ear experience as the Name Kṛṣṇa; for the tongue experience He appears as *prasādam*. In different ways our senses can have a corresponding relationship with Him.

Infinite Can Be Known by the Finite

Once, I went to preach in Karachi, in 1935 or so. The president of the Ārya Samāja came to see us, thinking he had an easy prey, and his first remark was, "If the finite can know the Infinite, then he is not Infinite. You are worshipers of dolls, idols—you say that you can know God, but you are a finite soul. The infinite can never be known by you." That was his argument. "You Vaiṣṇavas preach doll-worship, idol-worship. Your transaction is only within the limited world. You don't know anything about the Unlimited." With this basis, he attacked us. But I immediately replied, "If the Infinite cannot make Himself known to the finite, then He is not Infinite." This silenced him, he had no reply. So, in the Vaiṣṇava creed, or in any other creed, we should always keep in mind that everything depends on Him. He can come down to our level, but we cannot go up to His level.

We can only attract Him to come down to our level by improving our negative tendency. We should pray, "O Lord, I am so mean, I am the most fallen of the fallen, the lowest of the low. Without Your help, I am nothing. Please be satisfied, be propitiated with me." That is possible only through *śaraṇāgati*, self-surrender. Through *śaraṇāgati*, we can attract the superior plane to descend to the lower plane. He has the power. He can take me to His domain. He is all-powerful, but we cannot force our entrance into that domain. We have no natural right to do that. We are made of lower stuff.

He is *adhokṣaja*, transcendental. *Adhokṣaja* refers to that plane of existence which can keep the world of experience in a lower position—the world of experience is pushed down by the *adhokṣaja* plane. That subtle plane of existence can come down to us, but we cannot go up—only if He takes us there, can we go up. With a passport, we can go to the verge of our jurisdiction, to the border, but if we have a visa, if a visa is allowed, then we can enter into the domain of another land. So, the human mind and intellect can have no touch of the *adhokṣaja* realm.

A few days ago, there was a rumor of flying saucers. It was thought that from a more civilized land, they came in a small plane and wandered over this world. From earth, the air-force gave chase to the flying saucers, but they disappeared. Where they have gone, no one can trace and they returned disappointed. The flying saucers can descend here, to connect with this planet—the air-force can follow them to some extent, but the flying saucers disappear beyond their vision. The *adhokṣaja* or transcendental plane is something like that. There is a subtle plane that can come down to our gross mind and intelligence, but we cannot go up there.

Entering Krsna's Family

The Lord is not a heartless machine. We have come to a hearty Absolute. He has got heart, everything. I remember that one lady during Svāmī Mahārāja's lifetime delivered a lecture in this *naṭa-mandira*. She told that, "We have come from so far and we are so thankful and dependant on Svāmī Mahārāja—his call impressed me most. Here only can we live as a family member with our Supreme Lord. We live and serve as a family member and He also considers us as family."

martyo yadā tyakta-samasta-karmā
niveditātmā vicikīrṣito me
tadāmṛtavaṁ pratipadyamāno
mayātma-bhūyāya ca kalpate vai

A person who gives up all fruitive activities and offers himself entirely unto Me, eagerly desiring to render

> service unto Me, achieves liberation from birth and death and is promoted to the status of sharing My own opulences. (*Bhāg.* 11.29.34)

This *ātma-bhūyaya* (having equal opulence with the Lord) we find also in *Bhagavad-gītā*:

tato māṁ tattvato jñātvā
viśate tad-anantaram

> After this, they can realize Me and My real nature and enter into Me. (*Gītā* 18.55)

What is the meaning of 'enter into Me?' It is that, "He enters into My family." *Ātma-bhūyaya ca kalpate*—that they are given recognition—"They become My own family members. I consider them as My own and even sometimes more than Myself," as He says to Uddhava. "Uddhava, you are so dear to Me, than even Brahmā, Śiva, My elder brother Baladeva, My wife Lakṣmī-devī, even more than My own body. I love you even more than Myself—*prāṇabhūri varīyasi.*" It is mentioned in many places. "More than My life I consider you to be superior, Uddhava." So, such things are there and they are real, the standard of our ideal, our goal is of such quality. It is very, very high—but at the same time we should not think that I have attained it—I have got it, only to prove that it is imaginary, it is futile. It is there! It is the real of the real, but still I am fallen. Only with the help of the guru and Vaiṣṇava can we hope to attain such a great level where we can be one with the Supreme Lord. That is the most important quality of *prema*—love divine. It is the special qualification of *bhāgavata-prema.* It can raise the tiny soul to the level of the most favorite of the Lord Himself, such is the extraordinary qualification of devotion.

Sri Rupa-manjari-pada

Bhāgavata-prema in *mādhurya-rasa,* has been recommended by Mahāprabhu as the highest form of attainment possible ever for the faith of the *jīva.* Bhaktivinoda Ṭhākura has given a short description, a sketch of the type of confidential spiritual service in *mādhurya-rasa* under the leadership of Rūpa Gosvāmī in the camp of Rādhārāṇī.

Narottama Ṭhākura understands the substantial characteristic of *rūpānuga-bhajana* so much so that here in his song *Śrī Rūpa-mañjarī-pada,* he is expressing his aspiration: "When will my Gurudeva, Lokanātha Gosvāmī, take me by my hand and connect me to Rūpa. 'I am giving this young maidservant to you Rūpa, you take him.'" His guru is Lokanātha and his aspiration is, "When will my guru give charge of me to Śrī Rūpa." Rūpa's higher position as a *mañjarī* means higher dealings and different services, that are unique in the camp of Rādhārāṇī. This most confidential service is not generally given to other *sakhīs* and other servitors.

An exclusive concentrated attempt, an aspiration to enter, to have admission into the camp of Śrī Rūpa, is expressed in *Śrī Rūpa-mañjarī-pada* in earnestness—exclusive earnestness to get admission into the camp of Śrī Rūpa. *Śrī Rūpa-mañjarī-pada, sei mora sampada*—the characteristic of the aspiration should be like this. *Śrī Rūpa-mañjarī-pada, sei mora sampada.* I consider the holy feet of Śrī Rūpa-mañjarī as my only wealth—I don't consider anything else as wealth.

Sei mora sampada, sei mora bhajana pūjana—bhajana means internal sincere presentation towards the highest reality. And *pūjana* means the formal attempt—both formal and internal, *bhajana* and *pūjana. Bhajana* is more internal and sincere, *pūjana* is more formal. In the beginning of course, there is the formal attempt, formal respect and then there is the internal offering—*pūjana* and *bhajana.*

Sei mora prāṇa-dhana—she is the source of my life of sustenance. *Sei mora ābharaṇa*—she is the ornament of my life. *Sei mora jīvanera jīvana*—I also consider her to be the very life of my life, the essence of my essential existence.

Sei mora rasa-nidhi—she is the source of all my ecstatic aspiration—the ocean of my ecstatic joy. *Sei mora vāñchā-siddhi*—the fulfillment of my inner aspiration is there. *Sei mora vedera-dharama*—the *Veda* has so much position and hold over the society but I consider that Veda inspires me only to accept the position of Rūpa-mañjarī as the real meaning of the *Veda*. *Sei vrata, sei tapa, sei mora mantra-japa*—there is a fashion especially in the female society to accept many vows of different kinds, such as the *sāvitrī-vrata*. Sāvitrī performed that and is famous for her chastity. By her chastity she saved her husband from death. So, there are so many good ideals in the ladies of ancient times. *Sei vrata*—I have no other formal vow that I would like to take, other than that to Rūpa-mañjarī. *Sei tapa*—so many penances have been practiced to achieve their desired end, but my penance is only for her. If I do that then I think I have finished all types of penances.

Sei mora mantra-japa—refers to those who engage themselves in *japam*, the repetition of particular spiritual sounds for the attainment of some auspicious end. *Sei mora dharama karama*—her service covers all sorts of engagements to discover and serve the holy purposes. In all phases I concentrate on her feet—to achieve the service of those feet. Everything will be—*yasmin jñāte sarvam evaṁ vijñātaṁ bhavati, yasmin prāpti sarvam idaṁ*—all phases of life, all duties of life, yet I want only one point, the service of Rūpa-mañjarī.

Anukūla habe vidhi, se pade haibe siddhi—I only wish that the circumstances may be favorable, that the Controller of these worldly forces, may be propitiated by me. May He make arrangements in favor of such an attainment of life—if He desires then my fulfillment will be achieved. *Nirakhibo e dui nayane*—then what will be the effect if the administration becomes helpful to me? *Se rūpa mādhurī rāśī, prāṇa kuvalaya śaśi*—then I will be allowed to have a vision of her beautiful figure, her movement and serving attitude. That will come in me. I will be connected, rather I will see her feet, and direction, and will do some service under her guidance. I'll be allowed to have a vision of her beautiful figure which is like the moon, just as the moon is the source of energy and beauty of the *kumuda,* the red lotus at night. Generally the sun helps the lotus and the moon helps the red flowers that we find in the pond, the *kumuda,* which flourishes by the moonlight and is of red color. The lotus gets energy from the sunlight. But here are rays from the moon. *Praphullita habe niśi dine*—because Narottama Ṭhākura desires that the demand occur both day and night. So because here the moon is mentioned, this means that perhaps, the principle necessity is night for this *mādhurya-rasa.* So the moon refers to the night sustaining agency. Here also *kuvalaya* is mentioned, not *kumuda,* which means a particular type of lotus. *Praphullita haibe niśi dine*—that will be encouraged and sustained both day and night by the ray of that beautiful figure. That will inspire me day and night in the service of Kṛṣṇa's camp.

Then comes another stage, *tuwā adarśana ahi, garale jārala dehi*—after attaining this, I will consider it to be my own property. I have attained this, I shudder to think of losing it again, and I may not retain my position here. That apprehension comes. *Tuwā adarśana ahi, garale jārala dehi*—so long as I am dispossessed of such association I can't tolerate it any longer. After attaining these things I consider it to be my own home, but why was I forced to remain out of my home? Your separation feels as if a serpent has bitten me and my whole life is disturbed by the pain of the serpent's poison—that is your separation. *Cira dina tāpita jīvana*—for a long time I have undergone this pang of separation from you, my mistress.

Hā hā rūpa koro dayā, deho more pada chāyā, narottama laila śaraṇa—now I again come to your feet. Please grant me a permanent service in your camp, I am taking refuge under you. I have no other alternative. I fully surrender unto you and you should give me permanent service in your camp. Without this it is not possible to go on with my life.

Rupanuga Sampradaya

What is this *rūpānuga-sampradāya*? Mahāprabhu named this, the *rūpānuga-sampradāya*. The first disciple of Mahāprabhu is Rūpa Gosvāmī, although Rūpa Gosvāmī took his formal initiation from Sanātana Gosvāmī. But Mahāprabhu met Rūpa first, and later met Sanātana. So, Rūpa-Sanātana, and not Sanātana-Rūpa. Sanātana was originally the elder of the two brothers. But we refer to Rūpa-Sanātana, because the first recognition of Mahāprabhu was received by Rūpa.

Now, what is the real meaning of the *rūpānuga-sampradāya*? You are to mark it very attentively. *Mādhurya-rasa* is the total *rasa*, and the most intense of all *rasas*. It is all-accomodating. Twenty-four hours engagement of service with Kṛṣṇa is only possible in *mādhurya-rasa*. And there is the possibility of tiredness in *rasas*, other than *mādhurya-rasa*. Sometimes the father or mother may think, "I am too tired, I shall make arrangements a little later." But in *mādhurya-rasa*, there is no such reaction.

The differences between Rūpa-mañjarī and Lalitā-sakhī are of course things of the very highest order. We should not have the audacity to enter into these subtle points without proper guidance. When Rādhā-Govinda are privately in union, the *sakhīs* of the higher order do not approach that place, but the *mañjarīs* can go. The junior *sevakas* can go to perform any service necessary there, due to their lesser age. They are allowed, but the higher friends of Rādhārāṇī keep some respectable distance. So, when Rādhā-Govinda are alone in union, the highest quality of *rasa* is to be found in their *līlā,* and that is approachable by the juniors. That is for the *mañjarīs,* not for the *sakhīs.* So, the highest attainment is to be located in Rūpa, the leader of that junior group who has the advantage of the special service in that stage. So, *rūpānuga.* Wherever we are, we shall have to accept that this is the acme of our fulfillment.

Rupanuga-sampradaya Goes to the West

Our Guru Mahārāja was always *rūpānuga, rūpānuga, rūpānuga—rāgānuga,* and then *rūpānuga,* in particular. Generally *rāgānuga,* and then particularly *rūpānuga.* That is our *parivāra,* identification, our nature. Bhaktivinoda Ṭhākura says, "I run to get admission under the administration of Rūpa Gosvāmī." Who runs? He who has got such aspiration—he runs to become enlisted in the group of Śrī Rūpa—one who has such sort of prospect. And that will be the highest attainment of our fortune—Raghunātha Dāsa Gosvāmī has declared it. And still now, that is the highest point of ones achievement for the whole Gauḍīya *sampradāya.* Raghunātha Dāsa Gosvāmī is the *ācārya* of our highest necessity, our ultimate aim—he is the *prayojana-ācārya.* By the grace of all of you, and by the necessity, Prabhupāda has dragged these things from me, and I cannot but remember that he wanted me to go to the West.

Now, our talks are going to the west by the grace of Bhaktivedānta Svāmī Mahārāja. Kālī Dāsa says in the *Raghu-vaṁśa* when he is describing the dynasty of Raghu, in which Lord Rāma appeared: "I am a man of small literary experience; so many stalwarts have sprung from that great *Raghu-vaṁśa,* and

I am going to describe them with a meager attempt at poetry?" Many *ślokas* of Kālī Dāsa are devoted for this purpose.

athavā kṛtavardhare
granthe 'sminn pūrva sūribhiḥ
mano vajra samuthena
sūtresye vastune gatiḥ

> The previous renowned *kavis,* poets like Vālmīki Muni and Śrīla Vyāsadeva, have given a description of *Raghu-vaṁśa,* and they have made the path of entering into that sacred description easy. How is this? In a necklace of jewels, the jewel is a hard thing—the thread cannot pierce it, yet the iron needle drill has already made a hole through it, and now the thread is easily passing through.

Bhaktivedānta Svāmī Mahārāja was like a *vajra,* a powerful drill, the hard thing has already been pierced by him, and like a thread, I am passing through that. He was so great and so simple at the same time. Anyhow, Mahāprabhu and our Gurudeva have achieved through him a tremendous and inconceivable thing. One godbrother could not tolerate all these things. But the other day, when coming from Māyāpura, that *sannyāsī* said, "It is *acintya*—inconceivable." He did not want to give recognition, but from his mouth, the word came out. That, "What Bhaktivedānta Svāmī Mahārāja did, that is *acintya*: it is inconceivable." So, it is divine. It is inconceivable what he has done, what Nityānanda Prabhu, what Baladeva did through him, that is inconceivable.

Rūpānuga has been considered to be the highest attainment of the Gauḍīya Vaiṣṇava school. Bhaktivinoda Ṭhākura has written *Rūpānuga-bhajana-darpaṇa,* a small poem found in his *Gītā-mālā.* Here, he has made it clear what should be our aspiration.

So with that highest ideal in our heart we will go and externally will ask people to join Kṛṣṇa consciousness. All other attempts are futile in the world—all are temporary and reactionary, so join Kṛṣṇa consciousness! Mahāprabhu gave it to us and in this, the modern age, Bhaktivinoda, Bhaktisiddhānta Prabhu, and especially in the west, Svāmī Mahārāja, preached this Kṛṣṇa consciousness, which has such depth. The deepest concern in our innermost life is such.

We are of this nature—it may not be accessible or approachable for everyone, but in general this is Kṛṣṇa consciousness, this divine love. The Absolute Lord is the Lord of love and we can live in His family—such a prospect and hope we have been given and we should try and approach this in a scientific way. This is not an analogy, this is not hearsay, this is not imagination—you come and try and feel and get. It is a gradation, step by step—you should try to attain it. It can be attainable but it has its proper method and we have to try through that method. Everything requires a method, and in every formal education there is a step by step process. If I go for the visa, there is also a method. *Praṇipāta, paripraśna, sevā*—in this way we can go. This is the up-going current and not the capturing of the lower things—this is the capturing of the higher. So the process is different—only by surrendering can we make our progress towards that higher reality.

Pranama of Bhaktisiddhanta

Rūpānuga-dhara—dhara means line, lineage or current. So *rūpānuga-dhara* means the current of pure love that is coming through Śrī Rūpa Gosvāmī and his predecessors who are also of such a caliber. But he is the central figure. His position has been connected and scientifically arranged and through him it is passing. According to Mahāprabhu's advice, Rūpa Gosvāmī has been given the scientific form of that current. We are followers of that which is passing through him to this side. We want to take bath in that stream, and following that stream we want to go up.

I have also written a poem about Prabhupāda, a *praṇāma-mantra.*

gauḍe gāṅga-taṭe nava-vraja-navadvīpa tu māyāpure
śrī caitanya-maṭha-prakaśa-kavaro jīvaika-kalyāṇadhīḥ
śrī siddhānta-sarasvatīti-vidito gauḍīya-gurvanvaye
bhāto bhānuriva prabhātagagane rūpānugaiḥ pūjitāḥ

> That great personality who resides in Gauḍa-deśa on the banks of the Gaṅgā in Navadvīpa, which is new Vṛndāvana and is known as Māyāpura, has manifest Śrī Caitanya Maṭha and is the only person concerned with the real welfare of the living entities. He is known as Śrī Bhaktisiddhānta Sarasvatī who is in the succession of Gauḍīya gurus; resplendent as the sun in the morning sky, he is worshiped by the followers of Śrī Rūpa Gosvāmī.

Gauḍa-gaṅgā-taṭe nava-vraja navadvīpe tu māyāpure—in Bengal (Gauḍadeśa), on the banks of the Ganges, which is identified with Vṛndāvana, there is a new Vṛndāvana or secret Vṛndāvana—Gupta-Vṛndāvana. *Māyāpure*—in the village of Māyāpura. *Śrī caitanya-maṭha-prakāśa-kavaro, jīvaika-kalyāṇadhiḥ*—only for the benefit of the *jīvas,* he established Caitanya Maṭha in Māyāpura. *Śrī siddhānta-sarasvatīti-vidito gauḍīya-gurvanvaye*—in the lineage of the Gauḍīya Vaiṣṇavas his name is Bhaktisiddhānta Sarasvatī. *Bhāto bhānuriva*—he shines like the morning sun. *Prabhāta-gagane rūpānugaiḥ pūjitaḥ*—and is worshiped by the followers of Śrī Rūpa Gosvāmī. Bhaktisiddhānta Sarasvatī came and established Caitanya Maṭha on the banks of the Ganges in Māyāpura, in Gauḍadeśa which is a similar facsimile of Vṛndāvana. He did this in the name of the *guru-paramparā*—Bhaktisiddhānta Sarasvatī shines like the morning sun and is worshiped by the followers of Rūpa Gosvāmī—*rūpānugaiḥ pūjitaḥ.*

Sūryopāsana (worship of the sun) is done by Rādhārāṇī—Rādhārāṇī is a worshiper of Sūrya outwardly. All the true followers of Rūpa Gosvāmī surround him with their veneration and worship him with various items. *Rūpānuga janera jīvana*—it is written in Prabhupāda's own language, in the *guru-paramparā*:

mahāprabhu śrī caitanya, rādhā-kṛṣṇa nahe anya
rūpānuga janera jīvana

Mahāprabhu Śrī Caitanya, Who is none other than Rādhā-Kṛṣṇa combined, is the very life of the section known as the *rūpānugas. Viśvambhara-priyaṅkara, śrī svarūpa-dāmodara*—the very favorite of Viśvambhara, Mahāprabhu, is Svarūpa Dāmodara and, *śrī gosvāmī rūpa-sanātana*—and those Gosvāmī brothers known as Rūpa and Sanātana. Their names were given by Mahāprabhu Himself. *Rūpa-priya mahājana, jīva raghunātha hana*—then, the favorites of Rūpa were Jīva and Raghunātha and, *tā'ra priya kavi-kṛṣṇa-dāsa*—the next is Kṛṣṇa Dāsa Kavirāja, the writer of *Caitanta-caritāmṛta.* He is connected to Raghunātha. *Kṛṣṇa-dāsa priya-vara, narottama sevā-parā*—though Kṛṣṇa Dāsa's guru was Lokanātha, Prabhupāda saw that the *dhara* (the current), flowed from Raghunātha to Kṛṣṇa Dāsa to Narottama

Ṭhākura. From Narottama Ṭhākura a similar current—*yā'ra pada viśvanātha āśa*—then it came to Viśvanātha, then Baladeva, then Jagannātha, then Bhaktivinoda Ṭhākura. In him, he could trace that same current of the same high quality in Bhaktivinoda Ṭhākura. And then Gaura-kiśora Dāsa Bābājī Mahārāja also had it. Then he wrote, "I have the eternal aspiration to serve the holy feet of Rādhārāṇī."

śrī vārśabhānavī-varā, sadā sevya sevā-parā
tā'hāra dayita-dāsa nāma

And that servants' name is Dayita Dāsa. *Ei saba hari-jana*—"I am trying to do service to this lineage to satisfy Guru, Gaurāṅga and Rādhā-Govinda." In this way he is giving the knowledge of his position there.

Not Teaching Raganuga-bhakti

Pūjala rāga-patha gaurava bhaṅge—that is the motto of our Guru Mahārāja. That is the property of our Gurudeva, and we are serving that from one step lower. But we must be conscious of the fact that the real wealth of my Gurudeva is *rāgānuga-bhakti*. That is our aim. "But I am not particularly fit. I am to acquire my fitness for this aim by the servants of those that are within *rāgānuga-bhakti*. I pray one day I will be able to reach that standard." This should be our attitude, and if we think we are quite fit, then that is faulty. That progress will be indirect, not direct. Mahāprabhu says—*na prema gandho'sti darāpi*. "There is not a drop of real *rāgānuga-bhakti* within Me. That is infinite, that is an ocean. My attempt is a sham. It is artificial." He is blaming Himself in such a way—but from the background it is known that *rāgānuga-bhakti* is filling Him up, capturing Him wholesale.

Rāgānuga-bhakti is the very life of *prema,* the internal, irresistible attraction for service to Kṛṣṇa. It is continuous, not calculative of any gain or loss. We are to pray for that. It has come in such an irresistible way and captured us. As the ocean plays with a straw, it shall also play with me in that way. That is *bhakti.* That is *rāgānuga*—that *prema* is an ocean of love. You will have no initiative at all—but that is not a curse, that ocean is a cosmos. Harmony is there, and we are all in His hand. Yoga-māyā is making arrangements for all these things. We must look with a feeling of helplessness—we shall feel the emanation of the loving service, *prema*—love divine.

I am not teaching *rāgānuga-bhakti,* but I am making it clear that it is our goal. We must have that on our head—*pūjala rāga-patha gaurava bhaṅge.* We are worshiping this and our highest aim is *rāgānuga-bhakti.* With that object in mind we are doing work here in this world.

Raganuga

The different stages of development, *sambandha, abhidheya,* and *prayojana,* are also different stages of devotional service, like *vaidhi-bhakti, rāgānuga-bhakti* etc.

In *vaidhi-bhakti,* we generally see the constitutional position of the Master, the Master of the world. He is in cooperation with us, and we are guided by some law—that is Nārāyaṇa in Vaikuṇṭha. "This is a good thing, I get some special pleasure by His service. The *śāstra* also encourages me to do this." This sort of conclusion is held by the servitor in *vaidhi.* There is some awe, grandeur, and some apprehension that I may not do my service correctly—it is calculated devotion and calculated service.

But in *rāga-mārga* ones service is spontaneous and automatic. "I am helpless—I can't resist doing it." That service is fully dependent, just as in the inner workings of the body, there is some voluntary action, and some reflexive involuntary action.

It is involuntary that when we eat something, the process of digestion is automatic—I can't assist it. Without my consciousness the work is going on. So in *rāga-mārga,* it goes on without our calculated faculty—our voluntary faculty does not have much scope there. It must follow this internal, spontaneous energy which works there. Those in *rāga-mārga* cannot live for anything but to do their service. That is the position there. But it is not measured or calculated—it is automatic and spontaneous.

And in Vaikuṇṭha, the *sambandha* is Nārāyaṇa. We are rendering service, we are His servants, and He is our Master of everything.

But in *rāgānuga,* it is not that He is our Master. Sometimes Kṛṣṇa's friends are climbing on the shoulders of Kṛṣṇa and sometimes even giving a slap to Kṛṣṇa. Sometimes Kṛṣṇa is carrying them or climbing on their shoulders. They feel that they are very equal with Kṛṣṇa in their *sakhya-rasa* relationship. In *vātsalya-rasa,* Yaśodā thinks, "He is of lower capacity than mine and I must look after His welfare. He is destroying my things, I must punish Him." Such an attitude they have with the real Master in *rāgānuga.* This is arranged by Yogamāyā to give real and better pleasure to Kṛṣṇa. Not master and servant, but lover and beloved, in this way. That is the main thing there.

Raganuga-sambandha

In *sambandha-jñāna* one can also achieve the *rāga-marga* devotional service. *Sambandha* means, "Who am I? Where am I? What am I? I want a proper relationship with the environment." That is *sambandha* concern. He is my paramour, He is my son—in this way, it is as if it is in the mundane world. That is *sambandha.*

It is transcendent and this is the mundane—this is the distinction, they are the opposite. But they appear almost in the same way. The adjustment is very similar—it is very, very similar with this mundane world. But that is the highest and this is the lowest. This is self-centered and that is God-centered. That may seem self-centered and here it may feel that I am God-centered by my imagination. But there they are really God-centered but they think they have their self-interest. That is the position.

Raganuga-abhidheya

In the spiritual realm they do not recognize *abhidheya. Abhidheya* means that, "I just want to satisfy my friend Kṛṣṇa, by playing, or by supplying some peacock feathers. I want to satisfy Kṛṣṇa. Please take this!" In this way, that is their *abhidheya.* The *abhidheya* has become the objective. That is local *abhidheya,* the activities according to the relation between them. That is *līlā,* pastimes. Because they have attained their goal, the train-fare is not necessary! They have reached the goal. And there, if you want *abhidheya,* that is a local transaction, according to the local necessity of that position. That may be *abhidheya,* but they have attained their goal, and they are not passing through any way or road. They have reached the road already, and they have obtained their desired position. There, *abhidheya* means transaction—transaction in the perfect stage. You may call it *abhidheya* but actually *abhidheya* is finished—in the sense of what is applied here, that is to make a journey from one place to another. That is finished when we reach there, but it is in the form of a remedial transaction.

It may seem to be *abhidheya,* but it is not in the sense of a means to an end. The end is already attained, and we are already engaged in *līlā* automatically, designed by Yogamāyā.

Raganuga-prayojana

And *prayojana* is also immediate. "I want to satisfy, by my presentation, by my service." That is an immediate necessity. In the attained stage, *prayojana* is addressed to each *līlā. Sambandha, abhidheya, prayojana*—when the *prayojana* is in my hand, and the *sambandha* is established there along with my eternal and permanent relationship with Him—that is *abhidheya.* When I was far away, I had a general idea of what He was. Then when I came closer to that side, that is *abhidheya.* When I get that vision and attain their *kṛpā,* that is *prayojana.* My internal satisfaction is there. In a friendly circle, the two parties of Kṛṣṇa and Balarāma are fighting with each other. And in that fighting, they are feeling satisfaction, that they are achieving their object of life to the fullest extent, their fullest satisfaction. There is a mock fight between their parties.

Once Balarāma gave a slap to Kṛṣṇa, Who complained to Mother Yaśodā, "My elder brother has beaten Me, My mother." Balarāma was very much put to shame, after going a little distance away, He said,

"Yes, I did slap You, My affectionate brother, but should You complain to mother about that? Does it behoove you?"

"I ran to get some affection from My mother."

"Why did you put Me in such an awkward position by telling her this."

That is the *līlā.* Kṛṣṇa is doing this to see the position of Balarāma. That is also in a mood of enjoyment, the service of Kṛṣṇa. These appear as ordinary things, but the type of bliss which They enjoy is quite different and perfect. We can conjecture somewhat, according to our degree of surrender—we can have a deeper view into that, according to the degree of *tadekātma-rūpa*—how much we are of common interest with Him. That will help us to understand the reality underlying all these things.

Bhaktivinoda's Vision of Raganuga-bhakti

In *Caitanya-śīkṣāmṛta* and *Jaiva-dharma*, Bhaktivinoda Ṭhākura has written about *rāgānuga-bhakti*. It is originally written about by Rūpa Gosvāmī under the instruction and inspiration of Mahāprabhu—in *Bhakti-rasāmṛta-sindhu* and especially in *Ujjvala-nīlamaṇi*. The highest position is shown in *Ujjvala-nīlamaṇi* and the lower position of *rāgānuga-bhakti* has been given in *Bhakti-rasāmṛta-sindhu*. This has been translated into Bengali by Bhaktivinoda Ṭhākura in his own way—in *Caitanya-śīkṣāmṛta*, *Jaiva-dharma*, and in many other places.

That will be our object—we must not think that we are qualified fully for that. It is such a precious thing—*śiva viriñci vāñchita vedam*. Brahmā, Śiva, and all the higher candidates aspire after this, but have not obtained it. In a poem that I composed about Bhaktivinoda Ṭhākura, I have mentioned *śrī-rādhā-pada-sevānāmṛtam aho*—that is the nectarean service of Śrī Rādhikā—Rādhārāṇī. "Oh, very wonderful! You, Bhaktivinoda Ṭhākura, are the master to deal with that nectar."

Varam imaṁ pādābja-mūle bhavat-sarvasvāvadhi-rādhikā-dayita-dāsānāṁ—the highest thing of pure aspiration, the highest will of your heart is *rādhikā-dayita-dāsa*—the exclusive servitor of Śrī Rādhā, Dayita Dāsa, our Gurudeva. You please help me, that he may sanction and grant my admission within his group. *Gaṇe gaṇyatām*—you can recommend me, to enter into the group of Dayita Dāsa, our Guru Mahārāja—Vārṣabhānavī-Dayita Dāsa.

Always through Radharani

The *sakhīs* always want to unify Kṛṣṇa and Rādhā and therein lies their inner satisfaction. Always through Rādhārāṇī—they are so pure. The standard of purity is such that they sacrifice their own connection with Kṛṣṇa and they all centralize for the highest point which can give maximum satisfaction to Kṛṣṇa.

So within the highest attainment, getting direct association with Kṛṣṇa, they are so eager to seek the satisfaction of Kṛṣṇa that they do not rush to present themselves directly before Him. Kṛṣṇa's satisfaction receives the highest concentration and whomever can perform it, the *sakhīs* help them—this is their intrinsic nature. We shall try to aspire to take shelter of them—that is the highest attainment found in the *sannyāsa-mantra.*

The real potency is in Vraja—that is the dedicating Moiety towards Kṛṣṇa. Direct connection is there, and indirectly with Kṛṣṇa through Her—this is Rādhā's position. This is particular in the *sannyāsa-mantram.* In other *dīkṣā-mantras,* there is direct connection with Kṛṣṇa—in the *sannyāsa-mantra,* our spiritual connection is shown towards the *gopīs.* That is *rādhā-dāsyam*—that is above *kṛṣṇa-dāsyam.* The inner meaning of the *sannyāsa-mantra* is *gopī-dāsyam.*

Sannyasa-mantra

It is purely in *mādhurya-rasa*—*gopī-bhāvāśrāya.* In this *mantram* we find the main current, if we desire to be directed towards *mādhurya-rasa.* Other *rasas* give partial representation, but *mādhurya-rasa* contains all *rasas*—the *vātsalya, sakhya, dāsya,* and *śānta*—everything is included there. It represents the whole—and others are partial representations. Everything is good in its own position.

Still from the absolute consideration and from the line of our *guru-paramparā* and *mantram,* analytically we see very plainly that it is all pertaining to *mādhurya-rasa.* To be adjusted fully in the family of Kṛṣṇa, generally we have to transform ourselves according to the principle of satisfying Kṛṣṇa. Then when that is finally done, we will be adjusted in the different serving sections according to our inner taste, in a particular group, in a particular way.

Our guru is Rādhārāṇī and our *mantras* are within *rādhā-dāsyam.* Especially the *sannyāsa-mantra—gopī-bhāvāśrāya* clearly means that you take shelter in the service of the *gopīs.* We must throw ourselves in the ocean of ecstasy represented as Kṛṣṇa. After that, in the *sannyāsa-mantra,* we shall cast our faith in the shelter and the service of the *gopīs.* The *sannyāsa-mantra* means this, the *mantra* is there, *guru-paramparā* is there, they are all indicating our course towards *mādhurya-rasa.*

This *mantram* is given either to a *sannyāsī* or to a *bābājī*—the fifth *āśrama.* Both of them are given the *mantra* of the same nature. The inner meaning of the *mantra* which is given at the time of *sannyāsa* indicates not only *kṛṣṇa-dāsyam* but there it is mentioned about *rādhā-dāsyam*—that shows us the direction—your direction, your goal is that side. That is the meaning of the *sannyāsa-mantram.* According to our progress we will be able to understand this in the future. The specialty there that is in the *mantra,* received at the time of *sannyāsa,* is given in a nutshell hereby.

One of my godbrothers, Śrautī Mahārāja, once asked me what was the meaning of that *mantra.* He thought that it referred to Mahāprabhu, and asked me to put this question to Guru Mahārāja. He did not do it directly but he asked me, "You ask Prabhupāda," and I did so. Prabhupāda with some emphasis told, "No, it is not directed to Śrī Gaurāṅga but it is directed toward the *gopīs.*" He gave the explanation of the *mantra* in that way, and I also conveyed it to Śrautī Mahārāja, "Prabhupāda told like this and your suggestion is cancelled."

These things are mysterious to us at the present stage, and give a vague idea that we are to start in this direction and march towards our highest goal. Of course, it is most laudable that we have come to such a high ideal. But to have understood what is the real ideal does not mean that we have reached it. We must be careful there, in our journey—we must not be fooled. Do not think no one can fool you. We must be very careful in our journey, as there are many things to hinder our progress.

In this advanced stage I shall aspire not particularly for Kṛṣṇa, but for the mistress of a particular department where my service will be most suitable—that I may be engaged in general in that *mādhurya-rasa* service. I am seeking the help of Kṛṣṇa to gain entrance into a particular department, under the charge of the leader of that department—henceforth my aspiration will be to cast myself wholesale to their disposal for the shelter of my mistress. *Āśraya* means that I am inclined to throw myself to the aspiration of such an attainment under the departmental head, not directly under Kṛṣṇa—because it is mentioned in the scriptures that the *sakhīs* have no aspiration for direct union with Kṛṣṇa, that is their nature. They consider themselves to be branches and the duty of the branches is to give supply to the trunk. So the central trunk is considered to be Rādhārāṇī—and the *sakhīs* are so many branches, and their intrinsic nature is such that they don't want direct union with Kṛṣṇa for themselves.

Bhaktivinoda's Unique Gift

We can also appreciate to a certain extent that this was the inner tendency of Bhaktivinoda Ṭhākura. When I wrote my prayers to Bhaktivinoda Ṭhākura, Prabhupāda appreciated it very much. When I presented these *ślokas* to Prabhupāda in Darjeeling, Śrautī Mahārāja was also present there. Prabhupāda, read these stanzas very happily, and pronounced them in a very happy style. He appreciated the poetry, the theological augmentation (poetical decoration), and ontological augmentation.

lokānāṁ hita-kāmyayā bhagavato bhakti-pracāras tvayā
granthānāṁ racanaiḥ satām abhimatair nānā-vidhair darśitaḥ

ācāryaiḥ kṛta-pūrvaṁ eva kila tad rāmānujādyair budhaiḥ
premāmbho-nidhi-vigrahasya bhavato māhātmya-sīmā na tat
(*Bhaktivinoda-viraha Daśakam* - 6)

What you, Bhaktivinoda have done in general, Rāmānuja, and other great *ācārya's*, scholars, they have also done it. But your greatness and nobility transcends that—you went higher. Where?

yad dhāmnaḥ khalu dhāma caiva nigame brahmeti saṁjñāyate
yasyāṁśasya kalaiva duḥkha-nikarair yogeśvarair mṛgyate
vaikuṇṭhe para-mukta-bhṛṅga-caraṇo nārāyaṇo yaḥ svayaṁ
tasyāṁśī bhagavān svayaṁ rasa-vapuḥ kṛṣṇo bhavān tat pradah
(*Bhaktivinoda-viraha Daśakam* - 7)

Prabhupāda also appreciated the gradations in this verse—*yad dhāmnaḥ khalu dhāma caiva nigame brahmeti*—what is Brahman given by Śaṅkara. Then, what is Paramātma of the *yogīs*. Then, what is given by Rāmānuja—Lakṣmī-Nārāyaṇa, that is the highest course in all of them. But you, Bhaktivinoda, have come so far, so high, to show Kṛṣṇa consciousness, after passing and eliminating them.

What is Brahman as generally conceived by the so-called theist? *Yad dhāmnaḥ khalu*—that is only the halo of the spiritual world. The halo of the spiritual world has been called Brahman in the *Vedas* and Śaṅkara and his followers say that is the ultimate—the halo of the spiritual cosmos is an impersonal halo.

And what is Paramātma, what the *yogis* are running after? *Yasyāṁśasya kalaiva duḥkha-nikarair*—with great pain and penances, they are trying to find out the all-apprehending and all-permeating principle within. What is His attitude? Residing within, He guides the thing, the Paramātma—*yogeśvarair mṛgyate.* That is the part of the part of the part of Nārāyaṇa, that Paramātma.

And Nārāyaṇa Himself is in Vaikuṇṭha—*vaikuṇṭhe para-mukta-bhṛṅga-caraṇo nārāyaṇo yaḥ svayaṁ*—Nārāyaṇa, Whose part and Whose halo is all this, along with the liberated souls, many of whom are engaged in busy service of that Great Entity. *Vaikuṇṭhe para-mukta-bhṛṅga-caraṇo nārāyaṇo yaḥ svayaṁ, tasyāṁśī bhagavān svayaṁ.* He is *vilāsa,* and we are to aspire and enquire after the very source of Nārāyaṇa.

In following the quality and intensity of the *rasa,* we are to further approach the higher level, and there we can find Kṛṣṇa—*svayam-bhagavān.* You, Bhaktivinoda Ṭhākura, can give that to us, you are so great. By your grace, crossing the concepts of Śaṅkara, Patañjali, Rāmānuja and others, we are allowed to go further, higher, to Kṛṣṇa-loka—*sarvācintya-maye parātpara-pure goloka vṛndāvane*—which is the transcendental of the transcendental, where we find this *jñāna-śūnya-bhakti* of the *gopīs.* There, we will find *kṛṣṇa-līlā.*

A Passport and Visa to Vrndavana

You, Bhaktivinoda Ṭhākura, can give us the passport, or visa for that land of Vṛndāvana, where the inconceivably beautiful damsels, the *gopīs* reside. There, in those pastimes, Kṛṣṇa is giving Himself fully at their disposal. Kṛṣṇa has given Himself wholly to their simplicity, plainness, beauty and love. That, you can give us. You can take us to that layer, you Bhaktivinoda Ṭhākura—your writings, your advice, your grace, can take us so high.

śrī gaurānumataṁ svarūpa-viditaṁ rūpāgrajenādṛtaṁ
rūpādyaiḥ pariveśitam raghu-gaṇair āsvāditaṁ sevitam
jīvādyair abhirakṣitaṁ śuka-śiva-brahmādi-sammānitam
śrī-rādhā-pada-sevanāmṛtam aho tad dātum īśo bhavān
(*Bhaktivinoda-viraha Daśakam*—9)

Not only Kṛṣṇa in His *rasa-līlā,* but something more you have given us. What is that? *Śrī-gaurānumataṁ*—that which is granted by Gaurāṅga Himself, Rādhā-Govinda combined. He has granted *svarūpa-viditaṁ,* and the quality of that gift is only understood fully by Svarūpa Dāmodara. *Rūpāgrajenādṛtam*—the great Sanātana, the elder brother of Rūpa, the *sambandha-jñāna ācārya,* fully appreciated this gift and *rūpāgrajenādṛtaṁ*—Rūpa Gosvāmī himself imbibed the inspiration from Mahāprabhu by transmission, and *śakti-sañcāra*—he himself distributed that *rāga-rasa,* that love divine. *Pariveśitam raghu-gaṇair āsvāditaṁ*—and Raghunātha has tasted it fully, and developed it. *Jīvādyair abhirakṣitaṁ*—and Śrī Jīva and Baladeva, they have protected it, given protection to that gift with scriptural knowledge.

That it is the conclusion of all the revealed scriptures. They have proved it in connection with other *śāstras* also. That it is not a whimsical statement, it has connection with other existing spiritual scriptures, which in various ways are pointing to this. They do not express this directly but other scriptures are giving suggestion to this *Bhāgavata* truth. What is this truth?

Brahmā, Śiva, and Uddhava are only hankering and searching but have not found it. Such a thing is *rādhā-dāsyam*—the service of Śrī Rādhikā. And you, Bhaktivinoda Ṭhākura, are in a position to distribute that highest nectar of our *sampradāya* to one and all. You are so great—your position is so dignified. The comparative position of Bhaktivinoda Ṭhākura amongst all other *ācāryas* is mentioned here, and this is proved in a theological and ontological way.

Prabhupāda was very much satisfied with the critical, scientific, spiritual development, and also its poetic beauty. Always he expressed his satisfaction with this and was very much pleased to find this *siddhānta* in my *śloka.* And he expressed this also—that it is properly given in this *śloka.* He said that, "Bhaktivinoda

Ṭhākura wrote this through you (Śrīdhara Mahārāja)," that was the opinion of Prabhupāda. And to someone he said that, "Yes, what I came to give to the world, it is there, I am leaving it for the world." And he told to me, "You have written in a very happy style." He was highly pleased with this, finding that, what was the real necessity, it was expressed properly. So far as we understand, this is the aim of our life, wherever we are—we understand that our mark must be towards this.

Fortunately we have within us the capacity to understand and write about such things—*mādhurya-rasa, parakīya, rūpānuga. Kṛṣṇa-bhakti* is a departmental thing, so *rādhā-dāsyam* is another thing—a department within a department. It is *rūpānuga*. The *ācārya-paramparā* is in that way—its direct concern is with this. The consorthood of the Supreme Entity (*mādhurya*), has been delivered by Mahāprabhu and gives support to *dāsya, vātsalya,* and *sakhya.*

anarpita-carīṁ cirāt karuṇayāvatīrṇaḥ kalau
samarpayitum unnatojjvala-rasāṁ sva-bhakti-śriyam
hariḥ puraṭa-sundara-dyuti-kadamba-sandīpitaḥ
sadā hṛdaya-kandare sphuratu vaḥ śacī-nandanaḥ

May the Supreme Lord who is known as the son of Śrīmatī Śacī-devī be transcendentally situated in the innermost chambers of your heart. Resplendent with the radiance of molten gold, He has appeared in the Age of Kali by His causeless mercy to bestow what no incarnation has ever offered before: the most sublime and radiant mellow of devotional service, the mellow of conjugal love. (*Cc. Ādi* 1.5)

Anarpita carīṁ cirāt—that which has never been distributed before, so perfectly and so clearly, was not distributed in ancient times. I found this *śloka* in the *Bhaviṣya Purāṇa* written by Vedavyāsa. The *Bhaviṣya Purāṇa* was published in Sanskrit and I found a copy in Madras. We found three chapters in *Bhaviṣya Purāṇa* dedicated to Mahāprabhu Śrī Caitanyadeva. There also we found the names Rūpānanda and Jīvānanda mentioned—Jīva Gosvāmī's name has been given as Jīvānanda, and Rūpa Gosvāmī's name has been given as Rūpānanda. And Mahāprabhu's preaching center has been given as Śāntipura, so there is some difference. A discussion between Rāmānuja and Madhvācārya with Mahāprabhu on the Vaiṣṇava ontology is also mentioned there in the *Bhaviṣya Purāṇa*, though historically it is not possible.

But as Bhaktivinoda Ṭhākura has shown in his *Navadvīpa-dhama-māhātmya*—these Vaiṣṇava *ācāryas* came in the subtle world, not in the physical world. Madhvācārya came to argue with Mahāprabhu and establish his *dvaita-vāda*. Rāmānuja also came to argue with his *viśiṣṭādvaita-vāda*.

But Mahāprabhu answered in a mystical way—in such a way that they were struck dumb and went away in silence. This is found in the *Bhaviṣya Purāṇa*. Mahāprabhu only spoke this mystic *śloka* (*anarpita carim cirāt*) and they were silenced. This has also been discussed in *Jaiva-dharma* by Bhaktivinoda Ṭhākura.

Anarpita cārim cirāt—that which has never been given before is *rādhā-dāsyam*, the most secret object. The fulfillment of our life is there, because the intensity of Rādhārāṇī's service has no parallel. When that sort of service comes in connection with Kṛṣṇa, the quality and quantity of *rasa* from the *akhila-rasāmṛta mūrti* is drawn in and is used in such a beautiful and noble way. That is not to be found anywhere and everywhere. To those that are in that camp, the taste of the *rasa*—not simply *mādhurya*—but particularly that of *parakīya*, is superior both in quality and quantity, especially quality. And if you want to have a taste of that type of *rasa,* which only Rādhārāṇī can enjoy, you have no other alternative. That sort of *rasa* attracts Rādhārāṇī so much that the higher quality of the *rasa* must be there. And if you want to taste even a particle of that standard of *rasa,* you will have no other alternative but to get service in that camp. This is quite reasonable.

Radha-dasyam

Raghunātha Dāsa Gosvāmī boldly declared that *rādhā-dāsyam, rādhā-kainkarya,* is the highest end. There is *rādhā-dāsyam,* or *yaśodā-dāsyam* in *vātsalya-rasa,* or *nanda-dāsyam*—service to the leader of every camp, the highest leader, that should be our real concern, the point of our attention should be there. If we serve in this way we will gradually come to Rūpa, the leader of the younger servitors. And this has been clearly explained in Dāsa Gosvāmī's *śloka*:

āśā-bharair-amṛta-sindhu-mayaiḥ kathañcit
kālo mayātigamitaḥ kila sāmpratam̐ hi
tvam̐ cet kṛpām̐ mayi vidhāsyasi naiva kim̐ me
prāṇair vraje na ca varoru bakāriṇāpi

With that hope I am somehow passing my days, flagging my days, dragging my life through these tedious times only for that hope. That hope is sustaining me, the nectarine-ocean of hope is attracting me and sustaining me. Somehow I am dragging my days to my only safety. Otherwise, I have lost the direct association of Mahāprabhu, Svarūpa Dāmodara and so many other great souls, and still I am living. Why? I have a particular ray of hope. And the prospect and quality of my hope is very great and high. But my patience has reached its end. I can't endure it any longer. I can't wait. I am finished. I can't wait any more. At this moment if You do not show Your grace to me, I am finished. I shall lose the chance forever. I shall have no desire to continue my life. It will all be useless. Without Your grace, I can't stand to live another moment. And Vṛndāvana, which is even dearer to me than my life itself—I am disgusted with it. It is painful; it is always pinching me. What to speak of anything else, I am even disgusted with Kṛṣṇa. It is shameful to utter such words, but I can have no love even for Kṛṣṇa, until and unless You take me up within Your confidential camp of service. Such a charm I have come for. I have seen the clue of such a charm within the service of Your camp. Without that, everything is tasteless to me. And I can't maintain my existence even in Vṛndāvana. And even Kṛṣṇa, what to speak of others, has no charm for me.

Dāsa Gosvāmī is appealing to Rādhārāṇī, "For a long time I am cherishing the hope, this sweetest hope, *amṛta sindhu mayi,* my *āśā* (hope) is compared with the ocean of nectar. From faraway I am fostering such a hope, that I shall get the privilege of serving You."

"I am dragging myself on with this infinite and sweet hope of serving Your divine feet. But now, I think I have come to the end of my hope. No longer can I contain myself. No longer can I live. I cannot breathe any more. Oh my Mistress, I have reached the last circumference of my hope. If You won't be satisfied with me and accept me, then I can no longer sustain my life. I have dragged to the last moment of my life— to the final conclusion. Of what use is this Vraja, what is the use of my life, if I cannot reach this, the sweetest goal of my dream? What is the use of extending my life any further? Dragging, dragging, dragging on my life—what shall I do with this great Vraja-dhāma of such a renowned acquaintance?"

"Oh, One with the most beautiful feet, what should I do with Kṛṣṇa? I don't want Him. You will serve Kṛṣṇa, You have that capacity, it is natural for You, and if I serve You, that service may pass through You to Kṛṣṇa, and that will be the highest attainment of my fortune." Dāsa Gosvāmī declared this. And to this day, that is the highest point of our achievement for the whole Gauḍīya *sampradāya*. This hope has been accepted to be the highest end of our life, *rādhā-kaiṅkarya, rādhā-dāsyam.* When Guru Mahārāja used to come to this *śloka—āśā-bharair-amṛta-sindhu-mayaiḥ*—he would explain it with full emotion, sometimes with tears in his eyes. He became like a phantom. He used to explain this *śloka* amongst a select few disciples. When doing so, we could trace that he was quite at home.

Radha-kunda

First, we may be attracted by the highest peak of the Himalayas. Then when approaching, we see so many other beautiful peaks. At first we are attracted by Kṛṣṇa in general, then we come in contact with a proper Vaiṣṇava according to the necessity of our innate nature. In this way we progress, from Mahāprabhu to Svarūpa Dāmodara, and with permission of Lalitā we come to Rūpa, and at the point of Rūpa, that is the place of our highest attainment. This has been shown in the *līlā* of Dāsa Gosvāmī Prabhu.

tvaṁ rūpa-mañjarī sakhī prathitā pure 'smin
puṁsaḥ parasya vadanaṁ na hi paśyasīti
bimbādhare kṣatam anāgata-bhartṛkāyā
yat te vyadhāyi kim u tac chuka-puṅgavena

> O friend Rūpa-mañjarī, although you are a famous and important person in this town, still you cannot see the face of the Supreme Personality of Godhead standing before you. Your husband is not here, and yet there is a mark on the bimba fruits of your lips as if someone has bitten them. Did a great parrot bite them? (*Vilāpa-kusumāñjali* I)

Śrī rūpa-mañjari sakhī prathitā pure 'smin—these are the *ślokas* written by him, and he has been accepted as the *ācārya* of *prayojana-tattva*. That which is our highest necessity is in his hand. But the whole thing must be approached with the mood of divinity from the plane of dedication and not of enjoyment. This spirit of pleasure and enjoyment must not enter, otherwise that will keep us down in this plane of mundane relativity. Divinity reaches its zenith to the extreme with Śrī Rūpa-mañjarī.

vaikuṇṭhāj janito varā madhupurī tatrāpi rāsotsavāt
vṛndāraṇyam udāra-pāṇi-ramaṇāt tatrāpi govardhanaḥ
rādhā-kuṇḍam ihāpi gokula-pateḥ premāmṛtāplavanāt
kuryād asya virājato giri-taṭe sevāṁ vivekī na kaḥ
(*Upadesāmṛta* 9)

The highest place of our service is at Rādhā-kuṇḍa, as expressed by Rūpa Gosvāmī. Up to his last days he used to stay there in the highest sweet connection of *kuṇḍa-līlā* of Rādhā-Govinda. It has been preached by other *ācāryas* that *rādhā-kaiṅkarya,* (*dāsyam*) is the acme of our object of life, it is allowed by the grace of the Almighty. In his last moments, when he was about eighty, Raghunātha Dāsa was crawling on the banks of Rādhā-kuṇḍa calling, 'Rādhe, Rādhe, Rādhe,' in a half-mad state.

The Name of Radha

Śukadeva could not say the Name of Rādhārāṇī when he was speaking *Bhāgavatam* in that scholarly assembly, so there is no mention of Rādhārāṇī's Name there. Jīva Gosvāmī has given the explanation that the scholarly section could not appreciate that higher form of *parakīya* love—they were scholars, but not a higher type of devotee. So Śukadeva did not want to take the Name of Rādhārāṇī in that assembly of scholars, who would fail to appreciate the *parakīya rasa sevā*—the service of Rādhārāṇī and the *gopīs.* Their service is of an absolute type, which is not under any law or regulation, either social or religious. It is the complete unconditional surrender towards Kṛṣṇa, which is the highest position. So much risk to serve Kṛṣṇa with a whole heart is found there. So Rādhārāṇī's Name could not be taken in the scholar's assembly by Śukadeva Gosvāmī—this is the explanation as given by Jīva Gosvāmī in his *Sandarbhas.*

When taking the Name of Rādhārāṇī I always give some *praṇāma:* "Oh, please forgive me, I am not qualified to take Your Name. I am saying so much with my small tongue, by taking Your Name. Please forgive me for having the audacity of taking Your Name. Forgive me." She is so high, so great, so noble—we can't consider ourselves fit to take Her Name. Śukadeva Gosvāmī did not speak Her Name throughout the entire *Bhāgavatam,* where he has given the true perception of divine love. The plane of love is above knowledge, above intellect, above rationality. The vibration of that plane is love absolute, absolutely towards Kṛṣṇa ignoring all other demands coming from the material environment.

Parakiya-rasa

Rādhā-dāsyam means *parakīya-rasa,* where the utmost surrender is required. In *kṛṣṇa-līlā* in Gokula, the *gopīs* had husbands, but in Goloka there is only a pictorial representation of the husbands, otherwise *parakīya* is not possible. There is only a subtle representation, in order to create some panic in the mind of the *gopīs* to increase the intensity of their love, in the *milana* (meeting). In *mādhurya-rasa,* we can have a complete connection, and in order to enhance emotion, the *milana* must be very rare and very intense. So, the role of the husband is necessary to help. This introduces a shadow of fear in the heart of the *gopīs.* "Oh, I have got my husband! How can I go to meet Kṛṣṇa?" All these things are created in the mind and it will make the *milana* even more tasteful.

It is something like remembrance. That sort of consciousness is necessary to give it a *parakīya* character. And the *parakīya* character is necessary to make it very rare and also risky. So it becomes very intense, and that is helpful for the love of Kṛṣṇa.

This *parakīya* system has been evolved by Yogamāyā—to increase the union to its highest intensity is necessary. This is not found in *svakīya.* When it is admitted, socially and scripturally, that He is the enjoyer of all of us, then the enjoying intensity is of a general standard. But to make it more intense, the real position of union is necessary to be created in the environment by Yogamāyā. So Jīvā Gosvāmī has shown from the scriptures that Rādhārāṇī is in fact Kṛṣṇa's own sweetheart, but there is posing in Vṛndāvana that She belongs formally to someone else (*parakīya*). It seems that She has a husband. This makes it very precious, very risky and even blamable, increasing the intensity of union.

Parakiya Bhajana

An important point to conceive is the *parakīya* principle as applied to our present life. All our previous *karmika* obligations are analogous to the position of a husband (*pati*). In the Indian social system the husband has complete control or lordship over the wife. To withdraw one's gratitude from him, to disobey and seek comfort or pleasure from another (a paramour) is like getting free from the obligations to all the commanding forces beyond Kṛṣṇa.

The forces of our past activities have the right to exact their demand from us. Wandering in the world we have incurred so many obligations, in so many places, that cannot be neglected (*karma* and *jñāna*). They want to master us, to exact what they have loaned, to realize the debt. They should be viewed as husband, they have demands to be realized from us. To disobey them (the husband) and use our free will to go to Kṛṣṇa's side is like *parakīya-bhajana* (paramour devotion).

On one side is total demand from the environment, and on the other is to use our free will to take us towards Kṛṣṇa, ignoring external obligation. That is to deceive the husband (*pati-vaṣcayan*). Just as when we borrow money we are obliged to repay the lender. To deal with him publicly in such a way as to dethrone him, to overthrow and disobey, is not permissible—we cannot escape our obligation. But with free will, from the innermost region of the heart, we can side with Kṛṣṇa.

From our previous life we have acquired so many anti-Kṛṣṇa tendencies that hold us captive. Somehow we must take our free will away from them, unconsciously, without their knowing, and dedicate it to Kṛṣṇa. It is possible from our present position to do so. Wherever we are, regardless of how much debt we owe, however great the burden, free will can take us out of that obligatory circle and shift everything to Kṛṣṇa's side.

Our inner sympathy or prejudice should be in that direction. Our prayer is for that. We realize that we are in the midst of an unfavorable environment. The husband, the in-laws, society, even the scripture—all are against me. Deceiving them, secretly with my free will and the help of His devotees, I will approach Kṛṣṇa.

All prejudices are represented by society—even the moral codes of the scriptures, which includes almost everything—*sva-janam ārya-pathaṁ*. They are all on one side. And deceiving them, I will use my free will to dedicate my heart secretly to Kṛṣṇa. "My Lord, with Your own agent, take me out of here. Take me out!" We must be courageous and bold enough to disobey past obligations, approach with our innermost prayer and self-interest, and dedicate ourselves as *naivedyam* (an offering) to the lotus feet of Kṛṣṇa and His own.

It will be difficult for women because a similar, perverted thing will try to occupy the position of the genuine. It is a more dangerous position. Apparently it may seem that it will be easy because those that lack privilege receive more grace. But we should be cautious in our analysis not to mistake the womanly nature of the mundane world for the womanhood of the spiritual domain.

We are not enjoyers but we are to be enjoyed—this is the basic negative conception. We are not to handle, but to be handled. The posing is to passively offer ourselves—non-assertion. For preaching we are active, in the sense to convert misconception to proper conception, but when we turn towards Kṛṣṇa's side it is exclusively a matter of grace. Like a *cātaka* bird that lives on rainwater—whether the cloud throws a thunderbolt or rains water, he has no other shelter—*viracaya mayi daṇḍaṁ dīna-bandho dayaṁ vā*. While we are non-assertive, making no claim, underground a claim is being established. As much as we possess a non-claimant attitude, automatically our claim is established there. Dedication means that the degree of non-claimant attitude establishes a claim in that wonderful land.

There we thrive and here we die. 'Die to live!' Hegel's theory. That's a very good thing, the philosophy of Hegel: 'Reality is for Itself' and 'Die to live!' These two things have impressed me very much—comprehensive concepts. Kṛṣṇa is the consumer of all, everything is for Him. And 'Die to live!' If you want to live, you will have to die. Learn to die, if you want to live. 'Dissolve your ego!' Die means to dissolve our ego. And then the coverings of our soul, one by one, will be thrown off. The inner jewel will appear in its pristine glory, that finest valuable ray.

Highest Dedication is Union in Separation

Dedication in its highest state is union in separation. Outwardly we may be discouraged by this position, but at heart, our faith is nutured. Our bond becomes stronger and invulnerable—unbreakable even amidst any punishment or separation. Step by step we will go deeper and higher to our pure ideal.

Mahāprabhu, in His *Śikṣāṣṭakam* says, *āśliṣya vā pāda-ratāṁ pinaṣṭu mām adarśanān marma-hatāṁ karotu vā.* That type of love, that sort of attitude, can never make us separate from Kṛṣṇa. This is the acme of dedication—the highest form of unity in the deepest plane.

Even Rādhārāṇī Herself says that Kṛṣṇa is qualified in every way. "I can't blame Him in any way, still He is so cruel to us all, that He left Vṛndāvana. It is extremely painful to us—it is My *durdaiva-vilāsa.* I cannot accuse Him in any way." This is union in separation.

This is a peculiar type of achievement when, one who has the thing, says, "No, I do not have it"—this is the special characteristic of the Infinite. One who has possession of it says I have nothing. And when one says that they do have it, then they do not have it—it is such, because it is a statement from the negative for the positive. The negative who cannot assert at all, can attract only. Assertion is with the positive only, so the negative can hanker, they can express their own reality in the negative characteristic—they can express their position in the degree of necessity. The measurement is on the negative side—the depth of necessity, depth of attraction, but not of gain.

Without the quality of humility, none can enter the domain of devotion. Humility has its quality, from the standpoint of intensity and from the intent, or purity. Humility is a general thing. But Sanātana Gosvāmī's humility is of a high quality, and a high degree also, and this took him in direct connection with Mahāprabhu. Intense humility is the criterion of the negative side.

There, a slave may also have such a unique right, according to his degree of sacrifice, self-abnegation and intensity of hankering for mercy. There may be a gradation according to progress on the negative side. We are told that one who holds the highest position thinks himself to be the lowest of all. This is the measure of negativity. He or she who is rendering the greatest service thinks, "I am most unsatisfied, I can't do any service to Kṛṣṇa. I am the worst of all the servants. I can't serve properly."

In fact, that is the qualification for rendering service to the Lord. That dissatisfaction is the capital of service. "I can't satisfy my Lord; I can't work as directed." Such a devotee is always alert in this way to the highest degree. He is always suspicious about his own self. This is the ego of the negative type—never asserting, but always self-abusing. The combination of such servitors becomes very, very sweet. The atmosphere is very sweet—no aggressors, all contributors. The mathematical calculation is there. "I am a *taṭastha-jīva* and the higher sphere is made up of higher stuff than myself. There all are guru—the earth, the water, the air—everything is guru, cent-percent guru. And only as a slave can I enter there according to the degree of my free acceptance of slavery—and only with real earnestness for that." That higher sphere is subjective—we are subject in relation to this world of object.

Only I shall hanker, "You please come." He is positive, I am negative. So, I should encourage my quality of negativity that, "I am the most wretched. I am the most desperate fallen soul, that needs the greatest help, the best attention from You—so wretched that there is no other. Please come down to help me, to deliver me from this lowest position."

This is progress. Even Mahāprabhu Śrī Caitanyadeva says that, "I am shedding tears so much taking the Name of Kṛṣṇa, but I do not have a scent of love of God." Mahāprabhu says—*na prema gandho'sti darāpi.* "Not a drop of real *rāgānuga-bhakti* is within Me. That is infinite, that is an ocean. My attempt is a sham. It is artificial." He is blaming Himself in such a way. But from the background, *rāgānuga-bhakti* is filling Him up completely, capturing Him wholesale.

There is no other way—only to attract Him to come down to my level, by my negative side—that is my hankering. That should be improved—He is invited by humility, He will come down to take me. The negative side should be increased, but not asserted. He will have to take the initiative—humility, want, and dire need of this thing will attract Him. To come, or not to come is His free will. I cannot force Him to come with intense invitation from my side. In other words, I can force Him only by my earnest invitation. I can increase the earnestness of my invitation. "O Lord, You have to come to deliver this fallen soul. I can't live without You." In this way the negative should be increased to attract the positive. The Dominating, and the predominated are two aspects of the same thing.

Four Categories of Vipralambha

Divine separation (*vipralambha*) may be divided into four categories—*pūrva-rāga, māna, prema-vaicitra* and *pravāsa.*

Pūrva-rāga means before meeting—both the parties are not actually meeting but They come in some remote connection, through either the Name, a picture, or the sound of the flute. There is no real meeting, but only some idea of connection. This is *pūrva-rāga*—separation before meeting.

Māna means that after meeting there is some difference between Them in some small matters. "He is neglecting me—He wants to avoid me," this sort of sentiment comes—"Thereby I don't want Your connection!" Of course, real liking is there underneath, but temporarily these disagreements arise and one wishes to stay away from the other. "I don't like this association"—that is *māna.*

Prema-vaicitra arises when Rādhā and Kṛṣṇa are together but somehow think that They are not. This may arise when Rādhārāṇī is standing by Kṛṣṇa, and seeing Her shadow reflected in the body of Kṛṣṇa, She thinks that another lady is closely associated with Krsna. Jealousy springs up in such an intense way within that She feels great pangs of separation. These feelings of union in separation are called *prema-vaicitra.* Of course, this sentiment occurs only in *mādhurya-rasa*, not in other *rasas.*

Pravāsa arises when there is an actual separation for either a short or long time—two types of *pravāsa.* Kṛṣṇa may go to Mathurā for some time or go to a far off place. This separation is called *pravāsa.*

These four types of *vipralambha*—separation between the lover and beloved, are of a very high category. If we indulge in these topics carelessly, it will do some harm to our realization in the future, because the mundane characteristic may try to take us down. So we must approach these topics with much caution.

Union in Separation

The feeling of separation is normal and safe, and the feeling of union is mostly treacherous to the lower section. It is easy to mistake one thing for another thing. There is the possibility of going down. So Mahāprabhu Śrī Caitanyadeva showed for us the path of union in separation—it is the safest way. "I have got Him," that is dangerous. Mostly the cases are bogus, we must be very much careful about that. We should not think that getting anything and everything, I have got some touch of the Lord. There we must be very, very careful.

One disciple of Svāmī Mahārāja once told in a lecture that union in separation is the highest realization. I was very happy to hear this from him that union in separation, *vipralambha,* is the highest kind of attainment. Without *vipralambha,* nothing else can come to us. Kṛṣṇa and the opposite thing, antithesis, that will appear as *vipralambha. Vipralambha* is the most spacious thing pertaining to Kṛṣṇa consciousness.

And if we can have the grace of that plane, then we will experience self-forgetfullness. In self-forgetfullness also, if there is Kṛṣṇa connection then we are safe—we shall have Kṛṣṇa consciousness in the background and nothing else. *Vipralambha* is the safest and most fearless position.

Vipralambha Safer than Sambhoga

It is more dangerous to cultivate *sambhoga* than the mood of separation—that is a little safe. It is safer to deal with separation of the high type, but union is very, very dangerous to deal with. We may participate in feelings of separation a little, though we should not think that it is of this lower plane. The pain of separation is not of this plane, but still the separation is less injurious. With caution we may talk a little about that—but *sambhoga* will be very, very dangerous. When Rādhā-Govinda and the *sakhīs* are together and they are enjoying the company of one another, that will be very, very dangerous to discuss or to think or to deal in any way with this from this mundane plane—it will create a great offense—that is the idea. So direct handling is more injurious.

Indirect handling of separation, as Mahāprabhu is personally showing by example, is helpful. Mahāprabhu and the devotees are showing so many moods—they can't tolerate the separation of Kṛṣṇa. "Oh, I can't even tolerate my own existence without Kṛṣṇa—without His grace, without His company I can't maintain this undesirable existence." All these feelings may help us to a certain extent.

We are not to imitate that, but look respectfully at it as the highest ideal. And that will help us to brush aside our *anarthas*. Ones feelings of separation from Kṛṣṇa should be intense, but if some tears come we should not think that we have realized that stage. That sort of thing should be avoided. *Na prema gandho 'sti*—Mahāprabhu said that, "I have not a drop of divine love in Me, otherwise how can I maintain My mundane life."

Union in Separation is Proper Union

To dive deep into despair—that is the sign of one in the relativity of the divinity. In one sense, *viraha* is a positive thing, it is not non-existent—it is existent. Union proper and union in separation are two different things. The Infinite embraces everything—those who are not conscious of the infinite are also accommodated.

The nature of the freedom of the *jīva* is union in separation—that is proper union with the Infinite. To come in complete union depends upon Him, and that is very rare. The jurisdiction of the freedom of the *jīva* is in union in separation—it is not a question of intensity.

In *bhāva-bhakti* and *prema-bhakti* also, we find union in separation. This is a common ground, but when you have gone deeper you find it to be very, very intense. It will also have no limit. Dive deeper into *rasa*—the degree depends on that classification of union. The deepest union is possible only in *mādhurya-rasa*. That makes one almost mad. *Mahā-bhāva*—a madness in the highest sense—mad insanity. The highest form of sanity is madness—it is the opposite—this is *mahā-bhāva*.

"Please take me along with You, I can't tolerate Your separation." Mahāprabhu taught that, "You are always with Me and if you do as I say—then your presence is really with Me. This means that to be physically near is not really near. Nearness is a mentality—if we want to have association with a superior then only by serving them can we retain our close position. It is not achieved by any physical or mental process. Just be a patient servant—whatever instruction comes, we are ready to do that. That is the means to be in association. Nearness is calculated by *anugatām*, submission—submission is the way of measurement whether He is near or far. The unit of measurement is of such a character. Physically far away and spiritually very close. The opposite is to be physically very close, but spiritually far off.

Separation from the Devotee

In the discourse of Rāmānanda Rāya and Mahāprabhu, it is mentioned, that the greatest calamity, the greatest sorrow or most intense pain that ever has been felt by a Vaiṣṇava is separation from a devotee. *Kṛṣṇa bhakta guru viraha*—that is the deepest pain ever found in this world. So, this separation, *viraha* gives us purity.

Separation gives purity, and it is a test to our adherence to the cause. If in separation we feel so much pain, it is the standard of measurement, what sort of love I have for him. The intensity and pain of our separation is the standard. It is a real test, a real friend. There, the enjoyment cannot be present. The fallen souls are encouraged to observe separation and that will be helpful for them.

Sambhoga may have some misapplication for the fallen, so their safe path is with *vipralambha. Vipralambha* is really a guardian, a chastiser, a real friend—and with *sambhoga,* we may be deceived by it for our ill-fate, that possibility may be there. So, we are safer culturing *vipralambha* than *sambhoga.*

Our Real Wealth is the Fire of Separation

The burning fire of separation from Kṛṣṇa is the real wealth—just as with Śrī Caitanyadeva, His separation from Kṛṣṇa was so intense that He could not sleep or take food. His separation was so intense that at night He tried to get out of the house, though the doors were locked. He jumped over the walls of the house, practically unconsciously, and fainted in front of the Jagannātha temple. Such an intense degree of separation is found in Him! It is not possible for us to conceive this degree of feeling. Sometimes He rubbed His face against the walls because His could not get out to see His Lord.

A *sakhī* once related to Kṛṣṇa the pain of separation that Rādhārāṇī feels for Him. "Previously," she explains, "A continuous flow of tears was found in Her eyes, but it is not there anymore. Somehow She has managed to distribute them to Her friends. Now they are weeping like anything, but no trace of tears can be found in Her. She had some temperature in Her body, but now that is also gone. She has transferred this to Her intimate *sakhīs.* Her attendants are now saying many things—undesirable talks of mourning are found among Her attendants. Previously all those things were found in Śrīmatī Rādhārāṇī, but somehow She managed to leave them all with

Her friends. She had also been absorbed in deep thought, what will be Her fate? 'Maybe Kṛṣṇa will never come again—He is doing this and that'—so many thoughts were within Her, but now we find no trace."

"But Her superiors are burdened with those deep thoughts. 'O, the girl won't live. She will pass away very soon. What will be the fate of Vraja? If She passes away, Kṛṣṇa won't come here again.' What little is left in Her we see in the form of hard breathing and a beating heart—in a day or two that will also disappear. Now, Kṛṣṇa, You may remain happy here for Your misdeed. Your misdeed is the cause of all these things, but She has managed to relieve You—no complaint will come against You any more. Silently She is passing away—keeping You safe while You remain here and enjoy with Your own friends."

The Intensity of Vipralambha

Bilvamaṅgala Ṭhākura says, *anātha-bandho karuṇaika-sindho.* "These unfortunate days are impossible for me to pass. Without seeing You, I cannot stand to live any more. But You are a friend to the helpless, and You are an ocean of kindness and grace. Please consider it my Lord, how can I pass my days without You." The normal temperament of a devotee will be like that. Separation, of course, will be encouraging. If we find a person is always feeling genuine separation from the Lord, that will be appreciated, whereas anything else should be considered abnormal and dangerous.

These are extremely high transcendental subjects, and although this is not to be discussed in detail, this is the nature of divine love in union and separation. Both are interdependent, for one cannot stay without the other, and separation is created willingly to enhance union.

So you have all come from so far off and are engaging yourselves in these high talks of divinity. We are so grateful to you. In my old age it is almost impossible that I should be utilized by my Guru Mahārāja and in this way to talk about Mahāprabhu. And you, my friends, are coming and exacting from me whatever I could store from my Guru Mahārāja in my heart. I think I did something to give vent to the position of my Gurudeva today.

Verse Index